One *of* Them

One of Them

Norene Pavlik

Thanks be to God —
Norene Pavlik
Jenny Pavlik

Our Sunday Visitor Publishing Division
Our Sunday Visitor, Inc.
Huntington, Indiana 46750

The poem "Pain Withstood," © 1988 by Katrina Pavlik, first appeared in Creighton University's *Shadows* literary magazine in 1984 and is reprinted with permission. The epigraph poem is from *Maryknoll* magazine, Maryknoll, N.Y. 10545, and is reprinted by permission. All rights reserved.

Copyright © 1988
by Norene Pavlik
All Rights Reserved

With the exception of short excerpts for critical reviews, no part of this book may be reproduced in any manner whatsoever without permission in writing from the publisher. *Write:*

Our Sunday Visitor Publishing Division
Our Sunday Visitor, Inc.
200 Noll Plaza
Huntington, Indiana 46750

International Standard Book Number: 0-87973-420-5
Library of Congress Catalog Card Number: 88-61212

Cover design and photo layout by Rebecca J. O'Brien

PRINTED IN THE UNITED STATES OF AMERICA

For
the One who gives us life

A Family Prayer

God made us a family
We need one another
We love one another
We forgive one another
We work together
      We play together
           We worship together
Together we use God's word, together we grow in Christ
Together we love all men, together we serve our God
          Together we hope for heaven
  These are our hopes and ideals
      Help us to attain them, O God
           Through Jesus Christ, Our Lord,
                  Amen.

(Done in calligraphy by a "porch neighbor"
who saw it in *Maryknoll* magazine and
thought it described the Pavlik family.)

... acknowledgments ...

At age forty-six, I felt the awesome summons to write Jenny's story. I had never written anything except letters, journal entries, and occasional articles for clubs, nor had I experienced the emotions that would bombard me. I thank God for knowing my needs before I did and gifting me with unexpected, wonderful helpers, expecially Dolores Curran, Father John A. Simonin, Joseph Kemper, Theodore Rosengarten, Father Bernard Rooney, C.Ss.R., Father Joseph T. McGloin, S.J., Father Patrick Kaler, C.Ss.R., Father Michael Flecky, S.J., Father William J. O'Malley, S.J., Father Val J. Peter, Karen Lee, Terry Harper Luker, and Sharon Hagerty. Having a manuscript in hand meant nothing, however, without Herb Kramer and the Joseph P. Kennedy, Jr. Foundation. They and Our Sunday Visitor made possible the publication of *One of Them*.

Living with me through all this was my family, and that was no easy task. Despite wondering what strange bee had gotten in my bonnet, husband Kenneth subscribed to *The Writer* and *Writer's Digest* magazines, bought me books to help me learn how to write, and encouraged me to take a journal-writing course where I realized I could write about my feelings. He was marvelously supportive, and ever present for our children as they tolerated Mom's pursuit of this unexpected path in life that she often questioned. Ken's steady demeanor did more to keep our family's life on course than I can adequately thank him for.

While I necessarily relived the previous twenty years I described, Mark, Jenny, Paul, Katie, and Sarah kept steadfastly on their forward path. It seemed their actions must surely make my words unnecessary — actions that speak far more dramatically than my words ever could. Each of these is one of them who make a wonderful difference in today's world.

So many others remain unnamed. To them also, I extend heartfelt thanks.

...contents...

...introduction: Eunice Shriver... 11
...preface... 13
1 ...her name is Jennifer Lou... 15
2 ...she sees seashore... 21
3 ...setting our sails... 26
4 ...she'll be all right... 31
5 ...did I hear right?... 41
6 ...if so, so be it... 51
7 ...goals and no goals... 58
8 ...each problem has a solution... 67
9 ...aware of surroundings... 76
10 ...life is just now beginning... 84
11 ...progresses and regresses... 96
12 ...eleven and blossoming... 107
13 ...new chance to learn... 122
14 ...besides teenager, what?... 146
15 ...speaking in sentences!... 154
16 ...mountains and restless... 165
17 ...uprooting... 176
18 ...out of the cocoon... 186
19 ...proving and trusting... 203
20 ...culture shock... 224
21 ...into the challenging world... 239
...two tributes from Katie... 261
...postscript... 263

... introduction ...

By Eunice Kennedy Shriver, Executive Vice President, Joseph P. Kennedy, Jr. Foundation

Anyone reading this book will offer a sigh of relief and a shout of joy. The American family is alive and well. Family values are fresh and strong. There are still husbands and wives who love one another; children who are loyal and affectionate to parents and siblings; homes that are the centers of moral teaching, shared work and play, a strong sense of purpose, and a commitment to living fully rather than merely well.

And what is most inspiring and uplifting — at the heart of this family, challenging and illuminating it, is a special child, Jenny, who is not only "one of them" but one of all of us.

Norene Pavlik's family story is a textbook on how to receive, accept, nurture, and love a special child. It is a testament to the truth of the oft-repeated cliché — "adversity strengthens a family." Through the foundation of their religious faith, the Pavliks have fashioned a life that can triumph over pain and disappointment by converting the inscrutable into a pattern rich with meaning and beauty.

From the moment that Jenny's handicap is revealed, the Pavliks determine that she will be raised as "one of us." Although they are given no reason for her retardation, and no accurate diagnosis is ever made, the Pavliks accept Jenny with all her limitations and refuse to be discouraged in their efforts to let her develop to her fullest potential.

Aphasic? We'll persist until she speaks. Dyslexic? We'll stay with her until she reads. Stutters? We'll get her hours of speech therapy. Retarded? We'll keep her in kindergarten three years if we have to, but we'll see her graduate from high school. And all this time, through all these days and years, we'll honor her differences and her gifts with our love, for that is the meaning of family.

I congratulate Our Sunday Visitor for recognizing the significance of the Pavliks' story. It is not a ghost-written, self-serving tribute to material success of the kind that makes the best-seller list these days. Rather, it is the simple, unvarnished record of people who believe, quite literally, that character is more important than charisma; that service is more rewarding than success, and that in the day-by-day duty and sacrifice of family life we come closest to the will of God.

... preface ...

There will always be frantic parents who learn their child is retarded. Whether or not there is a cause found, the fact remains that their lives will be filled with emotional struggles and they will probably search, with aching hearts, for answers to their urgent questions, just as we did.

When it became apparent our second child was retarded, we had many questions and few answers. Libraries and bookstores held academic treatises, but I wanted to read personal accounts written by and about families who lived with a retarded member.

Because I looked for help, any kind of help, this revealing of our family life is offered in the hope that other families might realize that life with quality doesn't have to end with the traumatic diagnosis of Unexplained Retardation. To tell about Jenny's life, I had to tell about her family's life. Jenny did not live by herself. She lived with parents and brothers and sisters. We interacted daily, and we became what we are partly because of Jenny; she became what she is partly because of us.

We lived only as we knew how to live. Perhaps for other families to do things the way we did would be out of character. For that reason, I do not offer us as a model. My intention is that we merely serve as a glimmer of hope for other parents and families who must learn to live with retardation.

§§ 1 §§

... her name is Jennifer Lou ...

Awkwardly but carefully dropping the infant and purse inside the front door, I grabbed better hold of the sack and hurried to the bathroom mirror. "What will his reaction be?" I thought of the check I'd borrowed from my mother that he had ever so gently folded and refolded and then quietly torn in two. And then I remembered the donuts. So like him. How could I have possibly done this now? So unlike me!

No time for remorse now. He'd be home any minute and there was supper to prepare. The husky, brown-haired infant's insistent cries demanded my attention. The child followed me quickly on hands and knees and pulled himself up to the door of the bathroom, but I hurriedly left and went to the kitchen. His cries followed me.

Taking the grocery items from the sack, I muttered, "Liver and onions, that's good and cheap! And carrots'll go good with that; at least we've got carrots from canning last summer; thanks to Lud and Alice's garden. And this spinach. With home-canned tomatoes and the egg lady's eggs, that'll do for tomorrow."

Louder, I answered, "Yes, yes, Mark! Mommy's coming! Just a minute! And beans to bake. And juice. Yes, Mark! All you have to do is sit down again and you could crawl out here! You're going to be so-o-o surprised one of these days to learn you can actually walk across that doorway!"

His cry grew more demanding.

"Yes! Mommy's coming! Just a minute, Little Man!"

I hurried to retrieve him and took off his jacket. "Did you have fun at Donna's while Mommy was away? Just a sec, I'll be back. Mommy's gotta put our coats in the closet. I'll be right back, okay?"

Picking him up, I heard the car. "Oh, listen! It's Daddy. I hear Daddy! Let's go look!"

At the front window of our small prefab house that the realtor had guessed would be "perfect, just perfect for your needs," I glanced on down the street of neat, established, custom-built homes. The green 1947 Chevrolet club coupé turned into our driveway.

"See, there's Daddy!" Butched brown-headed Daddy gave heartwarming waves before he unfolded out of the small car.

He came to the window, intent on waving to his little son who so obviously was a miniature version. With a warm smile, his eyes met mine through the glass and continued upward.

The smile remained genuine as he came through the door. "Well, well, what have we here?" He reached an approving hand to my curly locks. So like him. It didn't make any difference whether or not I had curls, but if it was important to me, then it's what he'd want.

He listened to my story of a weak moment: ". . . and I just all of a sudden couldn't resist a little pampering, and there was this beauty parlor right there, and, and. . ."

"It looks really nice! I'm glad you did it. But to do it justice, we ought to go out to dinner. Want to?"

I thought of the donuts again. Last month he'd come home and handed me a bakery sack. "There wasn't enough money to put gas in the car, so I got donuts instead." So like him!

Now through my thoughts I heard him ask, "How're you feeling?"

"Fine. Really. I've had so little trouble this pregnancy. But I'll be glad when it's over. Won't be much longer. How was your day?"

"Busy. Let's go see if we can get Bob to watch Mark. Hop's been wanting to take Donna out; maybe they could join us."

I dialed the phone and remembered again the trip to the bank to take out a small loan. Also the protected feeling I'd had the day before, when he'd held the torn pieces of the check I had borrowed from my mother and lovingly said, "I want to be the one to take care of you and our children."

With this father of my children, I chose to settle into whatever kind of life came our way. I didn't think of life in terms of dollars and cents, but obviously, some of that check would have been appreciated to pamper an occasional weak moment.

Weak moments would come. Husband Ken's life was not destined to mesh nicely with my needs, because his career was dedicated to the needs of others. This young man had finished medical school and was now an intern. Since I'd met him in the line of duty, I knew firsthand the demands that would be placed on him, on us, and on our children. Our life would necessarily be a life of sharing with others. It would be up to us to carve out an individual style of living that could also include time to call our own.

When I look back, I realize how little I knew about what life could hold for us. Sometimes it was awesome. But Ken and I firmly believed that we had a choice — a choice either to accept or to reject challenges. In retrospect, I can unreservedly say we made a good choice. We chose to accept any and all challenges.

The next of those unknown challenges was eagerly anticipated and welcomed. The strength of my temporary curls had diminished to natural waves by the day I spent hours in maternity labor.

That was February 1, 1960.

We were happy, Ken and I. He was with me in the delivery room at 7:21 A.M. when six-pound, nine-ounce Jennifer Lou was spontaneously born. "She's breathing nicely, and she's got ten fingers and ten toes, and her body seems well-formed."

Later, the aroma of roses filled the hospital room at St. Elizabeth Hospital in Lincoln, Nebraska, as we accepted the new miracle of birth. I cradled the sleeping newborn and read to her Daddy a poem given to me by the Sisters of St. Elizabeth's after the delivery:

GOD BLESS YOU

> May every blessing this life can hold
> Be yours in the fullest measure.
> May this infant, that is better than gems or gold,
> Fill your future days with pleasure;
>
> Though clouds gather above your way,
> Some grief or gloom oppress you,
> May this infant that God has sent to you today
> Thru His love befriend and bless you.

Whoever wrote that poem spoke real truth. However, we

would not always recognize the blessing through the masks it wore. The clouds would be easier to see.

Gramma thought our new baby seemed rather scrawny compared to her other grandchildren. But Gramma was helpful. From having lived through her own experiences and those of her friends and relatives, my mother knew that bestowing love on our baby was more important than making comparisons.

I nursed Jenny and fed supplementary bottles when necessary. I loved holding her. Daddy nestled this child on his broad chest every chance he got. Dr. Spock's book was reviewed, but essentially we handled Jenny's development according to how our personalities meshed, sometimes ineptly. We had experimented with our first child and had settled into routines that were comfortable for us.

On Valentine's Day Jenny was baptized, with Uncle Buddy and Aunt Marguerite as godparents. At St. Teresa's church, Father Philip Rauth spoke the sacramental words, poured holy water over her forehead, and anointed with oil while Jenny slept peacefully. We had no way of knowing, then, that our child would probably never be capable of serious sin and, we believe, could therefore almost certainly be assured of heaven.

The infant smile at one month allowed Jenny to show special response. She developed into an even-natured, though slow-to-smile, baby. We quickly grew fond of her, and friend Hop teased, "Ahhh, you guys, how can you love that little thing that's only a piece of meat with a hole at both ends?" We had only to watch him love his own four sons to understand how deeply he, too, could love. His wife, Donna, laughing infectiously, held and loved tiny Jenny as though she were her own.

Every young mother should have a friend like the one I had in Donna. Despite our tight budgets, she taught me ways of homemaking that allowed for entertaining and for adding extra pleasures to family life. My heart still smiles whenever I extract a special treat that has been squirreled away, and I remember the day Donna sent our boys to the sandpile and then fetched a Coca-Cola from behind the water heater for us to share. Grocery money was meted out carefully from her husband's salary, so that Coke was a special treat shared over exchange of recipes, ideas, memories, and hopes.

Donna helped me understand that little children are not totally fragile. "Oh, c'mon, Girl, he's not going to eat the whole sandpile. He won't like it!" She even bundled the children and me off to search for treasures, pleasures, or necessities as the case may be, some of which I still use today. She'd call and say, "I'm coming by. Let's go to the Goodwill store!" Little did I know a Goodwill Rehabilitation Center would be a chapter in the life of the little baby I carried along on those forages.

Life was fairly carefree those days when Ken was preparing to be a general-practice physician. Following his year of internship we would go wherever the Navy commanded him to serve. In the meantime, major decisions were few. Perhaps the biggest was what to do with the car Ken had used during medical school. When we moved on we would take only the 1954 Plymouth I'd had before we were married. We finally sold it to our tall neighbor boy in exchange for baby-sitting service — forty hours at twenty-five cents an hour to equal ten dollars. We wondered about entrusting our tiny girl baby to that strapping teenager, but his mother across the street kept close watch. We didn't receive ten dollars worth of sitting because we usually took our children wherever we went, and I'm not sure Bob received ten dollars worth of car.

We started feeling questions about Jenny early in her life. Ken and I knew from our studies that most babies showed more eagerness by three months, whereas Jenny was content just to lie and watch her hands as she gracefully turned them round and round before her eyes. We unsuccessfully tempted her with colorful toys and hung them near to catch her interest. Toddler Mark, thirteen months older, entertained and encouraged her impatiently.

Any parent remembers some of the foolish things done in the role of entertaining a little child. Thus Ken's friends, who were already dads, were not surprised when he came to work with a perfect-circle contusion on his forehead: evidence of the bobbing suction-toy entertainment phase of life.

Jenny's abilities were slow, but her body started a fairly even development despite laggard muscle tone. Teeth started erupting at four months. No attempt was made to turn over, and by five months she still showed only limited inquisitiveness.

Routine medical checkups caused no concern. Immunizations

were started. There seemed little else to do, and in fact we chased doubts from our minds by assuming that Jenny was simply going to be slower to develop. Besides, Ken had heard from the Navy and we had to prepare for a move to California. Fitting in last visits to our relatives left little time to be overly concerned about little Jenny.

Our move to the West Coast of the United States was relatively simple because we owned few possessions. One packer wrapped and boxed our belongings within a few hours. One decorative item that has survived all these years is a picture I cut from a woman's magazine and stuck in a frame. It is a dark picture of a dove standing on the ground, with the words "Children, love ye one another." A fitting reminder of what we tried to instill in our children. Ken and I learned that love is one of the strongest, most necessary ingredients for family life.

§§ 2 §§

... she sees seashore ...

To live in California was an exciting prospect. Years earlier, Ken had visited there briefly on his way to Oregon, where he'd temporarily worked in a sawmill. I had traveled its length and shared the anticipation of living in the San Francisco Bay area.

Now with our little children we visited Auntie Lee and Uncle Russell in Oregon, then continued south through the Lake Shasta region until concern for Jenny arose and heightened when she spiked a high fever. There was no apparent reason. In Redding, California, we interrupted our trip to buy alcohol. Using the gallon thermos as a basin, we swathed our fiery infant in alcohol-water cooling diapers. Jenny's fever was relatively short-lasting, but her stools became soft and took on a terrible odor that lasted several weeks. Medical examinations found no cause, and change of diet brought no solution.

Ken was processed into the Navy at Oakknoll Naval Hospital, while I set up temporary housekeeping at a neighborhood motel. We found a rental house, called for our furnishings, and were told there was no record of them. Quickly we learned what so many military families had learned before us: events never happen as one might wish. Then Ken's orientation was cut very short because a doctor was needed on the ship, so while he sailed off on a ten-day trip to Alaska, I met the challenge of assuming responsibilities never before dreamed of.

His ship, the 622-foot-long *USS Breckenridge*, employed and transported more people than populated Ken's and my hometowns. Its usual sailing was to the Orient, on a schedule of about thirty-five days at sea followed by four days back in home port for debarking and reloading.

I had thought Ken would have a longer on-shore induction into the Navy before going away on this floating self-contained environment. But it was to return from Alaska and leave shortly, with my man on board, for the far Pacific ports. While I, alone, changed diapers on a five-month baby and entertained an eighteen-month toddler in a motel efficiency apartment, I wondered what on earth had happened to my life!

Leaving the children with a recommended sitter, I bravely said goodbye to Ken a second time, knowing I faced a whole month of who-knew-what. Breckenridge wives had encouraged me toward their camaraderie, so I gladly tucked myself under the wing of a fellow wife-in-waiting. While the ship started to ease away from the pier, my new friend Pauline said, "C'mon! We've got to hurry!" We rushed in her car to the Golden Gate bridge, that massive orange skeleton that ties San Francisco peninsula to Marin County. Quickly we parked, ran past the toll attendant, and probably left him wondering why two slim-skirted, spike-heeled, hair-flying ladies chose his bridge for their escapade. The immensity of that bridge! Shedding our high heels, we ran as fast as we could along the east railing and got only as far as the first tower to wave frantically as the gray ship, far under us, slipped silently past the bridge to enter the water of the Pacific Ocean. Clutching our shoes, we ignored the shredded-stockinged feet and tried to cross to the other railing, but faced a variegated rippling curtain of cars. Only then did we feel the ocean coldness sting our own emotional chill. Early astronomers guessed the earth was round, and so did we as we later sat in the car at an overlook and eyed only a telltale plume of wispy exhaust against the horizon. Crazy life-supporting memories!

How uninteresting, an APO address! While I addressed numbers of daily letters to Daddy, telling him about the growth and development of his children, he was docking at supposedly exotic ports in Hawaii, Taiwan, Korea, Japan, the Philippines, Guam, and Alaska.

There was plenty to tell about finding the furniture and settling into our rented house, and about inquisitive Mark, but progress notes on our blonde sparse-haired daughter were scarce. Sometimes her squealing grated insensitively on my longing for adult conversation. Generally good natured, she allowed me to hold her for all bottles, but pushed away impatiently as soon as she finished. Often she would not burp, and then her tummy distended with subsequent agony; when I tried to be helpful she angrily gulped more air in an exaggerated manner, which of course magnified the discomfort. Medical examinations and ineffective changes of formula indicated she would just have to outgrow the problem.

At Jenny's seventh month, she finally began to grasp offered objects. At eight months she reticently reached out for a toy, but more often preferred to watch her gracefully moving hands while she lay on her back or side. Her big blue eyes unsmilingly noted activities and people.

At nine months Jenny was seventeen pounds and 27 inches. At ten months she still resisted reaching out for my hand or toys, but loved to get hold of paper and tear it to shreds. She showed little self-motivation and made no attempt to crawl, although I tempted her with a prize of paper. She could not sit alone. Mark and I spent countless hours encouraging and entertaining her, as did Daddy when he was home. Finally I would prop her up with pillows and make toys available while I worked and Mark disgustedly went off to play.

Despite such limitations, Jenny had ways of proving her independence. She pushed away if I held her too long, gulped air when dissatisfied, and grinned when I scolded. She learned to cluck loudly with her tongue, and that began a communication bond between us. When she slept she had a scary habit of pulling the blanket over her face, which caused perspiration and fast breathing. I experimented with blanket pins and dressed her in blanket sleepers. She kept that habit for many years.

Days were counted until the ship's return. Mark and I conversed with Daddy's picture daily while he kissed and fondled it. Neighbor Ruth kept a watchful eye and passed on to us favors that had been granted to her when she needed them in earlier surviving-alone years. I appreciated her concern because my closest friend lived many miles away.

It is supportive for young parents to have adult conversation. Mine was limited. Some nights I felt guilty for being so glad to finally have the children tucked in bed. Just as frequently Mark was kept up past his bedtime to keep me company. His vocabulary was confined to toddler gibberish, but at least it was company. He begged to "sleep in mama big bed," but I remained adamant against it so there would be no resentful feelings toward his Daddy when he came home and shared my bed.

On Jenny's first birthday she giggled merrily when Mark plopped a cloth over her head and played peek-a-boo. She now sat like a Buddha, and he'd pull her leg from under her and demand, "C'mon, 'Kenny'!" hoping to topple her and make her crawl. He wanted so badly to have a playmate.

Finally, at about twelve and a half months, she developed a strange crawl, but she'd forget how to do it day to day. Even had Ken and I known about the theory of Doman and Delacato — that brain activity is stimulated by cross-pattern creeping and crawling — we could not have tried harder to help Jenny learn how to crawl. We even purchased a large oval braided rug hoping it might help her gain traction that the tile didn't offer. Knowing it could encourage a bad habit, we tempted her with paper placed beyond her reach. She'd get on her hands and knees and rock back and forth until the distance was covered, then balance on one hand while the other claimed her prize.

Jenny played with Christmas cards but didn't rip them. It seemed, since she could play with such a dexterity-demanding object, that she should be able to feed herself, but not until well past thirteen months did she put even a cracker or piece of cereal to her mouth. She ate whatever was given her, but had a pronounced choking reflex which caused constant watching.

For months I waited eagerly for the mailman to place my husband's gift of shared life in the red-flagged box. We could exchange letters only when there was a port to receive and dispatch mail.

I gained consoling strength by attending weekly church services. It was the highlight of my week, and I wouldn't have missed it for anything. Jenny could have sat anywhere, because she was usually like a silent china doll perched on my lap, face framed in a perky white bonnet. She made no attempt to fondle jewelry, shoelaces, hat, hair, rosary beads, or any of the usual enticements for her age. Mark, of course, made up for her sedateness, so we sat in the family room during Mass.

One day we shared that room with a family of four children, one of whom was spastic. While I was comfortingly lulled by the liturgy, my thoughts pondered the challenges and rewards of parenthood. Ken and I suspected that Jenny had problems, though nothing had been diagnosed. In the meantime we were being granted months to simply accept our now giggling, delicate, long-fingered infant. I thanked God that our children were so normal.

I wonder, now, what it must be like to know from the beginning, as that other family probably did, that heartbreaking problems would pepper the days.

I was content to let God guide our lives; truly, I could not have taken that responsibility from Him. Our belief in God was a strong foundation for Ken and me. It determined our acceptance of life and all that it held. Our problems seemed minor compared to the other young family's. In fact, it seemed we had few problems at all.

§§ 3 §§

... setting our sails ...

To maintain proficiency, Navy personnel must practice underway procedures. I was elated to learn that the *USS Breckenridge* would be at San Diego for its two weeks of training and families were invited to ride the ship there from San Francisco. Besides the chance to share Dad's work life and to be together as a family, that experience nourished in us a love for traveling and seeking new knowledge. Among other skills, Daddy learned how to move injured people from one ship to another. Mark, Jenny and I lived in yet another motel and welcomed him on alternate evenings.

San Diego memories flood me when I use a green ten-inch vase and remember it filled with red roses. In celebration of my twenty-seventh birthday, Ken took the children to a flower shop and Mark proudly presented their gift to me at the motel.

Traveling was not always easy with the children, but our trek of San Diego was the forerunner of a legacy that cannot be measured in frustrations, nor in dollars. Not always did we plan the benefits we would abundantly receive from our wanderlust. We say, "Thanks to the Navy days." It took us away from our families and forced us to be independent while being dependent on each other. It gave us an awareness of the broader world and its people.

The ship was anchored out in the harbor rather than at a pier, so for our return trip up coast the families rode a dinghy to its side, whence steep ladder steps ascended the multi-storied facade. Sailors carefully carried children, toys, diaper bags, luggage, piñatas, and large, brightly-colored souvenir Mexican paper flowers up those steep steps to the deck, while wives followed.

When we sailed under the Golden Gate bridge into San Francisco Bay, I thought of the day Pauline and I had achingly waved to our men. Looking up at the bridge towers, I could have thought of the little ditty my father wrote in my childhood autograph book:

    Standing at the bottom,

> Gazing at the top,
> How will you ever get up
> If you never try?

I have lived by that prod. It has served as encouragement on many occasions. Despite death, my father lived on with me.

With Mark in his size-four avocado-green corduroy suit, and Jenny in an apricot dress, aproned in frilly white, which Ken had bought in the Orient, I again stood at the bottom of the pier and gazed up at the top, where my man stood on the deck of his ship. The monthly goodbyes had resumed, and we tearfully waved through the strains of the National Anthem.

By now Jenny was fourteen months, cutting molars, and throwing her food on the floor instead of putting it in her mouth. I tried to teach her to fold her hands in prayer before she attacked her food, but would have to persist one and a half years for results.

She increased her mobility with a strange "scooching" motion. Her brother helped her maneuver down the step to the garage, thence to the backyard. I inspected the yard carefully to guard against injury, but snails proved their persistence. Though Jenny seldom put her hands to her mouth, she did taste in her curiosity over the snails. Ughh!

Jenny rode the fine line between playing and tormenting. Mark created snaking lengths of toys into trains, and Jenny, with similar determination, tried to destroy them. He tried to imitate her effective "scooch," but she would not imitate his walking, or even standing. The "scooch" became a jumping crawl with knees held fast together and since she discarded her shoes wherever and whenever, she protected her toes by holding them up in the air. We've wished we'd taken home movies to show her resourcefulness.

My mother visited, and one day when we were at a fast-food drive-in she excitedly exclaimed, "Jenny's standing!"

Sure enough, in the backseat of the car, on a platform that created a full level area, our reticent fifteen-month-old child was indeed standing and reaching over the seat for more french fries. Our exclamations filled the car! Had we been making things too easy for Jenny? Thinking it might be true, we denied her easy access to everything. To no avail. She would be at least seventeen months old before she tried to stand again.

On one of those hot June days, while I sat under the peach tree reading *Advise and Consent*, Jenny crawled to my lawn chair and knelt up to the arm. A strange sound caught my attention and I was appalled to see blood coming from her mouth. The little tyke had bitten the chair arm, and when she pulled away, the flange of the metal arm tore loose her two bottom teeth. They were sticking straight out from her lacerated gum. My startled inclination was to finish pulling the teeth so she couldn't swallow them, but in that split second I envisioned her living several years with no bottom teeth. Instinctively I molded them back into the gum, grabbed her, and holding her with head tipped down so she wouldn't choke on the blood, ran to neighbor Ruth's. I dashed through her front room and on to her kitchen, to the sink. Poor Ruth! Knowing of Jenny's easy choking, she thought surely the worst had happened.

Ruth quickly gathered her purse and her two children and offered, "I'll take you to the Naval hospital!" There the young dentist admitted, "I've not seen such a case." After consultation with a partner, he advised, "Leave well enough alone, keep the wound clean as possible, feed her only soft food, and come back if necessary. Other than that, there is nothing we can do. The laceration does not need stitching."

Jenny's teeth eventually settled in firmly, the gum healed nicely, and there was no dental discoloration. And to think how close I came to removing them!

New families from the ship entered our life, and because I was stimulated, our children had new stimulations.

That, however, stirred new emotions. I had feelings for Mark then that have subsequently existed for each of our children. When more than one child was present, it inevitably happened that one, often the younger, received more attention. Jenny now often claimed that attention. When Mark was slighted, I tried to give him extra care and companionship, and yet encouraged his self-confidence to know that he could entertain himself. He needed to know that he was important and capable in his own right, no matter how much attention he did or didn't get. And I needed to accept the fact that he and Jenny would receive varying degrees of attention from outside the family. I felt it was imperative that I help our child understand his self-worth in the eyes of God so that he need never feel alone and unimportant. It was his right to learn that as early as possible. To instill that, I used encouragement, discipline, and companionship as my tools.

While I pursued parenting alone, I even had to remind myself that I, too, had a self-worth. I didn't have the daily positive psychological strokes that Ken seemed so unconsciously adept at offering me. When he was gone I had only self-discipline, and a sort of companionship from the children, but I didn't get the encouragement. I did get discouraged. And scared. Among other sentiments, I longed for Jenny to be normal, especially when I watched my friends' children. I can't imagine what it might have been like if I hadn't had my own built-in sense of self-worth in the eyes of God. I felt that Ken had similar strengths.

Together and alone, Ken and I tried to channel the best character into our children. For Jenny, though, we still put much of our attention to hoping she would learn to walk. Finally at seventeen months she learned to climb onto furniture and crawl down the garage step without Mark's help. She needed constant watching but little entertainment. Her giggles were a delight to me and to her Daddy on his all-too-brief visits.

By eighteen months Jenny stood up to furniture, and her only problem was not knowing how to sit back down; so again we awaited new learning. She loved to play in the kitchen cupboard under the sink. She'd throw everything out of it and crawl in. I didn't then, nor do I now, keep potentially poisonous supplies there, or in other low-level storage spaces.

We so enjoyed both our children and wondered how parents could play favorites. We found each child to be a treasure for different reasons. I think I hoped our children would be average, but it became more important that each simply meet his own potential at whatever level that would be. What is an average child? Is any child really average? Or even if some are, does any parent honestly consider his child average? A child lives as he must — he is being himself. We wanted to give ours that chance.

Life's challenges were met on a day-to-day basis, and it was comforting to believe that God never gives more than we are capable of handling. Sometimes we doubt that; we tend to forget that if we place our trust in God our fear can be alleviated.

As I salvaged wet slippers and books from the toilet, I thanked God that it was the last month I had to face alone without the daily companionship of my mate. There were only two months remaining in my third pregnancy, and I was caught up in the process of moving to a different rental house. I cleaned our house carefully so that it would be ready for a Marine couple who would move in as soon as we left. I had learned that those next renters were also expecting a baby, that the wife was in and out of the hospital with hemorrhaging, and that her husband worked and also cared for their three little children. It seemed I never had reason to wallow in self-pity. There was always someone whose problems seemed worse than mine.

Mark packed his own toys, while I repeated the role of many of my military sisters before me. The moving truck arrived, we loaded our household furnishings, and the children and I followed it to San Pablo, to 1800 Espanola Drive. There, from a family room and patio that overlooked San Pablo Bay, we had a super view of houses, city, water, mountains, and sky. I pointed out the trains, ships, and airplanes to Jenny. Mark ran from one view to another. Probably Jenny didn't understand any of it those first days, but our world was definitely enhanced with all those visual aids.

Finally the long-awaited day arrived when I bundled the children into our tan-and-brown '57 Plymouth and merrily set off for San Francisco's Fort Mason to meet Daddy's ship for the last time. Seagulls graced the sky and docking posts. I mentally filed the sights for future memories. The mighty little tugboat nosed its oversized gray charge perfectly and smoothly into its berth while the Navy band played welcoming music.

The gangplank lowered, and the disciplined meeting of loved ones dominated the scene. Daddy took his bonneted little girl into his arms, but respected the abilities of his manly two-year-old son as he walked through the ship's narrow corridors and up steep steel stairs to his quarters to gather his luggage and the treasured souvenirs.

Mark climbed on the bunk and peered out the round porthole. Ken gathered his gear. Then with a solemn look he dropped a bomb: "I have to make another month-long trip. My replacement has not arrived."

What could we do but set our sails to meet another of life's inevitable challenges?

§§ 4 §§

. . . she'll be all right . . .

During my final weeks of pregnancy I was encouraged and supported by the close-knit group of ship's officer's wives, one of whom showed special interest. That older friend hesitantly ventured, "I've never given birth. You speak of your baby being very active in utero. I've heard about that, but what does it feel like?"

This infant was an especially active one, so I invited my friend to place her hand on my abdomen and just keep it there awhile. Before long her face broke into a surprised smile as she felt an exaggerated movement. "Oh, my goodness! It must have turned over! I had no idea they could move that much!"

I cherish a decorative tin can she gave me, filled with delicious homemade fudge. It was humbling to share my pregnancy with her. I did not take my blessings for granted. I stood in complete awe of the whole life-giving process, even though some days seemed interminably difficult to deal with.

That was a long month to handle alone. I didn't even dare assume it would be Ken's last trip.

Then one day, one grand, glorious day, Jan Pugh, the Captain's wife, called and said, "I've got some news for you and I don't want you to have to wait one more minute to hear it. Ken's replacement will be here, so this definitely is his last trip!"

"Oh, happy day! Is it for real? Are you absolutely sure?"

I felt liberated! With unleashed emotions, I gathered visiting clothes and dressed Mark and Jenny. That always made them eager with anticipation, and Jenny waved, knowing she was going bye-bye. Off to Vallejo we went to see a new acquaintance. At the Naval base her street eluded me. Up and down the streets I searched, until *nothing* looked familiar. I stopped to ask a lady who was doing yard work, but she apologized, "I just moved to this base and I haven't learned the streets yet. Why don't you come in the house and call your friend for directions?"

After the call, the Good Samaritan asked, "Where are you from?"

I opened my mouth to tell her, but nothing came out. I couldn't remember. All I could think of was Lincoln, Nebraska, but that didn't seem right. That was so long ago.

Ridiculously, I asked, "Where am I now?"

"Vallejo, California."

"Oh. Oh, yes, now I remember! We live in San Pablo."

We laughed over that. She warned me that after a few more moves with the military it could get worse.

Memories. Memories. I learned from the experience of mothering alone, and from watching others. I will never underestimate the value of traditional family life. Modern living styles flirt with temptations that embrace the demise of family life. I watch them in frustration as I remember how I willingly struggled through separations so that we could rise above them and resume our traditional life.

After that visit I settled into my final solo days. Daddy's picture never had such importance as on that twenty-sixth birthday, when we adorned it with red, yellow, and white flowers. Little fingers fondling it would soon be running through his hair instead.

Anytime I sat down, Jenny crawled to me immediately and clutched my clothes while she stood by my chair. It seemed she might stand there indefinitely. I wondered if she felt protected. She had learned a true crawl, except that it was backwards, which tickled her greatly. She couldn't seem to remember the forward crawling motion she had once learned.

Many times Jenny lacked understanding, and I wondered how much comprehension she really had. Imagine my elation one day when she crawled to me and I felt her diaper. "It's wet. Go get a clean diaper, Jenny!" Off she crawled to her bedroom. Following quietly, I saw her go to her diaper drawer. Then later, when I talked about Daddy, she immediately crawled to the window. I was sure she was looking for him!

Nonetheless, concerns crept in more frequently, perhaps because I was seeing other children more often. Beth's little boy was only five months and crawled all over the place. I made comparisons, even though I shouldn't have. Ken and I would have to learn, through the years, not to compare Jenny to her own age group unless we wanted to face heartaches.

I watched Jenny struggle to learn the simplest functions, even to feed herself with her fingers. Never would such accomplishments be taken for granted in subsequent children. During it all she was reprimanded for misbehavior. We persistently tried to channel her into good habits, and from the very beginning that was absolutely essential — although we didn't know it at the time. She grew to be a creature of habit, more so than the normal person, and she needed that groundwork of discipline. We could not have tolerated misbehavior from her any more than we could have from our other children.

Habit training needed consistency, and it benefited from each inception. Habit training needed example and discipline from Ken and me. For example, we cherished our quiet evenings for music and reading, so the children were trained that their after-supper hours could be quietly special also. When they were clean and tucked in their sleepers, they listened to records, looked through picture books and magazines, or were read to, depending on their abilities. By 7:30 they were in bed. It was good for them — and for us.

Of course, while the ship plied the Pacific, my evenings alone were too long, but the promise of the future aided my job of disciplining.

Three weeks before birth, we gladly became a complete family. But as fate would have it, Ken had the car and was on overnight duty at Treasure Island when labor commenced. At least he wasn't in Japan! We arrived at Oakknoll Naval Hospital with only an hour to spare before Paul was born at 5:55 A.M..

Mark readily accepted his nine-pound, four-ounce brother, although he'd had visions of an instant playmate. Jenny's first reactions were wonder and fright. Wide-eyed, she looked at the infant and then broke into frightened loud cries when Paul tested his own lungs.

There soon were new reminders that Jenny was slow. Paul developed by leaps and bounds. At two months he greedily reached for Christmas tree baubles while Jenny at twenty-two months finally took her first real steps alone. Glory hallelujah! It was the best Christmas gift we received. Still, there was a month of practicing before she accomplished an ease in solo walking.

With walking accomplishments, she seemed almost like a normal child, except there was no attempt at words, not even one.

Potty training resulted in much frustration for her and me. It took until three and a half years to know some success, which means I spent far too many unneccessary hours trying to mold that child into normal development. If only we had known then what we knew later: Neither her mind nor her muscles were ready!

Jenny's pursuit of pleasures followed various channels. Of course, it continued in the kitchen cupboards. What silverware Mark hadn't taken to use in the dirt, she slyly spirited off. And from the clothes hamper she adorned her neck and shoulders with an odd assortment of finery. Dolls, often naked, had seldom been out of sight, but now, as she watched me with the baby, she wanted to keep them clothed and bathed.

And Jenny teased, sometimes mercilessly. Not maliciously did she take toys, or wreck Mark's towers and trains; she was merely caught up in delight. That delight turned to screaming rage when the baby started crawling and, like a bulldozer, treated her like so much dust. That may have been the beginning of her preference to play alone, and usually only with girl-type toys.

Having been away from close relatives for two years, we were anxious to show them our hardly-like-a-baby-anymore. Could we manage a cross-country vacation with three little ones? We checked our budget and the car. And we checked our emotions. Short jaunts had seemed easy enough. The decision was: If we could tolerate the children at home, we could surely tolerate them for longer hours in the car.

With visions of Iowa cornland and Nebraska's Bohemian Alps in mind, we gathered the necessary travel accouterments. Ken made a platform to cover the backseat floor of the car, thus creating a two-tiered sleeping arrangement and play area. The baby's sleeping space was provided in the front seat.

One suggestion by well-meaning friends should have been scrapped. They lightly sedated their wee ones. We gave it a try. Never again! For a day we had hyper-crying, uncontrollable children. We knew what ours were like and were used to their personalities, so thereafter we dealt with them on trips as we did at home. No medication except an occasional pill for motion sickness.

The relatives showed proper interest in Mark, Jenny, and Paul. Perhaps more so in Mark.

"Why are his legs so short?" my brother asked.

"I didn't know they are." I answered. "What difference would it make, since there's nothing we can do to change them."

I acknowledged the source of the remark. Brothers don't change. The topics for teasing simply change with the years.

I did look closely at Mark. Concerns had hinged so much on Jenny all those months that I had unquestionably accepted Mark's steady progress. Yet, in comparison to his back, his legs did have a shorter appearance. It was obvious that his Dad was built the same way; even a tall man's shirt didn't always stay tucked in. I easily continued to accept our growing boy's physique and offered a prayer that he grow up in the likeness of his sensitive, caring father. Big shoes to fill!

Ken, with his usual practical wit, told my brother, "Mark's legs go all the way to the ground, so they can't be too short."

It was a good trip, and we took Uncle Danny, newly graduated from high school, back to California for a visit. We wanted our children to develop a sense of family beyond just our nuclear group.

We also were accompanied by chicken-pox germs. Mark broke out first. Then Jenny, with a harder case of many lesions in the diaper area and on the face. When hers subsided, husky Paul burst out with pox from head to toe. We encased his hands in socks and kept close vigil against scratching, but he scarred and carries those scars now as an adult.

Jenny at two and a half was a dainty twenty-six pounds. I sewed dresses for her, with pockets that she crammed full of anything that would fit or overflow. She learned to put on her socks — after they were found! Quietly she'd stash such small items into elusive sacks and boxes. She preferred to clump around in our bigger shoes.

We wondered anew at Jenny's faulty judgment, but watched in amusement when she contended with her training pants. If she happened to get both legs into one leg hole, she disgustedly yanked the pants off, tossed them aside, and got a new pair. Or if she looked in the new pants and the leg holes were vertical, she'd toss them away and keep checking clean ones until the holes were horizontal to meet her needs. It reminded me of the carpenter who rejected nails: "The head is on the wrong end — they're for the other side of the wall." The same kind of reasoning.

Many times in her life Jenny encountered difficulties because of faulty judgment. We counseled however we could at the time and were saddened when it became apparent she had reached her limit. Comprehension too often seemed unfulfilled, like a closed flower bud that for some unknown reason cannot blossom. The intrinsic beauty of the plant remained all-important, so nourishment continued.

Prayer life took on meaning of sorts. Jenny folded her hands during meal prayers. We were especially fond of post-meal prayers, because it was the signal to the children that they could leave the table. Much of our family communication is at dinner, and we've had some wonderful long conversations because they learned that discipline at an early age.

At cribside, Jenny knelt for night prayers because she saw Mark do it, and soon Paul. Also, she watched Mark lade his bed with toy trucks and cars. Paul filed his with books. So Jenny threw every doll she owned into her crib each night and threw them all out in the morning.

That fall we kept Jenny at our side when we attended the Seattle World's Fair and visited Mike Knowles, a man who had saved her Grandpa's life in 1920 when he fell down an ice crevasse on a hunting trip in Alaska. Pacific Northwest atmosphere caused Jenny an asthmatic reaction. She responded to medication from an area naval dispensary, but we decided not to press our luck.

Leaving the city, we stopped briefly to visit other friends at their home. Mark, not quite four, learned a valuable lesson that he told about through the years. He liked a little toy car at their house, so he hid it in his pocket. Many blocks later we saw him playing with it, and he reluctantly confessed. Back we drove through the streets, lecturing all the way.

"No, we won't go to the house with you!"

"But I don't want to go alone!"

"You will, though. Just tell them you're sorry you took the car."

That was the second and last time we were aware of any such pilfering. He passed the word on to his brothers and sisters: "Don't do it! You won't like it!"

Jenny's health improved the farther south we drove. Since Ken still had unused leave days, we bypassed home and visited Carmel-by-the-Sea. Upon our returning home, mixed emotions were prompted when we learned about the Cuban crisis. Had Ken been on duty, he might have been assigned to one of the deployed ships. At that time no one knew the situation would be relatively short-lived, so of course I felt relieved that he had been spared more sea duty; but we were not ones to shirk military duty. I was glad the decision had been out of our hands, especially since we had recently suffered a severe heartache when a dear friend of ours was an early casualty in then-little-heard-of Laos. His mother in Iowa had already lost a husband and son to lightning.

"Where on earth are Laos and Vietnam?"

"Why Jerry?"

Our children learned early about death. We tried to help Mark understand why Jerry couldn't visit us anymore. We remembered him during prayers for our deceased relatives and friends, and continued to pray through the years. We treated death as a part of life and did not make up stories. Now we're glad, especially for Jenny's sake. Her life has embraced older people and some handicapped children with shorter life-spans. She has lost some very close friends.

We settled back into routine, and what havoc one preschool child didn't think of another did. They kept mother on her toes. What Jenny lacked in originality, she made up for by squealing, inflections in her sounds, and nods or shakes of her head. There were no words. Dolls created much of that wordless child's play. Datt, as both boys called their Dad, built Jenny a sturdy white rail-sided doll crib.

The near flowerbed served as play arena for toy construction vehicles and doll dishes. Better to have the mess close than to wonder what they were doing. Jenny preferred to play alone but did consent to let Mark pull her in the red wagon. Invariably she fell sound asleep, even on short rides in the small backyard.

Birthdays became special occasions, always with choice of food, cake with candles, cards, letters, and gifts. A particular gift from Mark's godparents started a new trend. *A Fox in a Box*. Not a real fox, but the book. Our shopping purchases often included nineteen- or-twenty-nine-cent child books chosen by searching little hands; but Mark's gift was quality-bound and survived innumerable readings. Books were important to Ken and me, but now we were stimulated to join book clubs for our children.

We set a priority for books, but also needed other material belongings. Since medical education bills remained to be paid, I was glad that Donna had introduced us to Goodwill stores. For Jenny's third birthday we shopped at one and found the perfect little red tricycle at a price we could afford. (We didn't know it would be several years before she could ride a trike).

Three years old. Twenty-nine pounds. Thirty-eight inches tall. Waist twenty inches. Chest twenty inches. Head eighteen inches. Twenty teeth.

Jenny, with her brothers' help, excitedly delivered decorated birthday cupcakes to the neighborhood children.

On the surface much seemed to be all right with Jenny. So why the nagging doubts? Friends and relatives continued to assure us that some day Jenny would talk. They were reminded of other children who had been slow.

"Yes," I said, "But didn't they say at least some words? Did they not walk until twenty-three months? Sit before eleven months? Did they show relatively good judgment and reactions?"

Just what caused the persistent feelings? Jenny had learned to sit and to walk. She was eating well, and playing. There had been little success with toilet training. She desired playing alone. Routine medical checkups caused no undue alarm. Were we being overly-concerned parents?

While we lived these thoughts during our quickly passing final months in California, we were aware of our neighbors' heartache. After being driven from their home during the war, they had made the difficult decision to leave their loved ones and emigrate from Germany in search of a better life. They met varied obstacles to obtaining visas, but finally the father was allowed to leave. A year later the mother and two sons could join him in the United States. But when that time came, authorities refused to grant a visa for the five-year-old son, claiming that he was retarded. It was shocking news to the mother. Yes, she knew the child was slow, but she didn't suspect retardation. His slowness had been attributed to childhood illnesses of whooping cough, measles, and mastoid infection.

Relatives, friends, the consul, and other officials counseled. After receiving assurances that the boy would be taken care of and would eventually get to join them, mother and oldest son joined the father in the United States. They worked hard and saved their money, but there was always some reason why their son, with his special needs, was not allowed to join them. They became United

States citizens as soon as possible, knowing then, according to official sources, that they could have their son.

Such was not to be. Hopes were raised and dashed. Bills were introduced in Congress to no avail. A bill eventually was passed to allow special-needs children under twelve to join their immigrant parents. Unfortunately their son had just turned twelve. I wonder how our neighbors stood the heartache! The child never did get to join his family. To my knowledge he continued to live in a special home in his country, financed by his parents.

Many people do not understand the strong bond that can develop between parents and their handicapped child. But I, as mother of a special child, can guess how difficult it must have been for that mother to leave her child.

We were in a reverse situation from our neighbors in that we were the ones having doubts about our child's ability while others reassured us that she was probably normal. In a way we were grateful for those assurances.

When Uncle Don and Aunt Clarice visited, they gave Jenny a frilly blue dress and ruffled white hat that tied under her chin. Every Sunday Jenny proudly pulled the hat from its white square box and noisily indicated that she wanted it put on her head. She carried a little red purse and wore white dress gloves and was not satisfied until all was in order before she'd get in the car to go to church. She did seem normal in some respects.

While suspecting that she might have special needs, we found it difficult to plan our future. Ken's commitment to the Navy would soon be finished. So in April we admitted her to the naval hospital for a four-day checkup. We wanted to visit her but did not — we wanted them to have a chance to observe Jenny without us causing interruption in her behavior.

After the four days of observation and examinations, we were relieved to hear their diagnosis: Slow neuromuscular development but normal intelligence. They seemed to think she would outgrow any problems we thought she had.

The final weeks of Navy went quickly. We tried to decide where to settle next. We hoped to live closer to relatives. Letters describing medical practices and towns were studied. Some sounded good, some terrible, and some enticing. We had become fond of California, even the wintry morning fogs that so depressed one of my friends, and we wondered some days if we should remain there. At any rate, when could we return?

Our children were young, and we had not needed to get involved in the school or community. Those were our halcyon days. We're glad we took advantage of those early years for garnering free time for hikes, picnics, sightseeing, and whatever activity intrigued us. We set a pattern for life — a pattern that allowed for including our children in most of our activities. From other parents we gathered ideas on child rearing. When I heard a neighbor profess her goal of teaching her children to hate black-skinned people, I was appalled! I hoped our family would be accepting of all cultures.

We were on the threshold of an unrelenting life. Relaxation time would be at a premium once Ken started his medical practice and the children started school.

Ken suggested, "Let's go home through Canada! Let's have a summer fling. Let's even go to Texas and see Hop and Donna!"

We have not remembered all the ball games, television shows, shopping trips, or play sessions with friends, but our family conversations are peppered with reminiscences of trips, traveling visits, and new experiences. While the children learned to be perceptive travelers, Ken and I built up tolerance to deal with them in close confinement.

As yet we had not chosen a town for Ken to practice in, so we were heading for we knew not where in the Midwest. The continuing feeling that Jenny might need help caused us to consider small towns within easy commute of a university city. Out of hundreds of potential towns, it seemed awesome that one particular new place would become home. We prayed for a right choice.

Many days were spent in the car that summer, and Jenny seemed tolerant. Of course, she continued to have her same companions, including dolls, only in a confined area. Meeting numerous relatives and friends presented no apparent problems; she merely answered their queries with squeals, or more often ignored them. They noticed she had her own special world that none of us could enter, and that already Paul acted older.

We'll never know what her feelings were those months. Though three and a half years old, she could not talk. We could only guess her thoughts.

Jenny did seem to learn by seeing. How lucky for her that our family developed early traits that enhanced her life!

§§ 5 §§

... did I hear right? ...

We chose Edgerton, Wisconsin, a town of four thousand, about thirty miles from Madison.

The townspeople welcomed us readily; many made our adjustment to a new lifestyle easier and would see us through difficult days ahead. In fact, they started right away by lending us essentials for camping in our empty rental house, because once again our furniture was lost, this time for only ten days. The truck broke down in one of the Dakotas.

The first year and a half in Edgerton was one of the busiest and most emotional times in our lives. The time element was the first big challenge. In California, weekends had been a joy of family activities. In private practice, they were now sometimes a nightmare of emergency calls, especially during the summer. From the very beginning we stressed that patients must have first priority. I tried to wait meals until Daddy got home, but often had to relent. Some days he hardly saw his children.

While Ken reconciled to his new work, the children and I settled into new patterns as their needs changed with age.

Just when it seemed everything was nicely under control in our small three-bedroom home, Jenny all of a sudden exhibited a terrible fright, gathered her bed toys into her arms, left her own bed, and claimed Paul's crib. We never learned why. Thank goodness it suited Paul's fancy to be allowed to sleep in a big bed with his brother.

For a few nights that was satisfactory. Then Jenny suddenly reversed her decision and wanted the big bed. Naturally, Paul had his own conflicting ideas. And Mark, almost five, started having nightmares as so many young children do. Bedtime was a terrible ordeal. To top it off, one night Jenny screeched and screamed and cried in holy terror until I finally put her in our bed for soothing. That was a mistake. She liked it. And every night she pulled the same tirade. I resorted to rocking her to sleep out of desperation for a solution.

Shortly thereafter, Jenny developed a horrible gag reflex with vomiting. (That presented problems for years.) We looked for reasons. To begin with, she seemed to do it if we reprimanded her, or gave her too little attention. We wondered if the summer had been too strenuous, or if she was distressed with having to live in a different house. How could we know? Maybe she was reacting to the adjustments and rebellions that each of us was hurdling. Mark, though not a jealous boy, dealt with a tiger of a little kid brother and a little sister who now required much additional attention, and he was old enough to want to play with neighbor boys. I resented the too-frequent companionship between neighbor playmates and our sons. Also, Ken's life was no longer our own — we all had to play second fiddle to the patients.

Jenny withdrew into herself even more and spent most of her hours indoors. Then she took on an awesome fear of dogs, so Daddy or I had to accompany her outdoors whenever she would go.

Despite these obstacles, Jenny played, usually with her dolls and alone.

About that time the University of Wisconsin at Madison dedicated its new Joseph P. Kennedy, Jr. Laboratories for the study of mental retardation. Ken and I attended the symposium — not to learn about retardation, which hadn't reared its ugly head yet, but to keep abreast of what might be offered in the area of education in case we or any of Ken's patients might need it. We learned there was a lot of biochemistry involved in the study of retardation.

Two days later, President John F. Kennedy's assassination was indelibly etched with current happenings on individual memories. Because his sister Rosemary was retarded, he had promoted research in the care and education of the handicapped. We might feel it was long overdue, but everything does have to start sometime, and better later than not at all.

Adapting to our new lifestyle, and to the altered Jenny, was recognized by Gramma P. as not being very easy. Imagine our excitement to learn that she and Uncle Keith were coming for Thanksgiving and "don't buy a thing because we're bringing it all!" Two ducks, a goose, cranberry sauce, fruit salad, breads, kraut, candy, apples, and heaven knows what all. It was just great! We felt totally wrapped in love.

As the weeks passed we adjusted to the busyness. Ken showed an amazing capacity to find time for all facets of his day. Perhaps it seemed such because he rarely complained, so valuable time was not wasted carrying problems from one part of a day into another. He had noon lunch with us whenever possible. And the children were welcomed to be near him at every available opportunity.

Ken and I did not neglect our own adult needs for entertainment. Since the children were in bed by 7:30 P.M., we could socialize after that and not be missed.

New experiences evolved for Jenny. Before her first haircut, I pointed out, "Look, Jenny, that's the house where Mavis will cut your hair and make you pretty." I had talked to the beautician about Jenny's limited vocabulary and what to expect. Mavis scheduled her at a quiet time when the boys could go along. Jenny felt important. The preliminaries paid off.

Jenny, Little Jennywen. Wordless. Increasingly difficult to deal with. Now a severe test to our patience and resourcefulness. Her language of screeches and screams was as harsh to our ears as was Eliza Doolittle's cockney to Henry Higgins's ears in *My Fair Lady*. But Jenny was ours, and we had developed a strong love for her.

We teased that perhaps she could join the Discalced Carmelites, that order of cloistered nuns who remain essentially speechless and wear sandals — except Jenny would want to go barefoot. I gained strange consolation in thinking about those people who spend their days in quiet. They represented a peacefulness and reliance on God that I envied. I was sure we could all say much less and the world would not be a worse place because of our silence. Yes, there had been many times when I'd said words that I later regretted.

I was glad, though, that I had a choice of whether to talk. I wanted that same choice for Jenny. We must help her learn to talk and to overcome the fears that had recently pestered her. Ken and I both worked with her whenever she was near, and we often held her on our laps, encouraging mimicry of sounds.

Partly because of Jenny's fear of dogs, we got a mutt from the humane society. It shattered Jenny's world momentarily, but her emotion of fear was quickly displaced by anger and frustration because Brownie snatched doll things, Jenny's dearest possessions.

It was enough that she often had to retrieve them from Mark's toy tractor loader! That pet alleviated Jenny's fear of dogs, but the milkman, mailman, and visitors eventually feared for their lives, so Brownie didn't live with us very long.

Unexpected help for Jenny came when we decided to buy a set of Childcraft books and thus met the woman who taught nursery school. I wasn't convinced that a very young child needed to be in a school environment, so Mark had not attended, although his sometimes inaccurate speech patterns might have been corrected. And, of course, Jenny seemed totally incapable of surviving in a structured activity. However, at the teacher's encouragement, we enrolled Jenny for the final eleven sessions remaining before summer. There was no pressure put on Jenny to accomplish. The teacher offered her class merely as a trial to see what our child could do in a different environment.

At school Jenny stayed mostly to herself, but gradually became more receptive to others in the class and even in the neighborhood, though she still played solo. Her paperwork hung on our refrigerator despite total lack of creativity. She could only make meaningless marks with her crayons. When Mark colored with her and Paul, he continued to express impatient disgust with their ineptness.

I defended, "It's okay, they have to learn."

He replied, "It won't do them any good 'cause they'll just 'rurn' and have to die anyhow."

"Mark, that word is 'learn.' "

Here I was, concerned about a child who couldn't talk and one whose speech was not always proper, and he was already thinking about death? There was, obviously, much that I had to learn about children! He did not explain to me why he expressed that fatalistic attitude. He just kept coloring. I wonder if it had anything to do with his nightmares.

We passed up no opportunity for stimulation for ourselves or our children. But we learned quickly that if we wanted to be uninterrupted by patients we had to leave town for some of our pleasures. On Dad's afternoon off, with picnic hamper in hand, we followed the roads to one of the many interesting experiences that southern Wisconsin has to offer. Even when days were busy and there seemed little time for pleasures, there were still plenty available. We grabbed moments at every chance. Sometimes those moments were close at hand, as close as being greeted by a friendly hello after church.

Accordingly did elderly Mr. and Mrs. Welch enter our life and bring joy of friendship to Jenny's. Watching her initial reaction to him and to other men, we worried that Jenny might be too ready with her affection. Gently we guided her into acceptable behavior without thwarting genuine friendship. Mr. Welch and his wife became dear friends to Jenny and us, and often they came to our home for Sunday breakfast.

When summer came, there was no more nursery school. Jenny's problems seemed too big for us to handle alone, so we made an appointment with the pediatric department at the university medical center in Madison. That led to coordinated appointments in other departments that dealt with speech and hearing, neurology, and psychology.

When the reports started arriving, our emotions took on new dimensions.

A neurologist reported: Upper-body muscle hypotonia. In other words, those muscles did not have normal tone. Another said: There is definitely a problem. Not a matter of intellectual retardation, but a mental block which somehow must be penetrated if she is going to be acceptable to society.

Then we heard the words aphasia and autism. Words took on frightening aspects when they affected us personally. We started collecting articles from newspapers and magazines. We sent away for information. Our home library began to include answers from such places as Stanford University and the Institute for the Deaf in St. Louis. Jenny was not deaf, but some facilities overlap services.

Our concern was no small thing. The more we learned, the less confident we became. We felt we were badly lacking in patience to deal with Jenny's evolving, difficult-to-deal-with personality. Yet, the professionals with whom we dealt seemed to think we were handling the problem in a most satisfactory way.

While we waited for more reports, we continued to discipline Jenny as we did the boys, expecting her to do certain chores and exhibit as good a behavior as possible. She brought in the mail and the milk. She put away toys and helped set the table. She ran errands and developed pride in helping to take care of her own clothes. Though she couldn't speak, she did understand. At four and a half, she finally was completely toilet-trained, day and night.

Jenny's compulsive personality soon bloomed. Now things had to be just so. Bedtime brought out the worst. First she insisted her door be open and the bathroom night-light on. Later suddenly it was reversed; she'd run into the bathroom, angrily shut off the light, and then slam her door shut. Doll clothes had to be a certain way; so did silverware on the table, and so, it seemed, did everything! We prayed while she whined, cried, fussed, screamed, and never talked in words.

Through it all we continued to welcome houseguests and visitors, looked at potential homes to buy, snooped the countryside, admitted Mark for a tonsillectomy, and bought his clothes for kindergarten. And within me I was beginning to feel new life again. Ken and I recognized that our days were already busy, but it never occurred to us to reject this new pregnancy. We trusted God's judgment.

Eventually the summons came to hear the final reports concerning Jenny's testings. We hoped to hear some positive suggestions as to how to deal with Jenny. We didn't really expect that she had any physical disabilities because she always seemed so healthy. Her lab reports had revealed no problems. Perhaps there would be no reason for any real concern.

Leaving the household and child affairs to our competent sitter, Ken and I drove to Madison. We talked about various things, including our enjoyment of southern Wisconsin's scenery. We never tired of seeing it. We recalled we had chosen a proximity to a university city in case Jenny might need consultations. Ken said, "Well, here we are, going for another of those consultations. What do you suppose they'll tell us this time?"

I dared to hope. Months before, in California, we had been told that Jenny would probably outgrow her problems. In recent months our fears had been raised to fever pitch and then been allowed to subside. Sometimes Jenny seemed more capable. Yes, perhaps we were just being overly concerned. Or at least I was. Ken always seemed to have such a comfortable grasp on life. I felt protected in his presence.

We registered at the office, waited to be called, and were then escorted to a small consultation room. A woman entered. We had not seen her before. She sat across the desk from us and briefly scanned a file that was presumably Jenny's. She looked at Ken and me, and then it was her fate to say, "Your daughter is retarded; it is very possible that she may never even learn the alphabet."

Did I hear right? Could that be? I wanted to hit the woman so hard she'd regret saying those words for the rest of her life! She must have the wrong file! That couldn't be Jenny! What must Ken have been thinking? Did the woman even *know* our child? Did the stranger say anything encouraging? Did she even say *anything* after that? How dare she dash all hope!

We were then led to another department. I do not remember talking, even to Ken. Was it really black as a starless night or were there lights?

I tried to listen attentively when Dr. Klové told us about their findings. Somehow his words were gentler and held an element of hope while he guided us through the reports.

Essentially the reports stated that there had been organic brain damage; the reduction in language abilities was more pronounced in expressive than receptive areas of function; that she was a pleasant, cooperative child and her parents seemed to understand and accept her and were anxious to do whatever they could to help her. Her IQ was shown as sixty-six. Less understandable to us were her results of psychological testing: Basal age, twenty months. Vineland Social Maturity Scale, social quotient seventy-six. Developmental Drawing test, zero. Picture vocabulary test, IQ less than fifty-five. Parts of motor encoding subtest of Illinois Test of Psycholinguistic Abilities, age equivalent less than 2.6. What Ken and I clearly heard was that Jenny was diagnosed as retarded, with an uncertain educational potential.

The reports were bad enough but nothing so traumatic as the hatchet woman's. Dr. Klové at least held out hope. I have always been grateful for that.

In his report to us he wrote: "I don't think there is anything to be gained by considering a boarding school. You seem to love this little girl very much. That is a most important factor. You are disciplining her and helping her as best you can. I suggest you proceed along the same path. I do suggest speech and language training here at the University. Don't force her. Accept her noises as sufficient. As yet she seems incapable of forming words. Also, I think she should attend some kind of nursery school. After twelve months bring her back for re-evaluation. . . ."

At home we put less emphasis on making her mimic sounds. We read that two researchers, Doman and Delacato, advocated cross-pattern creeping and crawling for some handicapped people and for children. They believed that brain areas are stimulated by certain body actions, especially those provided by crawling. Recalling that Jenny, as an infant, never did develop a traditional crawl, we started crawling with her in her now acceptable cross-pattern style. If there were any truth to that theory, was it too late for Jenny? We didn't know but could try. Often, while I prepared supper, I watched the crawling giggling train of three little children following their engine Daddy. Throughout the day Jenny was encouraged in crawling.

Other stimulations continued. We kept Jenny at our side when we sought them within our own home or found them in Wisconsin's land and its people. Jenny stood on a stool at the clinic and watched Daddy put stitches in Paul's chin. She stood on the kitchen chair and watched me freeze or can foods and mix goodies. She cut out real cookies. Through it all I begged for fortitude.

One day it was time to hang tiny baby clothes on the clothesline to dry.

"Are we going to get our baby brother?" Mark asked.

"Hey, remember? We don't care if it's a boy or a girl. But God willing, we hope it'll be strong and healthy like you boys have prayed each night."

Our Saturday's child was born on September 19, 1964, eight pounds, six and three-fourths ounces. Katrina Maria. Katie. Little did we know how that child would enrich Jenny's life. What a loss it would be had she not been born!

Three wide-eyed heads bobbed over the seat of the car when we took our new treasure home from the hospital.

"She's so tiny! Can she play?"

Four days later Ken drove Jenny thirty miles north to her first speech therapy in Madison. After that I continued to take her. On those twice-weekly speech days I nursed Katie before leaving home, and again when I returned at noon after her morning nap. Mark was in morning kindergarten, so it was only Paul who felt a parental absence. He had to get used to baby-sitters, and we felt it caused him some tension.

Somewhere there is a speech therapist who deserves a great deal of credit. Jenny learned to call her TuTu. Susan Prather. Susan was successful if she maintained five minutes' concentration from Jenny during those forty-five-minute sessions. As the weeks passed, those minutes of concentration increased.

Miss Prather invited me to watch through the mirror-window anytime. I tried at first, but it was like watching a caged animal. Jenny banged the chairs against the table, sat down, stood up, switched the light on and off, opened and shut the door, busy, busy, busy. I cried and retreated to the waiting room. Intermittently through the weeks I went to the watching window. Out of all that persistence and play structure representing our household, I saw success happening.

"Baby. Eat. Up. Wet. Hat. Paul. Thank You. Poo. Shoe."

It seemed like a miracle. The words were not pronounced readily or clearly, but we could tell what they were. TuTu worked with determination and velvet gloves. In nursery school Jenny was free to enter play situations at her whim. But this one-on-one speech therapy demanded cooperation. It was very difficult for Jenny.

By Christmas we had much to be thankful for. With her Play-Doh Jenny spent hours slaving at the stove Daddy had made her, creating pan after pan of cookies for her family of eight dollies. We hoped she was listening to the fairy-tale and Mother Goose records that Paul played again and again on the little record player.

I didn't let Jenny's problems consume my entire thoughts or days, and of course Ken couldn't either. We hosted friends and relatives, attended church and cultural events. I worked with the church and hospital auxiliary, recruited for the Bloodmobile. Many of my activities took place in our own home, so the children were not excluded. Otherwise I traded baby-sitting so our children had playmates. I was stimulated, and I think it reflected in our children.

When I shared conversations with other mothers, it sparked new understanding for me and helped prepare for future steps of child rearing. A neighbor said her daughter expressed fear and refused to ride the school bus when she was young. She came to find out a brother had told her the bus was going to carry her away someday and never bring her back. Would Ken and I have similar tales to relate? Would we look for real meanings behind our children's aberrant behavior as they grew up?

I did not dream our tale would be about how we reared a retarded child we could live with. One who would learn manners and obedience. Who would learn to use her talents. Who would prove she could learn to write and read the alphabet, not just speak it. No small task!

We cannot take all the credit. There are dozens of teachers and friends and relatives who made a difference.

§§ 6 §§

... if so, so be it ...

Jenny had attended twenty sessions of speech therapy in Madison and was almost five years old. Her therapists definitely felt that Jenny was mentally retarded besides being aphasic. Aphasia is the inability to use or understand spoken or written language.

I wrote my mother, "If so, so be it."

If it was to be, we had no alternative but to accept and do the best we could.

The written report from the speech department stated:

> Jennifer exhibited a great deal of negative behavior in the initial therapy sessions and seemed unable to function cooperatively within the structure of therapy. Although she came willingly into the therapy room, she began to react negatively toward the therapist and the situation soon after the session started. Such behavior as screaming, spitting and turning out the lights was typical. Jennifer's infrequent and at times inappropriate vocalizations consisted of jargon and word approximations. To indicate her approval, disapproval and needs, she frequently used a high pitched whine with inflectional variations. Occasionally she was able to follow simple commands and directions. Inner language appeared to be intact on a concrete level, illustrated by Jennifer's ability to imitate routine household activities through play with doll furniture.
>
> Cooperation and attitudes of the parents: Dr. and Mrs. Pavlik have both shown considerable concern and are quite willing to follow any suggestions given. Dr. Pavlik appears to be more realistic about Jennifer's prognosis. Though both are frustrated with Jennifer's behavior, they feel her negativism should be met with firmness. Despite their frustrations, they show affection toward Jennifer and attempt to stimulate language development.
>
> Jennifer's behavior showed some signs of tolerating the structure of therapy. She became more sociable and attention held sometimes for almost thirty minutes. Quickly, though, she could revert to her

pre-undesirable actions. Those fluctuations of behavior were noted at home also. They seemed to occur if too much pressure was placed on her.

Recommendation: Continue speech therapy twice weekly and try to place her in a nursery school program for language-impaired children.

They did not think we could consider the possibility of kindergarten for the coming year.

Keeping in mind their suggestion to place Jenny with other language-impaired children, we kept her in the local nursery school for the rest of January until we could check out other possibilities.

Mark's days were filled with kindergarten, learning to iceskate, and playing, but he asked permission to visit Jenny's nursery school.

"Good idea, Mark!" I said. "How about if Dad takes you tomorrow?"

It proved wise to allow Mark to enter Jenny's world. He talked to her about her day's happenings. Because his speech usage still needed correcting, we had to keep alert to what Mark inadvertently passed on. We needed his good example for Jenny to learn from, and for Paul, whose pronunciation was precise and who picked up new words quickly, right or wrong. Paul was so precocious it seemed he could have shared some of his actions and knowledge with Jenny and each would have been normal.

It was interesting listening to Paul, and listen to him we must all his waking hours. He seemed to talk incessantly and asked questions by the hundreds. He apparently feared nothing except the tub filling with water, which caused him wide-eyed terror.

The search for a school for Jenny commenced. Ken heard about Kiddie Kamp in Madison, but it was for residents of that city. We found no other near ones except nursery schools for normal children. Then one day we heard about Happy House in Janesville and asked for an appointment to see it.

Mrs. Hopkins — Hoppy — that dear lady who created Happy House, recognized a need, moved her family upstairs, and turned the main floor of their wooden-frame two-story home into a nursery school for handicapped children. A makeshift ramp for the physically handicapped led to the porch.

When Ken and I visited Happy House I reacted with new personal heartaches. As a student nurse, I had toured a state mental institution and saw some of the malformed bodies and minds that lay behind those doors. Now at Happy House I was seeing children who presented similar problems, but these children were being cared for by parents in their own homes, not in institutions. While we talked, effervescent, middle-aged Hoppy placed a blind child on my lap. At the same time, I watched an aide and a volunteer help others with debilitating afflictions.

Frightened, I wondered, "Can it be that all this is to become a part of Jenny's life?" I felt like sobbing. But we weren't about to dodge the problem — it had been suggested that we try a school for children with language impairment. We knew of none other available to us.

Happy House had one opening, but it fell on the same day as speech therapy in Madison. Could we handle that? More importantly, could Jenny tolerate it? We would have to consider all the aspects and let Hoppy know our decision.

First we must celebrate Jenny's fifth birthday.

When Ken and I got up that birthday morning, Mark, Jenny, and Paul were sitting at the table in the dark with Mark's flashlight focused on Jenny's heart-shaped, yellow-and-green-frosted birthday cake. It was decorated with suckers and miniature doll toys that Jenny gingerly took off to play with. Jenny's favorite gift was a scrapbook that Mark had secretly filled with familiar pictures cut from catalogs and magazines. She spent hours looking at it while we reinforced word usage. Daddy made her a low wooden ironing board to sit at on the floor. I made a blue corduroy jumper dress. Paul and Katie gave her puzzle and paints.

Two days later we shifted into high gear to enroll Jenny at Happy House. Ken suggested, "How about if you pack a lunch and take Jenny to Madison for her morning speech therapy. She can eat the lunch on the way home, and I'll meet you at home and take her to Janesville during my lunch hour while you put the other kids down for their naps, and then later you can all go get her. do you think that'll work?"

As so often before, Ken accepted as much of the responsibility as his busy days permitted. He had become a full partner at the clinic, and also spent late hours studying for his medical National

Boards, but he continued to find time for his family. When he was not available at the noon hour, I made all the trips.

Jenny tolerated the tight schedule and learned more single words. Whether or not there was any connection, she and Paul became closer buddies, though repeatedly she teased him to the point of his screaming rage and then she'd giggle delightedly. They might as well have been twins.

Following the belief projected to us from university professionals — with proper exposure, these children sometimes rally round — we also kept her in the local nursery school.

Though Jenny thrived promisingly, we began to have doubts about ourselves. Speech-Happy House day tallied one hundred miles and constant effort. And I was wondering why my back and leg were hurting.

An orthopedic doctor gently informed me, "You have a spinal-disc problem. You must go into the hospital for rest and traction."

"Oh, great! How do I find time for that?"

We called Gramma to ask if she could come, and I called Happy House to tell them that Jenny could not attend for a week or so.

Lying in that hospital bed, I had time to ponder many things, including the fact that at that time only seven percent of our population were the farmers who fed the rest of the nation. I was glad my youth had been lived on a farm. There I'd had to overcome feelings that could not stand in the way of doing the daily chores. I hoped the discipline I learned would now serve a purpose.

We shifted gears again. I set different standards. We counted on our friends to accept an altered style of housekeeping. I don't think they even noticed. We had good friends.

A bonus from it all was a new style of finger painting. Oh, the joys of motherhood! Why don't we come equipped with all sorts of ideas from first conception on?

To the children, I said, "I've got some new paints for you. You get to use your fingers to paint on my back!"

Many, many lying-down relaxing hours were spent in that manner. What better place to finger paint with body lotion than on Mommy's back? And while I lay on the couch they combed and brushed my hair and put curlers in it, playing beauty parlor. They painted my face with makeup. My body rested but still I was with them in an active capacity. Perfect!

Little Katie was getting old enough for Jenny to enjoy and

was a true gift to our family. No hesitation in development for that child! She directed steady, determined hands to her crib toys and food. After Jenny, never did we take any such ordinary baby actions for granted. I spent happy moments, hours actually, watching this new child grow. Each action was precious. Each new accomplishment seemed a miracle.

"Kay-ke," Jenny hesitantly learned to call her.

As Katie learned, Jenny relearned and learned anew. When the baby did something, Jenny tried to do the exact same thing, even though she was almost five years older.

In January the recommendation had been against kindergarten for Jenny, but Jenny had made progress in some areas, and we wondered if there was a possibility she might be able to handle regular school. In the spring, on one of Daddy's afternoons off, we took the three youngsters to visit Mark's kindergarten, so Jenny could understand what we were talking about, and so we could all use the same visual images to communicate with Jenny. We went ahead and registered Jenny for the next school year just in case her progress continued.

Those spring days found us eager to resume family hikes. We walked along Saunders Creek and talked about the escapades in the book *Rascal* by Sterling North. A local boy turned author, Mr. North had chosen for our town of Edgerton the name of Brailsford Junction in his book about raccoons, crows, and youth. Scenery in that book existed in Edgerton.

While spring progressed, Jenny continued to attend regular nursery school and also Happy House, sometimes carrying apple blossoms to Hoppy. Through the years I have remembered Happy House, but more so Hoppy, who dedicated herself to helping the afflicted. I have prayed for her many times. We felt that Jenny benefited from going to that school, even though it was for a limited time.

In May, Jenny's progress report about her thirty-two sessions of speech therapy in Madison was encouraging. It said:

> Jennifer has made considerable progress, both in her ability to work meaningfully in therapy routine and in her attempts to communicate verbally. She attempts more words, but many of them are not yet stabilized. She appears to be ready now for actual vocabulary building. Jennifer shows improvement in attitude and has be-

come an active member of the therapy situation. She appears to be able to learn a task with repeated stimulation and reinforcement unless the demand becomes too great. . . .

With hope in our hearts, we gladly consented when Mark announced, "School's almost over and we can bring a guest. I want to take Jenny. Can I?"

Mark played his escort role like a perfect gentleman. A heavy morning rain let up just before the big yellow bus stopped at our corner for the slickered children. I wondered all morning how Jenny was conducting herself and if Mark was having to entertain her. Later, over lunch at home, Jenny's enthusiastic voice inflections, sounding like wordless sentences, proved that the morning had indeed been exciting for her.

After that most successful school year we felt we had earned a vacation. It didn't scare us at all to pack the kids in the car for two weeks and drive to Nova Scotia. Each child wore a light blue sweatshirt advertising Creighton University, Ken's alma mater. We fell in love with Canada's St. John River valley — "the Rhine of North America" — and with the Atlantic coast fishing villages piled high with lobster traps. After the Blue Nose car ferry carried us back to the rugged coast of Maine, we followed tufts of dancing clouds through tree-laden mountains of New Hampshire and Vermont. A fairy followed us to Lancaster, New Hampshire. We knew because Jenny lost her first two teeth there and she found two shiny dimes the next morning. Those same two pearly white teeth were the ones she almost lost in California when she had bitten the lawn chair.

It was a relaxing, enjoyable trip, though Dr. Falk may have wondered when he asked Mark how his trip was. Mark replied, "I snagged my Dad's shirt." We could never be sure which memories would dominate.

Jenny happily returned to TuTu for twelve more speech-therapy classes. Since Jenny's tolerance level had improved greatly, she now had hour-long sessions.

Summer held carefree hours, and Jenny learned to ride a tricycle.

Suddenly, in July, bedtime turned into another horror time. We never learned why. We should have foreseen something when Jenny emphatically began to insist that her door be open. She took up an intense dislike for going to bed. She cried. She screamed. She screeched. She vomited. We searched our minds for reasons. We could find no solutions. Ken and I took turns sitting with her until she fell asleep. If she awakened, the whole awful process repeated itself. Weeks and months of this wore on us. We finally took the easy way out and let her lie on the couch, even when we had company. When she was sound asleep we carried her to bed.

Then a night came when we were ready to retire before she had gone to sleep. Surprisingly, she tolerated our going on to bed, leaving the lights on. To our utter amazement, in the morning we found her in her own bed. We didn't know when she had tucked herself in. That, then, became her routine for many weeks.

A complex little child. We could never rest on her laurels because she held constant surprises for us.

I carried a diaper for her whenever we went anywhere — not for bathroom functions but for the exaggerated gag reflex. She would throw up at the drop of an emotion. We chose not to let it curtail our activities; that meant we had to insulate our reactions to embarrassment.

Jenny's speech report was positive except for noting more struggle and forcing behavior. That meant stuttering. Her therapist noted that Jenny was also showing some signs of self-consciousness, particularly when asked for a verbal response. Jenny had no trouble tolerating the hour-long sessions.

We made the report available to our elementary-school principal.

In the waning days of summer, we received a heartwarming announcement. Jenny had been accepted for kindergarten on a trial basis! Oh happy day! Even if it were to be on just a trial basis. We set no goals for our complex child. We merely wanted to expose her to as much as possible as soon as possible, and we were particularly happy that it could be in our own locale.

§§ 7 §§

. . . goals and no goals . . .

It was a much welcomed relief not to have to juggle the family's needs to fit around trips to Madison.

Wearing her favorite blue-and-white-striped dress, with a rest mat tucked under her arm, five-and-one-half-year-old petite blonde Jenny met the yellow bus for afternoon kindergarten. Because she couldn't talk clearly, she wore an identification necklace — a guardian angel engraved on one side, Jenny's name and address on the other. (Jenny wore this for several years.)

Just because the school had admitted our child, we expected no miracles. We respected the teacher who had to accept Jenny — that teacher was responsible for instilling learning in a large group of five-year-old children, each with individual untested potential. We intended to cooperate in any way possible.

Mrs. Gessert tried to guide Jenny toward learning without overstepping the sensitive pressure limits that brought on reactive misbehavior. Jenny gave forth little effort. Her only successful paperwork was trying to color within the lines of a circle. She made no attempt to try to print. Simple puzzles were assembled. She refused milk and crackers, threatening to gag when it was offered to her. Though her peers liked Jenny, she resisted their invitations to play and she stayed on the fringes while they enjoyed music, rhythm, and group games. Her vocabulary was extremely limited, but she seemed to understand what her teacher and classmates were saying. Jenny watched them closely.

We exclaimed over any paperwork she brought home, and hung it on the refrigerator and kitchen cupboards.

Jenny rode the same bus home as Mark, and often he complained, "Mom! She fell asleep again on the bus!"

It was no wonder. Despite her continuing going-to-bed problems, Jenny's morning started at four or five o'clock when her dolls rated motherly attention. She had retained her exasperating bedtime actions no matter who might be visiting. We had to get used to suggestions being offered by friends and relatives; why explain to them that we had already tried all of their proffered solutions? Their recommendations needed to be tempered with insight on our days' happenings in relation to personalities, other people, illness, activity, and children's whims.

That must be why Bob and Ruth were such soul-satisfying friends. They merely accepted us, and they accepted our children. Furthermore, they apparently accepted the fact that we must do things our own way. If and when they could help, they did, and we knew we could call on them anytime.

Jenny was barely holding her own that semester while Paul surged ahead. He enjoyed music, so we enrolled him in a weekly half-hour rhythm class taught by a local piano teacher. However, Paul's idea about that class differed from our intentions. During class he refused to join the singing, whereas at home he sang each of the songs over and over. At the recital, he sat with us in the audience.

Our hope had been to own a piano — in fact we had rented one in Nebraska and in California to help fill my recreational needs. We were excited now, because instead of getting a decent couch we opted to buy an Everett piano. It would arrive after we settled into a one-story house we purchased on the other side of town.

Just as Paul feared, the December 10 move to our new home occurred on rhythm-school day and he was sure he'd never see any of us again, ever, ever. He had to be reassured that Ruth would help him find his new house.

No longer could Jenny ride the bus. The school was close. I walked her to class at noon, and Mark met her after school.

After seven-year-old Mark walked Jenny from school the first day, he was eager to help unpack boxes, but only after he scouted the well-groomed neighborhood. Up the street and down the street he went, and then he was challenged. I happened to glance out the window and was shocked to see two boys, not much bigger, accosting him. One seemed to be threatening with what appeared to be a long stick or pipe or something. I raced for the door wondering how to handle this new problem!

Calling to them, I asked,"Would you boys like to come in for cookies and milk and take a tour of Mark's house?"

They came across the street with our son.

Good kids they turned out to be. They were merely testing the new kid on the block. A very close relationship developed with one boy.

Jenny ran through her new home checking each room. She knelt on the hearth with Paul and looked up the chimney, though probably with no idea why he said, "Santa sure will be glad we've got a chimney!"

Jenny took a budding interest in Christmas, but only in that the Christmas catalog was exciting. She'd bring it to Daddy or me with pages opened to the dollies and beg by holding out her tiny hands to indicate a length. "Den-nee, Ba-bee. Den-nee, Ba-bee." Each day the length expanded.

When Christmas arrived, Jenny showed a great sense of pride in giving us a gift she had made at school. We learned that Mark had helped her bring the painted-cardboard ice-cream-carton wastebasket home and hide it. He somehow made her understand that it was to be a secret. (A tear wells up now as I look at a salvaged five-by-seven-inch piece of cardboard painted pale blue with a small, narrow, thin-fingered hand imprinted on it with white poster paint. A cross-country household-goods mover could not have guessed my emotions when I saw that he had added the dilapidated wastebasket to the trash. I retrieved it long enough to cut a piece to save. After fourteen years of daily use, only this remains. It serves as a bittersweet reminder.)

We couldn't have asked for better teachers and school administrators. They kept Jenny's best interests in mind, and when offering suggestions they always gave us a chance to decline.

Jenny's teacher conferred with us. "I'm hoping to change Jenny to morning kindergarten for second semester. It appears she won't be ready for first grade after this year, and it might give her new understandings to be with a new group of children."

Luckily, that fit into our plans nicely. We had learned of a speech therapist in Janesville, ten miles south, who could give Jenny therapy in the afternoons. We felt more emphasis should be put on helping Jenny on an individual basis, but we certainly couldn't expect the school to be able to meet all our wishes.

Therapist Carol Gevaart suggested reinforcements for us to use at home — such as Lotto-type games where Jenny matched things, sounds, people. She recommended records such as John Ciardi's *You Know Who*, which quickly became a favorite.

Overseered by Paul and Katie, time to help Jenny was wedged among all the typical work, school, and pleasures that made up family living. Too often that time seemed limited; or I didn't feel like meeting the demands. Too many times my voice rose in impatience with the children. I could only hope the neighbors were understanding and tolerant. I often felt that Mark's friends saw me at my worst; perhaps they would remember that they also saw me at some very happy times.

One day Jenny brought a paper home from school. When I saw it, I grabbed her and hugged her and danced through the house waving the paper and excitedly announced, "Jenny prints n's! Jenny prints n's! Come and see Jenny's n's! Oh, Jenny, that's wonderful!"

Indeed Jenny printed small n's. She proceeded to print them all over the house. Everywhere. On every piece of paper that appeared before her pencil, and just everywhere! Even on the walls! Perhaps the current owners of that house still find n's.

Then one day Jenny drew a sun and people. Her people were just a circle with two lines drawn down and ending in scribbly round feet, but as far as we were concerned they were people, and Jenny seemed to know they were people. Our kitchen was never the same after that.

She kept messy piles of paper on the kitchen counter and used it often. Ken carried yellow x-ray liner paper home from the clinic and hospital by the armful. However! We had to be careful not to compliment Jenny on her drawings. If we did, she'd quickly and emphatically rip them to shreds.

Just as she did her fingernails. Jenny had been a nail biter for a long time but finally had quit and her nails were growing nicely. Unfortunately, I made the mistake of complimenting her and she promptly bit them all off to the quick.

"Oh, Jenny!" I wailed, "Why did you do that?"

On shallow footing, we minced along, trying to deal with her emotions. Luckily, there were friends who cared about Jenny with us, and she became a sociable child. On her sixth birthday, she readily shared M&M candies with her classmates, but that was one of the rare times she openly shared with her peers. Thank God for the elderly. She always felt comfortable with them. We felt blessed to have Mr. and Mrs. Welch as her close friends. There were others, but the Welches were special. They invited Jenny to their home, and when they came to ours they patiently listened to her run her fingers up and down the piano keys and try to sing. She needed that kind of attention.

We were also happy that Jenny's grandparents came and sometimes stayed for expanded visits. At those times tea parties abounded, and "Oh, Look!" when the children learned that Grampa had left a tip under his teeny-tiny plate when they were playing restaurant — even though his cooks never did get his make-believe eggs fixed to suit his fancy. The children showed great concern when Grampa told them he had a bone in his leg and he just didn't know what he was going to do about it. They felt so sorry for him and inspected his leg gently and tried to be ever so helpful. Then when he lost his appetite — they searched all over the house for it! Gramma loved to fuss over her little ones and easily entered their world. Ken and I did the disciplining and let Gramma and Grampa impart their special brand of love. Of course, they too could discipline.

We chose adult baby-sitters whenever we could because Jenny related especially well to them.

We rejected the television as a sitter. In fact, when arguments and commotion finally revolved around the TV, Ken carried it to the attic storage area. The children adapted easily and peace reigned. We wondered why we'd been reluctant to face the possibility of living without it. All we really needed was a good supply of books, boxes, paper, pencils, crayons, scissors, paste and sports equipment. If even those. Maybe we wouldn't have needed the books if we had been story tellers. We, like other families, had more toys than we needed.

There were many people who cared about Jenny. Father Ed Cosgrove, a Redemptorist friend, gave us phonograph records and visual aids to use in helping Jenny learn about her spiritual life. Also pamphlets about the retarded, written by Gerard Breitenbeck, C.Ss.R., and published by Liguori Publications. Father Cosgrove arranged for Ken and me and the grandparents to tour St. Coletta's School for Exceptional Children at Jefferson, Wisconsin, a large residential school directed by the Franciscan sisters. He suggested, "You can talk with the speech therapist while she shows you the school." Father knew we had wanted to have a chance to see the facility.

We were receptive to learning about every possible educational opportunity. Jenny's success in school was an unproven entity, and we wanted to be prepared for any eventuality.

I thought we had set no goals for Jenny. But I learned something in the immaculate halls of St. Coletta's. Obviously I had set goals. I had indeed assumed that Jenny would someday talk and be able to express herself. It was my constant prayer. It apparently had not settled on me that it might not happen. Perhaps that was why the Madison speech report had stated, "Dr. Pavlik appears to be more realistic about Jennifer's prognosis."

The therapist who gave us the tour through the large, impressive building of St. Coletta's School introduced us to a neatly groomed teenage student. The girl appeared to be normal. However, when a conversation was attempted we soon realized there were problems. The girl could not express herself. The therapist then handed her a stack of little picture cards from which the girl haltingly told us a story.

Again there were new thoughts to face! Could that possibly be Jenny's fate?

So far we had followed what had been recommended by the professional consultants at the university. And even more, our family activities always included Jenny. Other people reinforced the love and teaching. There seemed to be little else to do in offering Jenny every possible advantage, except to consider boarding school. We were impressed with what we saw at St. Coletta's. *Should* we consider it for Jenny?

We gathered information. We thought about it. We discussed it at length. We decided we rather enjoyed rearing our own child, difficult as it was at times.

We finally chose to continue our present course. That course kept in mind the temporal needs, and their rising costs, for our other children. We had now entered the years of eyeglasses and orthodontics. Private boarding-school education for Jenny would have been very expensive.

Jenny finished her first year of kindergarten with no astounding success academically. Or so it seemed at first glance. And yet for Jenny it was indeed a successful year. She tried to color pictures within the lines, but with only one color. She sometimes pointed to pictures in a book and tried to say the words. She was observant of activities in the schoolroom. She took good care of her wraps and obeyed the teacher quickly and cheerfully. She listened when others spoke. She even entered some of the singing games, though she didn't try to sing.

Her teacher had not exerted pressure on Jenny to accomplish, and that apparently was wise. We felt Jenny had definitely benefited from her first year of formal schooling.

Dr. Klové, the neuropsychologist at the University of Wisconsin department of neurology, was interested to find out how Jenny handled her year in kindergarten. We gave him our report, and after they put Jenny through a battery of tests, we studied his report.

The Stanford-Binet Intelligence Scale showed a basal age of two with a ceiling of seven and mental age of four to two. This corresponded to an IQ of sixty-one. Development Drawings — thirteen. Peabody Picture Vocabulary Test — IQ fifty-seven. Raven Progressive Matrices Test — fiftieth percentile of her age range.

Jenny preferred her right foot and right hand, and had a right ocular dominence. The finger oscillation test showed normal results for her age with normal relationships between the hands. Motor Steadiness Battery Test — unremarkable. Vineland Social Maturity Scale — eighty-two. Wide Range Achievement Test — no significant achievement levels.

Their impression was that Jenny appeared to have left-hemisphere brain damage and represented a case of differentiated intellectual impairment, with the main defects being in verbal-symbolic function. With the next year's comparison they hoped to be able to come to a conclusion.

Dr. Klové recommended more speech therapy. He felt it was apparent that Jenny could not benefit from entering first grade because she would have only failures to deal with, and he could guess what detrimental effects that would have on her personality. At least now Jenny showed no evidence of any serious behavior difficulties, and it seemed most important that we try to maintain that level of life. He advised against considering institutionalization of any kind at that time, if for no other reason than that what we were accomplishing was above what he had anticipated was possible for Jenny. He didn't think Jenny was exhibiting any unreasonable disruptive effects on the rest of the family. In fact, he felt that whatever we were doing was beneficial and he wondered about our methods.

I think it is important that we differentiate between reasonable and unreasonable disruptive effects. Jenny was often disruptive. But she had not prevented us from pursuing a stimulating life for our entire family. So for us to keep Jenny at home did not seem unreasonable. With encouragement from Dr. Klové, we looked forward to pursuing the same educational course.

That decision made, we proceeded with the summer interspersed with speech therapy in Janesville. Toward the end and excited with anticipation, we packed gear for all six of us and traveled by airplane to San Francisco. Katie, just under two years old, slept under the plane seat while the others pressed their noses to the window. A rental car carried us around the Bay area on a whirlwind of visiting relatives, friends, and former neighbors and seeing sights; then up the coast to Auntie Lee's, and on to Seattle.

While we were busily chatting with our former neighbor in San Pablo, Jenny must have quietly slipped out the door.

"Where's Jenny?" we remembered to ask.

"She's not playing with us," Mark distractedly answered.

Quickly Dad and I looked through the house and in the yard. No Jenny! This house was the second from the intersection.

Dad delegated, "Mark, go up the hill! Paul, go look that way! I'll go this way. Mom, you go down the street."

Most of the homes had six-foot-high privacy fences, so it seemed Jenny would be along the sidewalk somewhere. Just then the tall black mailman, who had delivered mail when we'd lived there three years before, pulled his motorized cart up to me and asked, "Did you lose your little girl? The lady at the end of the street has her in the house."

How frightening! That was the last house before the subdivision exit to the busy highway! Jenny had wandered into the lady's house and of course couldn't tell her who she was. The lady had started to dial the police when I nervously called in through the locked screen door. Thank goodness she had protected our child!

We kept *much* closer watch after that while we continued our visits and sightseeing. Always, we kept a cloth near at hand, because Jenny still gagged a lot and vomited occasionally. I never went anywhere without unobtrusively keeping it available. After seeing the West Coast through the eyes of little children, we flew home from Seattle two weeks later.

Back to reality. To catch up on the news, buy groceries, rush to the work world, put up with the play world. And then to make final preparations for another year of school.

That vacation was as important for our children as it was for Ken and me. It was a time to foster new thoughts and reactions. A time to store up memories and knowledge. A chance to forget the day-to-day pressures and routines.

For us, a time for special sharing.

§§ **8** §§

... each problem has a solution ...

The fall of 1966 Mark started second grade and Jenny started her second year of kindergarten.

School was crowded. An extra room for kindergarten was rented in the nearby veterans' building. Since Jenny was repeating, the teachers suggested she be assigned to that new classroom so it would seem like a new experience to her.

Mark and Jenny walked a block, crossed the street, took a footbridge across Saunders Creek, then climbed the school hill and went past the playgrounds. To get to the new kindergarten, Jenny proceeded on, with the help of school patrols, to cross two more streets. It was an easy route. Nevertheless, I hesitated to let Jenny come home alone at noon because of the streets and because she could not communicate well. She seemed so vulnerable. I met her at the main school building for the walk home.

After a few days, her teacher Mary Ellen Sill encouraged, "I'm sure Jenny can handle the walk alone. Why don't you let her try? I'll stay with her to the top of the hill."

The next day I waited for Jenny at the foot bridge where she could see me from the top of the hill. Then after a couple of days I waited on our side of the street. When it seemed that Jenny could handle crossing the street alone, I waited at the end of our driveway. As Jenny gained confidence, so did I.

There have been lots of Mary Ellens who took the extra step to force Jenny to an element of independence. When Jenny or we wavered, they were there cheering her and us on.

One day Mark stayed home sick. Jenny's tears fell at the change in routine, and she had no reason to think she could get to school without him. Every day she had relied on him. Not to lose the ground we had gained, I insisted that she walk to school alone. Though frightened and crying, she mastered that task. From then on she was proud to walk alone, and Mark was free to join his own friends. He had been faithful and had never complained.

It wasn't just injury from cars I was protecting Jenny against. I didn't trust all people. On occasion I'd gone to the protection of a young special-ed boy who was fending off normal kids, so that, too, I feared for Jenny. What is it that makes us ready to taunt anyone who is not like us? Does it give us a sense of superiority? Dull or even bright — it doesn't matter — none of us escapes jeers if in some way we are different. Did our parents not teach us that a purpose of life is to reach our highest potential and that we each attain that potential at a different speed and to a different level? It's all right to be oneself! And we must likewise allow all others to be themselves.

I hoped that Jenny might be allowed to pursue her education with the least amount of friction from others.

While Jenny was at school those mornings, little Katie had a chance to imitate Paul's quiet, creative play; but the minute Jenny came home, all bedlam broke loose. Surely her teachers would have been surprised to see what a disruptive force she exhibited at home. Apparently she was not that way at school. She extracted our Jekyll-and-Hyde personalities, especially from Paul and me. Then I'd feel guilty, even though I recognized that guilt feelings were worse when dealing with a child like Jenny. I had to remember that all of our children had ways of getting to me in the course of a day; it wasn't just Jenny.

So I would settle the children for their lunch as quickly as possible. Jenny needed that because she had not eaten anything to speak of since the night before — not that we hadn't tried to feed her. I actually looked forward to weekends and free days just so I wouldn't have to force breakfast down her before school. No matter what food was offered, she went through a horrible gagging, crying repulsion. Eventually I'd give up with the attitude, "If she eats, okay; if not she'll just have to go hungry." And usually she didn't eat. Furthermore, she refused mid-morning milk and graham crackers at school; when it was encouraged, she retched.

Lunch was successful. After Katie was tucked away for her nap, Jenny liked to build with the red American toy bricks. She constructed unusually appealing creations with intricate designs. She learned to cut out paper dolls. She listened to story and music records and especially enjoyed Winnie the Pooh — "E-E-E-Pooh."

Jenny's school papers were proudly shown, and she verbalized the color she'd used to scribble a page full. No longer did she rip them to pieces when we complimented. That was small but meaningful progress.

Three days a week she went to school a half hour early for speech therapy. We were grateful that therapy was available on a frequent and regular basis. It positively affected Jenny's progress.

Printing was still limited to small n's. In September Jenny chose "geen" colored paper to create a birthday card of lines filled with n's for her Daddy. While she recklessly constructed n's, Paul methodically gathered his brightly colored paper and pencils, arranged them carefully on the floor by my feet, laid on his tummy and with pencil in hand, looked up and asked, "How do you spell Happy Birthday to my Dad?"

"Oh, Paul," I praised, "Daddy's going to be so pleased. It starts with H."

He eyed his paper carefully, positioned his pencil to the paper and said, "How do you spell H?"

I printed the words and Paul copied them onto his card, but he got them mirrored. Should we have worried about that? In some children that reveals an abnormality in the ability to learn. In our searchings about Jenny we had become familiar with dyslexia and other learning disabilities. If parents are alert to their children's possible problems, they should be brought to the attention of the teacher when the child starts school, or at any time during schooling.

Daddy loved the tale about the birthday card. And we did watch Paul's paperwork, but saw no further cause for alarm.

Despite Ken's busyness, he found time for his children. He played their games, read books, helped them make my yearly birthday cake, swam and ice-skated, taught them how to plant seeds and trees. He joined them in music, hikes, and comedy. His influence was endless. That fall he helped them build a tree house in the backyard.

The tree house attracted friends. When the five o'clock whistle blew, it meant playtime with friends was finished unless special permission was granted. We stumbled onto that gem of discipline quite by accident, but it made our life much more manageable. It made for a relatively serene household for Daddy to retreat to after his day with the public. It brought our family close because there was time to play with one another; or there could be solo quietness before supper. It allowed a leisurely pace for school homework and music practice. It nourished a satisfaction for being in the cozy confines of home in the evening hours, so when our children reached their teen years they were settled comfortably into a pattern that didn't presume they had to be off to a friend's house or wherever.

Evenings were a peaceful pleasure. Jenny was going to bed quietly. To be sure, she still had a compulsive routine! Every doll she owned was tossed into bed, and cherished possessions were placed just so around the bed. We didn't criticize her, but merely let her go about her compulsions before we went in and prayed with her and tucked her in bed. It had been a frustratingly long year, sleepwise, interspersed with all variety of bedtime quirks. Could we hope, since we had survived them all, that we might be able to survive anything?

Katie had routines also, but they were not so binding. Her speech developed nicely, and once more our parental hearts suffered as we watched this child, like Paul, pass by Jenny. We wouldn't want it otherwise, but even so it was difficult to be reminded anew that Jenny was very slow. We would have rejoiced had we suspected that Jenny would soon emulate Katie, learn from her, share play and friends, and benefit tremendously from her steady temperament.

Our friends who had similar-aged daughters invited Jenny to birthday parties. I hope they know how much that meant to us! Since Jenny didn't play well to make her own friends, she missed out on many childhood pleasures.

For that reason we were thankful for such events as when Bob invited Mark, Paul, and Jenny to the Lions' Club Christmas party for children. "I'll help them with their meal."

Ken asked, "Are you absolutely sure you want to take Jenny? You know how her gag reflex is."

Yes, he knew. And yes, he was sure. Jenny liked the experience, and Bob survived, though we delightedly tried to imagine the scene he told about when his young son scrambled up on the table to better see Santa Claus.

We had decided to give birthday parties only on eighth and twelfth years so our friends would not frequently be faced with buying gifts for a Pavlik, and so I could maintain an element of personal sanity. We wondered, though, what Jenny would be like next year when she should have her party. Would she be capable?

We knew what she was like now as she approached her seventh birthday. But what would it be like next year when her peers would be in second grade and we knew not where Jenny would be? Would those peers still want to come to her party then? And what about subsequent years after that? We had no way of knowing how Jenny would progress. We knew no one to compare her to, and I had not found books in the library to gain insights. What should we do? It seemed if we took the opportunity now, at least Jenny could have a party experience.

Questions without answers; they caused the greatest fear. In fact that was the only thing we really feared — things we didn't know enough about.

That year Bob Stricker gave us our answer. Bob was a carpenter in town who said, "I can start remodeling your kitchen tomorrow."

So. The kitchen would be torn up. The carpenters surely didn't need little birthday guests underfoot!

But we should have been able to make the decision without extenuating circumstances. How much easier it would have been had we known what we knew later: each year presents its own problems but it also presents solutions. Each day that we lived with Jenny, we had to meet the demands of that day, and thus meeting them, we found solutions. There were always people who cared about her. We could have had a birthday party any year we chose. I wish we would have known that. Each year I might have had to plan a different kind of party, but yes, we could have had a party any year.

That year her birthday was a quiet family celebration. Her white cake was dressed with frosting grass and sucker flowers. Clothes, paper dolls, and animal rummy were her gifts.

Jenny's school days were going well. A spurt of new words warmed us, and Jenny accomplished her first real schoolwork — crossing out pictures that didn't match. The smiling faces on her papers held no candle to the ones she earned from her family.

After picture-taking day at school, Jenny started to comb her own hair. The photographer provided a comb for each child, and Jenny apparently realized that other children combed their own hair. Subtle things were learned at school.

Sometimes she seemed so normal, only to shatter us by an unexpected reaction to just about anything. Mealtimes were the hardest, and occasionally Katie attempted to imitate Jenny's retchings if she didn't like something. We didn't interfere, except to warn Katie that she wouldn't like the results because she'd have to clean up after herself. In so many ways we affected one another. Each child had to be dealt with individually, according to his own personality.

Recognizing Paul's increasing inclination to worry, we gave him only one day's notice that he was scheduled for a tonsillectomy. He packed his own suitcase, rechecked it often, and kept it within his sight all day. If he went to another room, he took the suitcase with him. He helped me prepare for guests, and while I hosted a meeting that evening, Daddy took him to the hospital and got him settled into bed, interested in TV and the activities of the nurses, and promised him a supply of popsicles. Though wary-eyed, Paul handled his first hospital experience with dignity, and it was a turning point in his young life. He had attended rhythm class and played in the neighborhood, but was definitely not pleased with the prospect of starting school. Now he took an interest and asked about kindergarten. Perhaps Paul learned he could survive without his Dad and Mom?

Lazy days caught us unprepared for disturbing news. Ruth said, "Bob got the grant for study in veterinary pathology. We'll be moving soon. We'll miss you."

Not nearly so much as we would miss that family! We had relied on them in many ways. But families must do what they must. All we could do was host a going-away party, wish them well, and hope our paths could cross frequently.

That summer's legacy to our children was a car trip to Tucson, Arizona, to visit Uncle Keith and Aunt Theresa.

A friend asked, "Why go to New Mexico or Arizona? It's nothing but desert!"

How wrong we found him to be! Much of it desert, yes, but we came back with every intention of traveling all that interesting country again someday. We even subscribed to newspapers from two small New Mexico towns we traveled through so we could better understand their mixed cultures.

Returning through cousin country, we showed eight-year-old Mark St. Peter's church in Omaha where Aunt Mary Ann and Uncle Francis were his godparents when he was baptized as a baby. It seemed that age was about when our children became interested in knowing more about themselves.

In Iowa, Gramma asked, "Would you like to leave Jenny with me for a while? I could fly home with her whenever you want." Gramma added, "I think it would be good for Jenny to have some quiet days and not have to keep up with your overly active family."

We considered the various aspects, pro and con. I don't know that we were more active than any other family, but Gramma certainly thought we were. Of course, she heard about our activities through my letters, and when events were summarized into a few paragraphs, no doubt she was left breathless. I needed to write those letters, to share with my mother, just as I hoped our children would some day share their lives with Ken and me.

Jenny did stay. She had her own bed and kept it neat. Gramma said she took pride in choosing clothes from her suitcase. Jenny stayed contentedly happy and kept busy playing and trailing her dear friend. She developed a lasting fondness for Gramma. And Gramma learned a thing or two. She learned that environment was not the only answer to Jenny's needs. She decided, "Perhaps Ken and Norene do have a bigger challenge than I thought."

Jenny's appointment at the university speech clinic determined her return date three weeks later. For several months afterwards, Jenny inflectively babbled about her airplane ride to anyone who would listen — friend or stranger. Always with interpretation from us. (Years later when we tried to establish Jenny's earliest memory, it became apparent that she had no recall of her stay at Gramma's or of the airplane trip, though she was already seven years old and it had made a big impression on her.)

The results of the speech and language reevaluation were what we expected. There were no structural or functional deviations that should prevent her from producing speech sounds. Her hearing was good. She was able to correctly produce or closely approximate all consonant sounds with the exception of "s." Her speech intelligibility ranged from poor to fair. Her expressive vocabulary had increased since the initial evaluation, but her language usage and structure were still severely delayed.

In past reports her right hand, foot, and eye had dominated. Now she favored her right hand, left eye, and left foot, but used her right foot for kicking. She could not skip or hop on her right foot. Her balance was notably precarious, and she had to hold onto something when kicking. She was unable to balance on one foot for more than a few seconds.

Jenny could copy geometric forms correctly, except for the diamond. She could not trace a line within two guidelines, nor would she circle a picture that was the same as a sample picture, though she could identify objects that were the same. While she was being tested, she stamped her feet and banged the table if she faced a particulary difficult activity which caused failure. There was suffering.

The clinicians felt that the significant gap between receptive and expressive language suggested a symbolic language impairment over and above a general delay in language development. They assumed it was due to a general retardation and specific brain injury. It seemed that we simply had to accept the fact that Jenny had some disabilities she might not be able to overcome.

Summer wouldn't be complete without an appointment at the neuropsychological department at the university. This was their third examination, and they came to no other conclusions than that Jenny continued to function in the mildly retarded range of intelligence. She tested out to an IQ of fifty-six on the Stanford Binet Intelligence Test. They encouraged placing her in a class for educable mentally retarded as soon as possible, with special emphasis on language-enrichment exercises.

With Jenny's reports in hand, we had a conference with our school administrator. There would not be a special-education availability for Jenny until the following year when our school would incorporate a third room to accommodate more learning disabilities. In 1957 they had created one room, and in 1964 they added a second room. This was 1966. With the addition of the third teacher, they would have separate classes for high school, junior high, and elementary learning-disabled students.

We felt fortunate that our school offered special learning facilities for the children with exceptional educational needs. I suppose until you have a child of your own who needs help, it doesn't seem important. It's easy to say, "We never needed that in the past. Why do we now? What was wrong with teaching them all in one room?"

Well, I remember what it was like for children who couldn't

learn easily when I was in elementary school. They were teased unmercifully by other kids and sometimes not played with. They were held back grade after grade until they finally felt embarrassed or ineffective. If they started dating when they reached the right biological age, they stuck out like a sore thumb. Finally they just quit school. There were never kids like that in the upper grades because they didn't make it that far.

I thank God that schooling was different for Jenny! At least she would have a chance at succeeding in life without always facing failures from the very beginning.

The administrator read Jenny's report from kindergarten. Jenny would attempt most projects. Her listening and attention spans had strengthened. She joined most activities without being urged. She was showing improvement in becoming more independent. She could print her name relatively well, despite some trouble with letter formation. She recited numbers one to ten and could identify most of them visually. And in speech therapy she was more willing to try new words.

We weren't sure where else Jenny could go to school to attend the recommended class for educable mentally retarded, so we stayed with the local school system. They planned to put stronger emphasis on speech therapy and suggested that Jenny attend full days of double-session kindergarten. To make it more interesting for Jenny, they wanted her to go to the morning class in the veterans' building and to the afternoon session in the elementary building, and with different teachers than she'd already had. She would walk home for lunch. We felt comfortable with the plan.

Jenny was unaware of all the decisions revolving around her by people who cared. All she knew was that she had learned to tie her shoelaces and was looking forward to going back to school.

§§ 9 §§

... aware of surroundings ...

"Jenny really *is* exceptional! She'll finish four years of kindergarten in only three years!" It helped to keep a light approach.

Jenny's kindergarten teacher in the morning was Paul's in the afternoon. Blond, lithe Paul came home the first day most indignant. "We had to listen to some guy named Rubinoff play a violin. That's not school! I didn't learn how to read!"

Our enthusiasm that night at the Rubinoff concert counteracted our son's professed lack of interest.

Paul had put up with Jenny's torments all his life and often chose to ignore her, sometimes seeming almost heartless. But his depth of caring became apparent when he gave us reports about one of his classmates. Angie was a slow learner, and some days Paul came home very pleased because Angie had learned a new procedure. He didn't tell us about other students. Already Jenny had made her mark on her brother.

Mark's and Paul's artwork overflowing the refrigerator and cupboard door stimulated Jenny into higher production of duplication. Ken extended the kitchen cupboard for a sit-at counter. Jenny could more easily work near me — drawing, cutting, pasting, and practicing alphabet letters to her heart's content. There she looked and re-looked at library books that Mrs. Zaborek encouraged her to bring from school.

At the beginning of her third year of school, Jenny drew a picture of her family members. Her teacher kept it, added subsequent drawings, and presented the assembled booklet to us at the close of the school year. The drawings seemed to indicate that Jenny was becoming more aware of her surroundings. Jenny's first people consisted of only a head with simple eyes, nose, and mouth; rectangular body, short stick legs, round, scribbly feet, long V-shaped arms, but no hands.

The drawings improved as the year progressed.

Jenny looked forward to her class Halloween party and to

trick-or-treating. Socially she had come a long way. While we were cleaning out the insides of pumpkins, the phone rang. It was Father Earl Toups. "There are two girls from Mexico visiting here at the Seminary. They're taking six months teacher training at St. Coletta's School. Could I bring them to your home to see what an American family's Halloween is like?"

Father knew what a mess our kitchen was, but if he was willing, so were we. Time was getting short before the witching hour, and there were still pumpkin cuts to make. They joined us in the kitchen, where Ken and I continued to help little hands carve their jack-o'-lanterns. Jenny showed Dad the pencil marks on her pumpkin where he should cut eye, nose, and mouth. Some of our jack-o-lanterns were unusual. We carved off just the skin of the pumpkin to create eyes, nose, mouth, teeth, scars, hair, wrinkles and eyeballs. Then we scraped the insides and saved the pumpkin meat to cook for pie fillings. Our real purpose for scraping, however, was to make a thin shell. Because we didn't carve completely through the shell, an air hole for the candle was cut in back. When the candle was inserted and lit, our elaborate, sometimes criminal looking, jack-o'lanterns always drew a second or third look from the young ghosts and goblins. Some asked for directions on how to make them.

After putting their lit lanterns in the front yard, the children quickly ate hamburgers, chips, and apple pie with their guests. Then, masqueraded as Thor, Casper, Goldilocks, and a Rabbit, they scurried off to spook the neighbors and beg for treats. Our South-of-the-Border guests thought it more than fulfilled their idea of an American Halloween.

Ken and I gladly shared in such ways, but attending meetings was another, less appealing matter. We were aware of the County Retardation Council. Many unselfish people on the local, state, and national levels changed the dark world of the handicapped child and adult because they recognized deficiencies and worked together to educate the public and effect legislations that allowed for funding of programs. Without those willing people, we would still be hiding our retarded children at home and in institutions.

At one meeting they discussed the need to develop a local listing of where parents could get information about existing facilities. That had been one of our struggles! We had scanned phone books and newspapers and constantly kept an alert ear. We shared our gleanings, but relied on others to follow through.

Ken and I had to accept our own emotional and physical limitations. We lived daily with Jenny, and though she was not severely handicapped, she needed constant supervision. It seemed that she had potential for learning, so we wanted to offer her stimulation. We wanted time, also, to guide our other children correctly so they could lead fulfilling lives. Ken's days overflowed with professional duties, and I had personal needs. So ultimately we had to choose what was right for us. We chose the stay-at-home position; but we felt truly grateful to those who publicly aided the world of the handicapped. They are the ones who created a new world for the less fortunate.

Though we were reluctant to go to meetings, we would not miss a teacher's conference.

At our conference in November, we heard Miss Slinde's initial remarks about Paul and Jenny with wonderment. "Those aren't our children you're talking about!"

She said both Jenny and Paul were concerned about keeping the classroom neat. How could those same two wreak such havoc at home?

New words from the teacher soothed our ears and eyes. "Attentive listener. Can concentrate on one task. Watches how others do a project and then does it. Very particular about own work. Has good attitude about self and others. Courteous. Shows interest in books. Will participate in music-rhythm activities. Can understand and interpret meaning but cannot always express ideas clearly. Shows some creativity. Knows colors."

Those observations weren't about Paul. They concerned Jenny! In that third year of formal schooling, Jenny was showing them some real success.

Besides full-time school, Jenny's days were busy. She entertained us with songs, especially "Polly Put The Kettle On," in her garbled diction. She drew simple ships and filled papers with them. She picked up and sorted toys and attempted to keep her room neat and clean. She liked to watch me cook, bake, and sew. She did errands. No wonder she started asking to go to bed right after supper. Her body simply needed more rest. Usually her bedtime was uneventful, but sometimes she retched if things didn't go just right.

In January, Jenny's drawings of her family were more complete. Our bodies were triangles. She drew round hands with stick fingers. There were eyelashes and ears. Each person was a different color and we now had straight rectangle legs with circle feet.

All of Jenny's paper work improved a great deal. She printed her entire name, though often backwards.

By February her drawings included hair, triangle noses, and a variety of hands. Some hands had petal-shaped fingers, some were sticks, and some were scribbly circles. Straight double-lined legs curved to form feet. Her drawings always had happy-looking faces.

Jenny turned eight years old, and we celebrated quietly without the traditional eighth-year party because I was recuperating from back surgery. The children helped me make an owl-shaped cake, and we decorated a little white-branch tree with plastic flowers and candy and set it among her gifts of clothes, a weaving loom, and a musical Winnie-the-Pooh bear.

Jenny, a babbling child of eight, was approaching a level of comprehension. But Katie, at three years, was definitely her leader.

Katie's days were filled with joy because she spread joy. She was never cross, never begging, always loving and patient, easily entertained. I could take her everywhere and know that she would be well-behaved. She spoke G's for J's; otherwise her speech pattern was good enough for her age. We called her Gumper because she jumped a lot; for no particular reason — she merely liked to jump.

We'd ask, "What are you doing?"

Sturdy, full-legged, knock-kneed Katie, with short blond pigtails flying, happily answered, "My gumping!"

There was one area in which we did have to discipline Katie. She pulled the bark from our birch tree, and she couldn't resist the temptation to keep doing it.

One day, while drawing a picture at the kitchen counter, she matter-of-factly announced, "My don't pull bark from tree no more."

I commended, "That's good, Gumper!"

"My pull from Mr. Genson's tree."

"Oh, Dear!"

We could easily understand Katie's language, but not always Jenny's. Children, though, have a way of comprehending one another. Katie sifted through Jenny's lack of consonants and multilated words and responsibly assumed leadership roles.

Jenny attended speech class with another child. All of Jenny's consonant sounds were omitted or substituted except "k" and "p." She was hesitant to imitate and had very little spontaneous speech. The other child's presence helped, because that child was talkative and quick to imitate. Whenever all the attention was focused on Jenny, Jenny became hesitant and tense and seemed to have a block against speaking; but if everyone spoke together, the tension gradually disappeared and Jenny imitated without being asked. Often it was necessary for the therapist to separate words into parts and ask Jenny to whisper before she felt secure enough to try. Jenny tried simple sentence construction such as "It's a. . ."; "what's that?" or "I see. . . ." But she would not incorporate it into spontaneous speech.

Jenny's family portrait in April showed a distinct change. Daddy, Mark, and Paul were all on one page and had trousers and rectangle feet. Shirts were one color, pants another. Arms were colored and ended in circle hands with stick fingers. The girl figures were colorful, with each dress different. At the top of the page she correctly printed "Pavlik Jenny."

Improvements were noted in the daily papers she brought home. Yes, Jenny was changing. Slowly, but surely.

She took her jump rope to school, content to only share it since she couldn't master the steps herself. Mrs. Zaborek, Jenny's afternoon teacher, told us that Jenny enjoyed singing with the class group but often drowned out the others, especially when they sang "You Are My Sunshine." When she sang that song and others, some words were distinct, but most were a slurring of various sounds. We could distinguish "Twinkle Twinkle, Little Star" and "Pledge of Allegiance" and "Brother John." Those she tried to teach to Katie when they were in the bathtub playing in the water. The "Brother John" song came out "ringing in the doorbell" — Katie could interpret only as far as her experiences allowed. It was fun to watch and to help Jenny's experiences unfold.

Traditionally we started the month of May by making and delivering May baskets. A pretty little basket filled with sweets and flowers was stealthily delivered to a person's doorstep. Anyone who knows that old European custom tries to catch the child and give him a kiss. The custom was seldom celebrated, much less known, by some of our friends and neighbors — a fact that Mark had learned the year before in our new neighborhood. That was why I now found him secretly making a special basket out of a paper cup and construction paper.

"Shhh . . . I want to make sure Jenny and Katie get a basket. Don't tell them!"

He filled the basket with candy and a flower, and spirited it to the front door when the girls were scurrying around delivering their own. They never learned whom their basket was from. For that we could almost forgive Mark for being forgetful. His Cub-Scout den mother's husband offered him, "I'll pay your dues for any week you come that you haven't forgotten something." Every week Mark had to pay his own dues.

We considered the school year a most productive one, although Paul had not completely reached his goal of learning to read. We knew because one day he and Jenny arrived home before I did, and when I got home he came running to the car with the news, "We got the note you put on the back door!" Daddy really liked that tale, too, because he had tacked that note to the screen for the plumber.

Jenny's final family drawing was similar to the previous one, except that she had us all on one page. We hoped Jenny could maintain her new accomplishment level over the summer. She was accepted for a summer speech program at school and would attend daily sessions for five weeks with two other little girls.

There were some who thought surely Jenny would go into first grade, that she seemed socially ready. But Ken and I knew that wasn't the only consideration. Neither of us thought Jenny was academically ready. Jenny had diligently accomplished self confidence and we were afraid she might lose it if challenged beyond her abilities with the pace of first grade. We remembered how much new material was constantly thrust on Mark all through first grade. It would have overwhelmed Jenny.

We were interested to hear what Dr. Klové at the University would recommend.

Jenny was tested for several hours. The WISC yielded a verbal IQ of fifty-three. Performance IQ, sixty-one. Full Scale IQ, fifty-three. She'd gained in psycholinguistic development by ten months in the past year. Most of her development was in spatial relations and positions-in-space skills, while eye-hand coordination was less developed. She indicated definite preference for the right hand.

They felt that Jenny's social behavior was much further developed than what they usually saw in children with her psychometric intelligence level. For that reason Dr. Klové stressed that it was important to recognize that Jenny's intellectual potentials were lower than her present social-development status. With her psychometric results, he felt it was contraindicated even to try her in a regular first grade; that it would probably be a traumatic experience for her. In intellectual areas, Jenny tested out as holding her own without evidence of regression, and she showed gratifying improvement in her overall behavior. Dr. Klové felt every effort should be made to maintain that status.

We always came home from those meetings feeling that we were apparently doing things as well as they could be done for Jenny. For that we were indebted to our school system. Of course, home atmosphere played a role, too, and should not be underestimated.

Since February, Mark had been studying maps and library books to choose a vacation trip. He sent for travel brochures. But faraway places of intrigue were overruled. Dad said, "My patients talk about going up north, and that means anywhere from forty miles to three hundred miles. This year we're going to find out what's up north."

While waiting for Dad's vacation days, we registered Mark for a week at Rotary camp, thinking it would be a good reprieve from his siblings and from his constant neighborhood companion. And whom do you think we found in the top bunk of his cabin when we delivered Mark to camp? You guessed it! The neighbor boy! We suspected a well-kept secret.

We found a marvelous country "up north": Milwaukee with its multiethnic culture, and Lake Michigan's seashore like the ocean's; Door County, like Cape Cod; Washington Island with its similarities to Prince Edward Island. Upstate lakes abounded with fish and whistling pines, and the deciduous trees matched New England's beautiful foliage that turns brilliant colors in the fall. Michigan's Upper Peninsula sported hills covered with trees, offering beautiful vistas. We ate cheeses and cheese curds, known as

Wisconsin popcorn; Cornish pasties like those miners carried to work in their pockets; bratwursts and belgian tripp. We saw ore-loading docks and ships at Superior. We swam in lakes and stayed in cabins; snooped in villages, then in neighboring Minneapolis, and toured its modern art gallery. Hundreds of dairy farms with traditional silos dot Wisconsin's rolling landscape. Apple orchards march up and down the hills east of La Crosse. Small mountains frame reflecting lights along the Mississippi River. Wisconsin truly is a beautiful state.

We returned refreshed and filled with the knowledge of what's up north. Jenny attended summer church school with her brothers and joined most of our activities. Even so, she lost some ground, and we were glad she would be enrolled in the new elementary special-education program for the coming year.

She would need lots of careful help and tender guidance.

§§ 10 §§

... life is just now beginning ...

Normally Jenny would have been in third grade instead of starting first-year special education. She could not speak in sentences, her language was very limited, and what words were articulated came out too loud.

Edgerton was experimenting with elementary special education, as were many schools in the 1960s. Ken and I embraced it with open minds and hearts. It would allow Jenny to learn at her own speed without prohibitively consuming time of a regular classroom teacher who must also meet the demands of aggressive students. Some parents cannot accept the concept of special education for their slow-learning child. Perhaps they think it brands their child as a slow learner; perhaps they think that having a slow learner reflects on their abilities as parents.

We have not had such feelings. God gave us this particular child, and we assumed the responsibility of rearing her to the highest level of her own potential. There need be no guilt in having a retarded child. The only guilt should be if we reject that child or if we pursue a course of education that does not best benefit that child.

When our school asked permission to include Jenny in photographs for possible newspaper pictures, we readily consented. Children love seeing themselves in pictures. Jenny was no exception. Jenny was as important as any of our other children. It made no difference to us that she would be in special-ed news. That was her world, and she should be allowed to feel comfortable in it.

Jenny had no clear way of describing her four girl and seven boy classmates, so we were glad her teacher sent home a roster to aid communication. Since Jenny had problems communicating, it was important that she have other ways to make good first impressions. We kept her neat and taught good grooming habits and good manners. She could feel good about herself.

Principal Mr. Brotzman greeted Jenny whenever he saw her.

"Good morning, Jenny. How are you today?" He usually heard, "Fine." He, and other school personnel, encouraged Jenny's friendly nature into bloom.

At open house Jenny proudly introduced her family to Miss Kozak. "Kay-tee, KAY-tee." Also, "Pau" and "Mock."

Jenny quickly settled into the routine. Each day we asked many questions to allow us a glimpse into her day; at teacher conference we learned that Jenny was giving her teacher glimpses into our days at home. Jenny enthusiastically chattered to tell about home life — though not always understandably. Jenny used a larger vocabulary and often spoke out of turn, so now she had to learn to raise her hand for permission to speak. When she did speak it was usually too loud. The poor tyke! New accomplishments presented new problems.

She mainstreamed in art, music, and physical education. Those classes were kept unpressured. It was good for her to have exposure to normal children in a non-competitive atmosphere.

The speech-therapy goal was to increase the length of Jenny's responses and to build correct sentence patterns. Miss Lindgren did that by using short phrases over and over in games. Jenny was encouraged to use prepositional phrases and in most cases would imitate as much as she could remember. Sample sentences were kept simple and slow so she would not become frustrated. As the amount of Jenny's spontaneous speech increased, she seemed to become more friendly and outgoing.

At home we carried through any suggestions her teachers made, but mainly we just incorporated Jenny into our life and interrelated with her in any manner that seemed right at the moment. I do not intend to give the impression that our household was smoothly quiet. Far from it. Ken and I were supportive of the children's ever-increasing activities, and in return we expected them to be supportive of ours. Life took on new dimensions each year, and it left no room for selfishness by any one member. Mark's play world revolved around preparing for Vince Lombardi's nod from the Green Bay Packers football team. Mark's orthodontia and glasses could not detain the juvenile Pack; however, piano practice must!

Paul read avidly, and Katie's zeal of rhythm school overflowed at home. For Ken and me, community action increased. He became Cubmaster and eventually "appointed" me a den mother.

Neither of us felt our boys needed scouting, but if some of us didn't help unselfishly, then boys who really did need such a program wouldn't get it. When we worked with the young boys, it was easy to recognize the rewards of those families who worked together as a complete unit. Of course, not all parents could give of their time, but those who could be counted on made a difference in the scouting program.

Jenny helped set up chairs in the church hall for the monthly pack meeting, watched the skits, interviews, and awards presentations, attended the Blue-and-Gold banquets, and helped me bake goodies for one event or another. (In later years Katie remembered resenting those boys coming to her house right after school, but there was no indication of that at the time. She presented only an accepting nature.)

From the beginning, the children watched Dad and me pursue new endeavors. There was never a question that mother had any inequality. Whatever I wanted to do I could. I was lucky, though, and so was my family, because first and foremost I wanted to be a full-time mother. Ken enhanced my days with constant support, often handing me bouquets of enrichment. If he saw interesting or beautiful sights when he was out and about town, he phoned it to my attention. More than once I scooted a child or more into the car to go see something he recommended.

One evening he handed me a lovely rose and said, "Marie Gullickson sent this to you. She says what good is beauty if it isn't shared?" I didn't even know Marie. She was an elderly patient of Ken's who, in her caring way, also added beauty to my day.

Ken allowed me freedom to be whatever person I needed to be. I read in the local paper that a flying club was going to form, and he didn't act too surprised when I said I'd like to learn how to pilot an airplane. As a little child, I lay in the grass under the maple tree in our yard and wanted so badly to have one of those planes way up in the sky come down and land in our yard. My brothers scoffed at me, "Those planes can't possibly land in this yard! They need lots of room to land." I didn't believe them. The planes looked so tiny way up there in the sky. Of course they could land in my yard! My yard was the whole universe! When my sister graduated from college, my Dad treated us kids to airplane rides at the Omaha airport. By then I understood.

Autumn spiced the air when Ken and I took to the skies to

learn how to fly a Piper Cherokee 140. Jenny went along to the grass strip at Albion and watched us get the airplane in and out of its hanger. The children respected our need for quiet time to do book study for ground school. They delighted over the cutoff shirt-tail commemorating first solo flight. Not so happy was Paul when I forgot to go to his parent-teacher conference because I was up in the sky making lazy dips. He was sure his entire academic career had been ruined. Luckily his teacher understood the lure of the skies — it was her brother who instigated the flying club. She rescheduled the conference, and my credibility as a mother was reestablished.

I tell these things to explain the type of life that surrounded Jenny. We shared our living with her even though she could not easily share hers with us. Jenny thrived. She became interested and cheerful.

Jenny had attended Uncle Keith's wedding and could now understand when we said that Viola was getting married. I suppose the children thought Viola, who had lovingly taken care of them on occasion through the years, must be close to a hundred years old — because they thought Dad and I were plenty old. She wasn't, but she had a grandchild Katie's age, and some even older.

Katie exclaimed, "I didn't know older people get married!"

"Of course they do," Dad said. "Love knows no age."

Jenny and Katie helped me entertain Viola's friends at a linen shower.

Older people helped our children understand the progression of life. Since their real grandparents lived several hundred miles away, we felt blessed that there were others to take their place. Years later the children loved to reminisce about some of those friends.

"Remember when Mr. and Mrs. Welch took Jenny and me to the Oasis for breakfast?"

"Remember when Linda and Billy were living with us and we made a birthday cake for Mrs. Welch?"

"Remember when Mr. Welch got too sick to come to church anymore? Was Mr. Price her cousin?"

"Oh! Remember how Mr. Price used to reach in his pocket after church and give us those miniature Hershey bars and he wondered how on earth they got in his pocket?"

"Remember when I dropped Mrs. Welch's cookies all over the ground? I wonder if she knew!"

"Remember I was *so happy* when Anna called *me* and thanked me for the May basket! It was my first very-own phone call!"

"How about that old guy on crutches in church? Do you remember him?"

Oh, yes, we remembered. All those and many more. The old man with canes — we never knew when or from whom a new source of encouragement would come. Through the years so many people cared about Jenny. Their theme to us was usually, "Don't give up hope."

When we first saw Joe, the old man, we could not have imagined that he and his wife volunteered as adopted grandparents to the mentally afflicted children of Central Colony Home in Madison. Joe was an inspiration to all who saw him laboriously maneuver his arthritic body with canes. When we watched him, our days seemed painless. Going to Central Colony represented an extremely generous character.

Joe and Florence were transplanted from Chicago, where Joe had been known as a happy singing bus driver. Our hearts were lightened when we received this note, with its hope-filled message, from Florence.

> Quite often at Mass we see you and your lovely family, never knowing that you had a special child. We, too, had a special child who couldn't talk, walk, or even crawl until he was four years old. He couldn't keep food on his stomach most of the time and was very frail and couldn't hold his head up. One day when I had him in the treatment room in the Children's Hospital in Chicago a very famous Doctor came through and took an interest in our boy. After much treatment and x-ray the Doctor found he had a small defect in his heart which was affecting his brain. He would have as many as six or seven spasms a day. It was quite a few years before he was normal. He could never find a playmate because the children thought he was odd. He was cured. He is now taking his master's degree, is married, and has two lovely children.

Joe and Florence held our child in their hearts and prayers. We are glad they told us. We never felt alone.

life just beginning • 89

That year Jenny was almost lost in the shuffle of Christmas preparations, but somehow either Ken or I made time to help her have a gift for each family member.

To emphasize good grooming, Katie and Jenny received a Suzy Homemaker vanity to set on their dresser — complete with combs, brushes, curlers, and barrettes. Coincidentally, Jenny's school exchange gift was powder, lotion, and perfume. Paul gave her play cosmetics. We practically had to abandon the house when the girls lavishly played beauty parlor. Sometimes a quick scrub of fragrant girls occurred before we could leave the house to go somewhere.

Jenny printed her own Christmas thank-you notes for the first time. Each was a major accomplishment that required days and days of work. I printed brief sentences that she copied at her counter in the kitchen. That took us into the quietness of January when snow covered the ground, and we harbored no guilt feelings about staying inside. Playing bingo helped Jenny learn numbers. She often beat us at concentration, a game played by spreading out all the cards from a deck face down on the floor or table; players take turns turning up two cards at a time to try to find a pair. If a match isn't made, the cards are turned face down again. If a match is made, that players gets another turn. We played Lotto and worked with words and sentences and ideas, as we had done multitudes of times before and would do many times to come.

Jenny continued to attend weekly religion classes. Her teacher understood Jenny's situation, but assured us that Jenny's behavior was good. We like to think that God keeps special children in the palm of His hand.

We didn't always plan the things that made up Jenny's life. Sometimes they just happened to evolve, such as the day Katie and I chanced onto a new activity.

Katie was an emotionally solid child who always kept herself entertained or followed my steps inside the home or out. Often she set up tea parties for her dollies, using Jenny's yellow plastic dishes. As I distractedly watched her, my mind meandered back to the farm of my youth.

"Katie, I was just thinking. Your Gramma and I used to have tea parties. We sat at the kitchen cupboard by the window, and I watched for Papa to come home. She gave me a bit of coffee with lots of cream in it. One Christmas I found a china tea set under the tree. I wonder if that tea set might possibly be with that stuff we brought from Gramma's. Let's go up to the attic and look."

Sure enough. There was a box. Carefully unwrapping each tiny china piece, we found a paper dated 1947 — twenty-two years before! The cream-colored pieces were edged with golden orange and decorated with green-leafed cadmium red flowers.

Excitedly I said, "Let's dress up and have a *real* tea party! We'll put on our best company manners and invite the Queen. Let's entertain at the coffee table in the front room!"

We used the fancy silver tray and carefully arranged my tiny china tea service, sugar and cream, real tea and dainty thises-and-thats of cereal, marshmallows, and cookie pieces. A precedent was set. Katie could hardly wait for everyone to get home from school.

"Mama and I had tea today, and we invited the Queen, but she never showed up! We used special dishes from when Mama was little. And we used a silver tray! And we dressed up!"

The boys were all ears. They fondled the dishes delicately as if they were pieces of treasure. As usual, Jenny seemed not to comprehend the whole tale. The time would come. She could be shown. Jenny and Katie eventually received their own china tea sets and held *many* tea parties.

Jenny learned by doing. For that reason we were glad that our school offered field trips. Sometimes clubs in town made the outings financially possible, such as for the Shrine circus. Mark came bounding in from school calling, "Fourth graders get to go to the Shrine circus and the special-ed kids get to go too!"

Mark cared about Jenny. We didn't have to ask him to keep an eye out for her; it seemed to come naturally. His friends tolerated her and always spoke to her. She had no desire to join their play, but liked to watch them.

On circus day, Jenny's teacher and chaperon would take good care of her. Even so I felt concerned. She clutched her coin purse containing fifty cents. I repeated, "You can keep it in your pocket, Jenny. If you want to buy a treat, your teacher will help you. Be sure to stay right near your teacher and don't go away unless she says you can. If you have to go to the bathroom, she'll show you where to go."

I did have concerns for Jenny. She looked so normal. From appearances people might not guess her needs. Retarded children with identifiable body features are related to right away because it can be understood they need help. We couldn't protect Jenny's every moment. We had to trust others to assume some of her care. There were many who truly did care.

Several weeks later we learned about some of the conversation of that day.

The doorbell rang.

"Is Jenny home?"

Jenny recognized elderly Mr. Swenson. She and her wheelchaired friend Nonie had ridden with him to the circus. Mr. Swenson ran the greenhouse. He handed a box toward Jenny and said, "Here, Jenny, these are the plants I promised to bring when the soil was ready for planting. Now's the time to plant them."

How thoughtful! Jenny understood. Daddy helped her prepare the soil and plant the flowers in the front-porch planters, and that year we referred to them as "Jenny's flowers."

Jenny's first year of special ed was a full year. As I study memorabilia from her ninth year, I realize it was a turning point in her life. It was the beginning of her memories. What if we had given up on our child before that? Just what if! I shudder to think of it! When I encourage other families to hold on to hope for their retarded children, I do so with the full knowledge that perhaps Jenny was lucky. Our family had a particular structure that other families might not have. Jenny's brothers and sisters were indispensable in her process of learning, just as our lifestyle enhanced it. Even though we were uniquely ourselves, perhaps other families dealing with retardation might look at us and pick out shreds that could give them hope. No, we had not given up hope for Jenny. Nor had we set unreachable goals. Essentially we accepted her for what she was.

Jenny's ninth birthday was finally party day. We didn't want to force an unwieldy situation on her, so only four friends were invited. They played games that Nonie could play from her wheelchair. Gifts were opened with self-conscious giggles, and then Jenny gave her guests a ceramic miniature animal and a cactus. Her special souvenir from the party was a ceramic February angel that topped her red, white, and pink heart-shaped cake.

When spring blossomed we had to get used to the fact that Mr. Welch would never again be at our breakfast table. The seasons come and the seasons go. With no way to stop it, life went on. We understood when we discussed the migration of birds and geese along with the loss of our friend.

Dad's current news was, "The geese are landing on Muskrat Marsh. Let's go see them!"

We grabbed the binoculars, some young and old friends, and walked through plowed fields to get a closer look at the winged creatures that offer the same faith in the renewal of life's cycles as does the hint of fresh spring air. When wavy-haired Jenny sat on the fertile ground in her blue trousers and teal-green shirt, we would have been heartened to know that it was her real spring also. It was as though Jenny's life was just now beginning, never to reach full bloom, but budding enough to add beauty to the world's garden of people.

Nine years it had taken Jenny! Her beginning now wasn't just because she was in special ed. It was because all through her years people had cared enough to give her a chance. It had simply taken Jenny much longer than others to get started.

It would be a long struggle yet, and Ken and I would have to deal with much impatience and unsureness. Results in Jenny would not show overnight nor over months. We lived the months and could not see her improvements day by day any more than we could see her physical growth, yet they were there. Much of our awareness came retrospectively.

Jenny now gibbered about her adventures as they happened; about the picnic that heralded the close of the school year. Jenny's teacher mustered courage and took her class for an overnight tent camping on the banks of the Rock River. Each child contributed food and supplies and later received snapshot reprints to give visual reinforcement to a much enjoyed experience.

Some mothers groaned when summer arrived and the children were underfoot. Not I! That's the time I could leave the world of adults and enter the child's world, if only vicariously.

As far as we were concerned, summertime meant travel. This time we headed for Washington, D.C., in our first air-conditioned vehicle, a station wagon. Everyone had a window, and that meant fewer disagreements.

Dad's Father's Day card from Mark, drawn while riding in the car, was a rendition of the capitol of Kentucky. Paul's printing promised, "I will try to be a good boy." Jen's was a picture of a

life just beginning • 93

person. Four-year-old Katie printed the alphabet from her own knowledge.

Kentucky bluegrass country; a glass factory in Weston, West Virginia; the battlefield at Gettysburg; Pennsylvania Dutch food; the chocolate factory in Hershey, Pennsylvania, where the street lights look like chocolate kisses and street signs like candy bars; Valley Forge; Philadelphia, with the Liberty Bell in Independence Hall; Annapolis — and finally the familiar and exhaustingly interesting sights of Washington, D.C., that we had seen so often on television news. Thence to George Washington's Mt. Vernon; the Blue Ridge Parkway, and Thomas Jefferson's fascinating, invention-laden Monticello; the capitol at Richmond; Williamsburg and Yorktown; the Smoky Mountains; Pigeon Forge pottery; Nashville and Paducah.

We *loved* that trip to historical sections of our country. We encouraged all of our traveling friends to make at least one pilgrimage to our nation's capital.

Jenny kept pace with us. She didn't need a cloth for her gag reflex anymore, but her loudness was a constant problem. We wondered how much Jenny would remember. Up to that time she expressed no memories, not even when we expected she might.

Jenny's summer was happy and rewarding, with swimming lessons at the city pool. Katie led her to new heights of learning. We could not have anticipated the blessing that Katie would be to Jenny, or to us. When we strained with impatience, Katie steadfastly went about the day doing quietly what came naturally, with Jenny shadowing two steps behind. They played house often.

Imagine their delight when I injured my knee playing tennis with the family; while I hobbled on crutches, our little women had a chance to play with my real toys. They vacuumed, dusted, and helped cook; ran errands, gathered the wash, and put it away. They washed dishes and ironed simple items. Their months of playing house came to fruition.

The boys assisted, but continued their sports and the tree fort with its inevitable fictional good guys versus bad guys. They took care of the yard, garden, and rabbit. Mark played little-league baseball.

"C'mon, kids," I'd urge. "Hurry up! We don't want to be late for Mark's game. Daddy'll meet us there if he can."

There we were, living our mundane life while Neil

94 • *One of Them*

Armstrong, Edwin Aldrin, and Michael Collins probed the skies to the moon. July 20, 1969. "That's one small step for a man, one giant leap for mankind."

Neil Armstrong, one of many capable human beings, had the privilege of being the first man to put foot on the moon. Why him? I suppose he has wondered, just as John Glenn may have wondered why he happened to be the first man to orbit the earth. (I've read about Annie Glenn's open struggle against stuttering and see a good answer. She has given hope to many.)

We are on earth not for our own purposes. We are to use our talents to help others. The space program is a fantastic test of talent that allows the imagination and intellect to soar. If we are wise we will use it only for the purpose of helping others. We and our children heeded TV in wonder as the real planet Earth was encircled and photographed by a space ship.

After the moon landing, Mark and Paul sat on the back stoop looking at the sky. They were encouraged to reach for the moon; to use their talents wisely. The girls would be encouraged similarly. We hoped our country would be ever free to allow their talents to soar. We wished that every child in every country could be teased with dreams to be achieved.

It was important to Ken and me that our children understand all God's children deserve opportunities. Ken learned as a young boy when his parents shared their home with Indian children during the summer. I learned it unconsciously when our family welcomed foreign college friends. And I cherish a set of Japanese paper dolls that my sister's pen pal sent me from Kobe, Japan, in the 1940s. My parents obviously did not discourage that exchange, even though those years represent international conflicts. It was only natural that Ken and I teach our family that all people are important.

We taught our children that if they were self-motivated they could thrive anywhere; but they should know that poverty, ill health, and prejudice can cause awful limitations. Retardation too, if allowed.

We welcomed high school AFS foreign exchange students to our home. Anne Gazengel from France lived with the family across the street and accompanied us to church on Sundays followed by breakfast. Anne learned that American people differ; indeed, that families living in the same block differ. Not that they

life just beginning • 95

differ in major ways, but in subtle ways. When Anne returned to France, it would be unfair of her to report, "All Americans do it thus and so." She garnered experiences and then had to form her impressions. She found unifying ties, but recognized that people are individuals, not just a nationality or a color or a religious denomination. Even in our family, Anne found unifying ties, but saw each of us as an individual.

So many things there were for a child to learn. We hoped that even Jenny could someday grasp some of the deeper meanings of life. That year it was possible to hold that kind of hope.

§§ 11 §§

... progresses and regresses ...

Posted on the refrigerator was:

JENNY'S READING LIST — Summer 1969

>*Tip*
>*About Friends*
>*Sally, Dick and Jane*
>*Bigger and Bigger*
>*Under the Sky*
>*What Is It*
>*My Little Red Story Book*
>*Little Brownie*
>*My Dog Laddie*
>*Awake and Away*
>*Where Is Everybody*
>*Ten Apples Up on Top*
>*Green Eggs and Ham*
>*Going to School*
>*We Went Looking*
>*Energy*
>*I Want to be a Homemaker*
>*I Want to be a Librarian*
>*I Want to be a Fisherman*

Jenny was proud. She had struggled to pronounce the familiar words in those books. We helped with the ones she didn't know. She was anxious to get back to school to show the list to her teacher.

We juggled clothes until each child was presentable enough to start another year of learning.

After the first day of school, Mark was sure his fifth-grade teacher, Mrs. Bruni, was the best in the whole school. Paul didn't know about that, but he knew his Miss Peterson was the prettiest. Katie wouldn't agree. She swooned, "Did you see the beeeee-u-tiful dress Mrs. Semrau was wearing? She's from Hawaii!"

We laughed when Katie asked, "What's that grade I'm in? A girl asked me what grade I'm in and I said second because I couldn't remember that word."

"It's 'kindergarten.' "

"Oh, yeah, that's it."

When Jenny walked to school with Katie, she was exposed to new kinds of socializing as she watched Katie talk to new and old friends. Another situation arose, and my heart threatened to break the day I realized it.

I saw Jenny sitting at the kitchen counter with big tears in her eyes.

"What's the matter, Jenny?" I asked.

She just shrugged her shoulders and looked to where Katie and a friend were busy in play. I understood immediately. When the boys had started school they made new friends who came to the house to play. Jenny had been content to remain on the perimeter. She was not able to relate to schoolmates well enough to establish her own visiting friendships, but she'd had Katie for her constant companion. Now that was changing. I was sure the tears gave an insight into Jenny's unexpressible feelings.

We could not suppress Katie's natural inclinations. It was important that she have new friends and enter an increasingly sophisticated play world. So our role took on new dimensions. When Katie had certain friends in to play it was my cue to create a recreation or necessary job for Jenny in the kitchen. She learned to do minor meal preparations and took pride in them. If Daddy was around he read with her or somehow incorporated her into what he was doing.

I must say that some young children were amazing. Lisa Henry, for instance. That child created play that Jenny could handle and it never appeared that Jenny was an extra. Some other children included Jenny, but only insofar as Jenny was capapble of joining. Lisa, however, made sure that Jenny was in the circle of play.

Oh, my. There would be heartaches. We couldn't protect Jenny from everything, nor should we have. She learned that each family member has responsibilities to the other members of the family. We reiterated the idea of respecting other people and reinforced that teaching through the years.

We never get too old to receive parental example. Ken and I continued to be influenced by our parents. We recognized subtle ways that they showed respect for others without giving up their own freedoms.

For instance, when Gramma and Grampa arrived, it was "*lutefisk* and *lefse*" day at one of the churches in Stoughton.

"What's that?" Grampa asked.

"Well, Grampa," his son explained, "it's not exactly like your Bohemian meat, kraut, and dumplings, but it's dear to the Norwegian heritage. From what we've gathered, the old-timers used to dry whitefish to make it last through the winter. A soaking process made it edible again. That's called lutefisk. Lefse is a pancake-thin bread made from mashed potatoes and flour. It's rolled thin and cooked on a grill or skillet like the flour tortillas of Mexico. Some of the churches in this area earn money from lutefisk and lefse dinners. It's usually served with meatballs."

Ken continued, "We're going there to eat tonight so we can learn what it tastes like."

The children ate with varying degrees of interest while we discussed national customs. Placing his napkin back on the table, Ken asked, "Well, Grampa, how'd you like it?"

Grampa answered, "I'm sure glad I'm Bohemian." But he ate it without complaining. Grampa thought the lutefisk and lefse could never take the place of kraut and dumplings, fruit dumplings, and kolaches, but he wouldn't expect a Norwegian to believe that.

Gramma and Grampa saw that our household was becoming more and more a den of activity that Jenny took interest in. For a child who couldn't verbalize clearly, she was certainly inquisitive. She hung around Paul's eighth birthday party and watched the pirate-dressed guests walk the plank, pin the patch on the pirate's eye, and vie for gold-wrapped chocolate coins. She went with us to art fairs, punt-pass-kick contests, soccer games at the seminary, and whatever the boys or Katie showed interest in.

Katie, Jenny's leader. I can't imagine what Jenny's life would have been like without her. They raked leaves to jump in, and when ours weren't enough they accepted Mr. Jenson's invitation to use his. They played tetherball and jumped rope to singsong rhymes; played school, house, restaurant, beauty parlor, church, and the gamut of life situations that intrigue a child. Up and down the stairs they played, Jenny learning how to do things by watching her five-years-younger sister.

Since they played so well together, I had an element of control over my days, though some mothers might question whether anything can be called controlled when there are children of any number or any age in a home. Perhaps my control existed only in relation to Dad's brimful days. Despite the demands on his hours, he made time for his family and even managed some minutes for himself. But patients remained most important.

There are relatively few real medical emergencies, but when anything happens to us personally it indeed seems an emergency. Ken kept that in mind when caring for his patients. However, I think we parents need to teach our children that much of what happens to our bodies can be taken care of by ourselves. We have become a nation of media-believers who expect instant cures for just about everything. We have forgotten there are home remedies; that our bodies are remarkable works of art that function very well if given half a chance; that we don't need all the medications advertised; that often the body needs only time to shed aches and pains. Sometimes we expect doctors to prescribe medicines that we don't need.

There are, of course, some real medical problems in children, and we need to be alert to telltale symptoms. But we live with our children; we know them; we soon learn how they act when they are merely trying to get their way or want to stay home from school. We can recognize when they are truly feverish or suffering malaise. What we teach them about sickness and health when they are young is what they will know when they are grown.

We taught our children that they should not abuse their bodies with unnecessary medications, not even simple home remedies. They were not allowed to use their health wrongly for getting out of undesired activities, or to miss school if they didn't have homework completed.

They learned in school about well-balanced diets. When I served those foods I felt perfectly justified in telling them, "Sorry, guys, you don't need those vitamins they advertise on TV."

Ken helped teach our family nutritional values by being an example. I could serve any food and know it would be eaten. And our children learned early, from their Dad, that if they didn't eat a little bit of everything that was served for a meal they could expect a second helping of whatever they begrudged. Since most new flavors were tolerated after two or three eatings, our children quickly developed a taste for a wide variety of foods. We warned them that if we traveled to exotic places they would certainly want to be able to eat whatever foods were placed before them.

Immunizations were considered of vital importance. Jenny, for no apparent reason, had retardation with subsequent learning difficulties; so we knew there were traumatizing problems without flirting with the known, preventable causes. There are some tragic consequences from communicable diseases that could be prevented by immunizations. (I do realize that there are sometimes reactions to immunizations.)

Jenny was lucky. She remained remarkably healthy. The one health problem most difficult to deal with was her teeth. Because of her gag reflex, she did not develop good dental hygiene. Continuing to teach her activated the gag reaction. When Jenny was younger, we had finally resorted to a general anesthetic to get some needed work done on her teeth.

Now our dentist friend, Dr. Henry, took Jenny under his wing. He invited her to his office to "just sort of look around." He showed her his treatment rooms and let her ride up and down in his chair. She liked that. She saw a patient who had his mouth open and was getting his teeth checked. Then Dr. Henry invited her to choose a trinket from the treasure chest. And that was all he did her first visit.

"You come back again sometime, Jenny, and visit me."

She did go back again, and that time he showed her some of his tools and told her what they were for. He let her handle some of them.

Then he asked, "Someday would you like me to look at your teeth and see if they're all right?" She wasn't quite ready for that. Someday. But not today. So that was all for that visit.

After considerable reinforcing at home we could suggest, "Dr. Henry is wondering when you're going to come visit him again. Would you like to have him look at your teeth, Jenny!"

His friendly persuasion paid off. Despite her traumatic experience in the past, she accepted his care. He guided her through the worst of her gagging years; and she came to accept routine dental care and assumed daily brushing and flossing.

He was another in a steady stream of people throughout the years who helped Jenny learn and have new experiences; just as our older friend Anna Olson did when she gave Katie and Jenny a special invitation to her house for lunch. They dressed in their favorite school clothes and assured me they would remember their manners.

We're not sure why Jenny was finally ready to accept learning, but she was. Persistence and consistency — perhaps those are the keys in teaching special children. They were necessary for Jenny's learning. We knew her teachers practiced those qualities.

Her teacher used varied methods to reach her students' reasoning powers. Jenny couldn't explain fully what new activity was pending when she brought a note from school requesting four eggs.

"Cookies, cookies!"

I decided her teacher must be a glutton for punishment. It took much care and patience to help Jenny in our kitchen, but there was a teacher with ten slow learners, four girls and six boys!

The next note requested a rolling pin and cookie cutter. Rolled cookies? Now that demanded real courage! I could really understand the final note: "If you have the time, would you like to come and help the children frost cookies?"

I did go. It was a good learning experience for those students — and for me. They dealt with measurements, procedures, and coordination. A simple task for me took major concentration for some of them. Frosting the cookies demanded a close test of their coordination when they maneuvered knives around the cookie surface. Creativity was expressed by putting sprinkles on top, or by adding contrasting-colored frosting. Then they had the pride of sharing. They wrapped their cookies to take home to mother and dad. I hoped all the parents were receptive and recognized what that gift represented.

Another school activity for Jenny was looking through magazines to find pictures that started with certain sounds. She had a hard time grasping that, so we all helped her — our vocabulary sounded like hissing animals as we emphasized consonants. Imagine the gratefulness I felt when, cooking a pheasant that our friends had given us for Christmas, I heard Jenny at my side ask, "F?"

I dropped the bird, hugged her excitedly, and said, "Yes, Jenny! Yes, oh yes!"

Oh, happy day! Later she could learn that "ph" is also the sound of "f".

It was eighteen degrees below zero that night when I tucked our complex child into bed, with a warmth of heart that belied the frigid temperature.

As cold as it was, her dad went out at midnight to add another coat of water to the parking area by the garage. He had built up the edges with snow to hold water for an ice-skating rink. The kids loved having a rink right out our back door.

The boys' friends joined them for hockey and ice-skating basketball. Our back porch was a jumble of water hose, ice skates, and winter apparel — and Jenny's chair. She tried to skate but lacked confidence, so she pushed the chair around for balance.

Winter is a magical time of year, especially for children. Ours learned to ski but envied their friends their snowmobiles and accepted rides whenever they were offered. We resisted the temptation to buy that noise that would mar the environment. Instead we walked in the beauty and serenity, and that was the winter activity that Jenny tolerated best. The others felt the wind at their faces when they rode sleds and toboggans down the school hill. When they came home shivering but exhilarated, they settled down with hot chocolate and sometimes roasted marshmallows at the fireplace; or they rushed back from play to hurry and do their piano practicing or studying. They were flexible enough that if routine was broken it didn't cause undue setbacks.

Jenny, though, must have routine in her life. The rest of us had traditions. Jenny had routines. She kept routines and needed them just as surely as she needed food. When her routine got disrupted, she needed someone to guide her back to her comfortable niche again.

One of her routines at school continued to be speech therapy. That year Barbara Sternberg used a different approach. Instead of stressing articulation, she concentrated on language work, feeling it was important that Jenny have more to say than just words and short phrases.

In a local newspaper article, Jenny was pictured with her therapist working with picture cards. I was reminded of our visit — how many years before? — to St. Coletta's School, where I saw the teenager try to speak by using cards. No longer was I afraid. Quite the contrary. Now I felt intense gratitude!

Special education seems costly to the tax system, but it educates people who can eventually enter the work world and become a credit to society and to themselves.

Our school, thanks to teacher Naomi Strasburg, initiated a one-room special-education class in 1957 for fifteen students. In 1970, the town of four thousand, with three special rooms that schooled forty-five to fifty students, gave Naomi its "citizen of the years" appreciation award. Her caring had affected many families!

Jenny is just one example of the type of handicap that benefits from special schooling. We cannot assume that just because someone is in special ed he is retarded. It is also for other kinds of learning and emotional disabilities.

In special ed the students can be kept with their peers while being allowed to function at a level at which they *can* function. Teachers gear the classes to individual attention and to repetition that is very necessary. The child can and does learn. It is heartbreaking to measure such accomplishments by dollars-and-cents value.

What would *we* have done without special ed?

Perhaps empathy for my fellow schoolmates when I was young helped prepare me for having Jenny, and prompted my recognition of the value of special ed.

We had definite reasons that year to appreciate special ed.

Suddenly our hope for Jenny nosedived when she started stuttering so badly she couldn't communicate with us at all. We thought it must surely be caused by a new situation that had entered her life over which we had no control. Some days Jenny was notified not to come to school because there was no substitute teacher to cover for her ailing teacher. Finally it became necessary to reassign the special-ed students to other rooms, and Jenny was placed in a regular first-grade room.

We felt that Dr. Klové was being proven right. He had warned against placing her in a situation where she couldn't succeed. He was sure she would react adversely. She certainly was reacting adversely!

We considered keeping her at home, but didn't. As at other times through the years, we pushed on despite the uncertainties, because we didn't know if alternatives would solve the problems.

While we were in the throes of new emotions over Jenny's stuttering, I received consolation from birthday cards. Katie drew a picture for me — of a house with arms on it. A guidance counselor friend told us it was evidence that Katie thought of her home as a happy home. Jenny's card was a picture of an Easter bunny or a cat — we were not quite sure which. Paul's card said, "The good time of the year came because it is your birthday." And Mark? It seemed that was the year he needed to tell Ken and me how he felt about us. He was eleven years old, and long ago we had quit thinking of him as being only thirteen months older than Jenny. He was years older!

For my card he drew a map of where our next trip would be. There was also Lucy, from the "Peanuts" cartoon, holding a birthday cake with scads of candles on it labeled, "Happiness is a cake with lots of candles." Inside he wrote a note: "To a great Mom who keeps our clothes clean and mended, feeds us at every meal time, irons our clothes, takes care of the dog when we are at school. We like her especially because she does things like playing basketball, ping-pong, football, baseball, croquet, and tennis. She does things other mothers don't do like fly an airplane, take French lessons, Cub Scouts and skiing."

How do children know when we most need a warm blanket of affection?

Often when caring for Jenny I felt totally drained of every ounce of patience in my body. I was sure our children would remember me only as "that woman who yelled at us all the time." Their birthday cards to me were a loving reassurance that maybe family life was going smoothly enough.

Ken seemed always to be a pillar of patience. I knew what his days were like in the medical world, and yet when he walked into our home an air of peace settled over us all. The children responded to his gentle guiding. He has said a most important aspect of his days was being able to come home from work and know his family would be there to greet him.

That year Mark won a Father's Day prize, offered by the local newspaper, for writing about his Dad. I think Ken was as pleased as I had been with my birthday note. Mark wrote: "I think my Dad should be Father of the Year because he always plays sports with me. Dad belongs to the flying club and gives me airplane rides. He helps me with my homework when I need help. My dad puts in time as being a Cubmaster. He helped me make a float which won a grand prize at the school. Every summmer my dad takes our family on a long trip. I am proud of him because he is a doctor and is always willing to help other people. Dad finds time to play with my brother and sisters. He is awfully nice to Mom. I like him especially because he cares about the family and wants me to grow up and be a good person."

Our days and emotions revolved so much around Jenny. Or so it seemed. It was good to know that our other children didn't see it that way. Indeed, we had found time for everything. Somehow there *was* time for our work, for community action, for all our children, for friends, and for ourselves.

It had been a frustrating end to the school year for Jenny. We definitely learned that she slid backwards when the pressure was too much.

Conferring with her speech therapist, we discussed Jenny at some length. She felt there might be hope for Jenny if someone could break whatever barrier was holding her back. Well, we had been thinking that since her infancy. There always seemed to be some sort of a barrier that a specific key might be able to unlock. But what was the key?

There was little else we could offer Jenny beyond what she was already receiving, so we kept repeating what we had always done.

That summer we refreshed her with another traveling adventure, this time to the western states. Our French AFS friend, Anne Gazengel, accompanied us from Billings, Montana, round about to Spokane. All of Montana captivated us, and San Francisco captivated Anne, but she was absolutely amazed that there could be so many hundreds of miles of desolation between Salt Lake City and Reno. Our children collected picture postcards, advertising brochures, and the memory of new experiences to share with their next classmates.

We returned to the busy pseudo-routine of Wisconsin summer. Jenny was still stuttering, but we could communicate.

Jenny's summer held a special highlight.

"Hey, Jenny! Uncle Buddy's are coming!" They were her godparents.

They seldom came, and we wondered if Jenny was prepared well enough to receive First Communion while they were visiting.

We had tried often to help her learn her relation to her Creator. The study guides, records, and booklets given us by Redemptorist friends were helpful. One was *My Guide to Heaven* by James W. Fieder, published by St. Coletta School for Exceptional Children. That booklet was graded to suit different levels of intelligence; the first ten pages giving simplified specifics about God.

We took Jenny to visit our parish priest, Father Wayne Turner. Father asked her questions and determined that she understood enough and could receive the Sacrament of Holy Eucharist. Because of Jenny's occasional gag reflex, he practiced with her with the unconsecrated host.

There would be no special ceremony for Jenny. It seemed best to keep it simple and not put her under any extra pressure. She would go to Mass with us like always and simply leave the pew with us and approach the Communion table with no undue attention. We practiced at home and in the church. She would have a simple white short-sleeved dress with touches of teal blue accenting it. She would not wear a veil. We wanted nothing to distract her. Her godparents and five cousins arrived the day before from Nebraska.

The big day dawned. We were excited for Jenny, and she knew it. She looked pretty in her simple dress. On her wrist was a dainty corsage from Dr. Boulet's family. (Jenny has it among her souvenirs.) Word had spread to parish friends, some of whom gave her cards, and little gifts, and of course congratulatory hugs. It was a special day for her and for us. She handled it all very well.

The spiritual aspects of Jenny's life were as important as the academics. It all fit together nicely.

Jenny's life was following a pattern of sorts.

The next groove in the pattern was her final visit to Kr. Klové. Her psychometric levels tested to essentially the same scores as those obtained the summer before. He felt she clearly belonged in a class for educable retardates and saw no indication for any kind of institutional placement. He again stressed that she would encounter unreasonable difficulties in a regular grade placement.

We agreed because we had seen.

We were reassured that there would be a teacher for elementary special education when the fall term started. They also planned to continue Jenny in speech therapy.

Jenny's stuttering was one more problem to handle patiently.

§§ 12 §§

... eleven and blossoming ...

In the fall of 1970, Jenny was ten and one-half years old with these measurements: Chest twenty-five inches, waist twenty-one inches, hips twenty-six inches, height fifty-five inches, weight fifty-eight pounds, shoe size three, inseam twenty-five inches, hand six inches, head nineteen and a half inches.

She started her sixth year of schooling, walking to and from with Katie, who was in first grade. Rooms in the elementary school building had been reshuffled to create a permanent special-education facility. Her new teacher, Mrs. Webb, had recently earned a degree in special education — an academic specialty we were beginning to hear about more often. Increasingly, there were media reports concerning the rights of the handicapped. Physical facilities, academic possibilities, and medical research were being reevaluated. Doors to real life were opening throughout the nation for physically and mentally handicapped students.

Jenny truly enjoyed school and ate lunch there because her teacher hoped it would encourage social interaction.

Speech therapy remained an integral part of Jenny's schooling. Without it the years might have been a waste. Even with it, it was a long hard struggle for our child. Her new therapist, Mrs. VandenNoven, worked on all areas from articulation to sentence structure. She used colorful cardboard train cars to represent parts of a sentence, and it was Jenny's task to try to make a complete train by forming a complete sentence.

Jenny read and sounded out new words. Her spelling improved as she figured out beginning sounds and words that rhymed.

Math, requiring abstract thinking, meant mistakes in simple addition and subtraction problems. If there weren't enough fingers to count on, she was stymied. Jenny probably will never learn the intricacies of math but has proved that she *can* accomplish routine procedures. Perhaps such children should master a computer instrument to gain some independence?

To give Jenny opportunities to be with normal students, her teacher suggested she attend social studies with a first-grade class. It would be followed up with tutoring in her own room. Even though Jenny had that adverse reaction to the first-grade situation the year before, we concurred with the suggestion, since it would be for only one class.

For home we bought simple workbooks to fill her hours. No longer was she content to do just art work or to play; she wanted to apply her knowledge of words.

Jenny consumed a lot of our thought but increasingly less of my actions and more of Katie's. Through Katie she reached for greater achievements, because what Katie did Jenny imitated. Katie reveled in reading anything and everything. A reading contest in her schoolroom was so much pie in the sky. She needed no incentive, because as far as she was concerned reading was her God-given right and she must get on with it. Whatever I was doing, Katie was often at my side reading aloud. So, therefore, was Jenny on my other. I listened in stereo.

Motherhood is such constant giving of oneself. Our children should be able to rely on us, even in ways like Mark, in sixth grade, who attended junior high school several blocks from our home. Sports and music enhanced his curriculum and his forgetfulness enhanced mine. Was it my imagination or did it always happen on the coldest days of the year?

Over the phone I heard, "Mom! I forgot my trombone and I can't come home to get it because I have class. I wish I could. Is there some way you can get it to me?"

"I don't know. The car didn't start today."

"What am I going to do?" he wailed.

Motheringly, I said, "I'll see what I can do. Go to the front office before band class and see if it's been delivered. If not, you'll just have to skip band today."

Hmmm. I wondered what Dad's schedule was. I called the clinic. Wouldn't you know, he was scrubbed in surgery.

It was well below freezing, and I hesitated to call out any of my friends whose cars might not start either. So I faced the alternative. I thought nothing of bundling our children in warm clothes each morning and scooting them out the door to school. If they could do it, I guessed so could I. I chose the warmest clothes in the closet, donned a ski sweater and Ken's down-filled coat, planted a wool cap on my locks, and set out to brave the elements with Mark's bulky trombone case in hand.

By the time I walked those several blocks I figured I deserved any compliment that came my way! I also relearned why kids cavort in play while they wend their way to school in the winter. It keeps them from freezing to death!

When we cared for our children or anyone else, our children learned to care. They watched as Ken and I showed special caring when we received a call revealing his parents had been in a car accident in Iowa. They were in a hospital. We drove to their assistance and brought them home. Katie and Jenny gladly gave up their bedroom and assumed the role of nurses.

While Gramma healed, she cooked us Bohemian delicacies. And in beautiful, unselfish, simple ways she entered the world of a child. When she made desserts she told Jenny and Katie, "Go get your doll pans and you can make tiny pies." Or cakes, or cookies, or whatever. She served full course meals in tiny doll dishes. Her gifts were of herself. Or they might be as simple as a personal letter that included a stick of gum, a shiny penny or a balloon. She knew gifts did not have to be expensive.

When our children received gifts, we made certain they wrote thank-you notes, even if weeks inadvertently passed. Jenny's correspondence endeavors needed much encouraging from us and persistence from her. Her accomplishments served as an example to her siblings. Occasionally, though, she got one of her notes returned with a message saying, "I think Jenny put the wrong letter in my envelope." Her correspondents are patient, and so were the mailmen who deciphered her addresses.

And speaking of gifts. My oh my, we had to be sneaky at Christmas. An article in the *Liguorian* magazine caught my eye and I read to Ken, "Santa Claus giving is the greatest kind of giving because it is anonymous."

"Well," Ken replied, "If we don't find a better method, ours isn't going to be very anonymous anymore."

The children were on to us. Paul raced to the window immediately whenever he heard the car drive in, and Katie was half a step behind. Jenny followed, but her non-abstract thinking could not draw any conclusions. She was to have many years of childlike Christmases yet.

Jenny had a hard time keeping anonymous when she prepared for the family gift exchange because it was exceedingly difficult for her to make decisions. In fact, it was almost impossible. Decisions of all sorts challenged her severely. So we helped her select gifts, using what allowance money she had saved, and what coins she had earned doing special chores around the house. It seemed good that our children exchanged gifts: while they did their own choosing and shopping, they had to think about what someone else might enjoy; they learned how to budget their meager income and shop prudently; they learned that good gifts don't have to be expensive and can be purchased in all types of stores, even grocery stores. Jenny wrapped her own gifts; sometimes the packages were not very neat, but they were always well received.

Christmas traditions increased yearly. We heard requests from all quarters.

"We're going to make plenty of pecan tassies, aren't we?"

"How about the bonbons?"

"Let's make sure we've got plenty of Mexican wedding cakes!"

"Do we get to frost cookies?"

Besides those requests, there were new recipes to try. We didn't need all those cookies so we gave some away, and thus another tradition started. On Christmas Eve day we filled plates with the assorted delicacies and went, as a family, to deliver them to friends. Sometimes we carolled the recipients, and always we hoped for snow.

Traditions entered our family life so subtly we sometimes were unaware that they had started. I recognized the value of traditions some years later when our post-college son spent the pre-Christmas weeks with us. During college he had been unable to get home until just a couple days before Christmas, and he'd had to suppress his longings to be part of the preparations. When he could finally be with us for an extended visit, he found that in some ways we had changed. We weren't like what he had remembered from his elementary- and high-school years. Well, neither was he. We were keenly aware that he had changed out of adolescence to maturity, and we had expected that change. But he had spent only brief holidays with us since then, and we had been so busy that he hadn't noticed we were changing. As our children matured and needed less of our time, Ken and I had developed new interests, some of them very time-consuming (such as writing this book). Our son could now see this for himself, and it took time for him to adjust to our new image. Those who were still at home felt comfortable with us and defended our actions. They were used to us. But our returned graduate said, "Not all is as I remembered it."

Our children changed and we expected it. We didn't see the change day to day, but it was there and we merely accepted it. We parents have a right to change also, to broaden our ideas and interests.

During those Christmas weeks I began to see the lasting value of traditions. Despite the disrupting emotions caused by learning that change occurs in each of us at all ages, our family retained a strong continuity. Traditions as simple as delivering plates of cookies to friends, or singing them carols, held us together as a family. Our continuity was strongly bound by traditions. We repeated activities again and again. We reminisced and dreamed ahead. We shared a quality of life that has subtly evolved through the years in a way that is right for us. We could see that we have changed, but we could still come back together as a strong family. Traditions made it easier.

Our traditions don't recur just at Christmas. They permeate the entire year. They are material, and they are spiritual. Tradition is part of the reason why we beat all odds to attend church services while we are traveling. It is why we celebrate birthdays. It is why we are close to relatives though we live far away. It is why we feel especially sad when a particular dish breaks. It is an important part of our life.

So anyway, this year that college son had turned twelve and we wanted to surprise him with a different kind of birthday celebration. Unknown to him, we invited several of his friends for early Sunday morning breakfast of his favorite: pancakes with butter and syrup, topped with strawberries and whipped cream. He was surprised, to say the least.

When Mark celebrated his birthday it meant Jenny's wasn't far behind. That eleventh year we gave her warm ski gear. The boys had become proficient on downhill skis, and with their help we worked with Jenny and Katie. It took many tries for Jenny to comprehend what she was supposed to do for a snowplow maneuver. Ken guided her up the tow rope between his legs, and Mark, Ken, and I took turns encouraging her down the slopes.

Sometimes we wondered if we should push her so hard to attempt the things we found pleasurable. But if we never pushed ourselves beyond our suspected limits, would we ever rise to new heights of learning? It seemed all of Jenny's life we pushed her beyond her limits, though at the time it only seemed we were pulling her along so we wouldn't have to leave her behind. And yet she, too, derived pleasures from our activities.

Perhaps the biggest struggle was the patience it demanded of us. We met that demand because it kept Jenny with us. It was hard for us to accept letting her stay home while we were out having fun. That loomed as a big problem in our minds.

We wondered if there would come a time when she simply could not keep up with us or would not want to. We feared that possibility.

We pushed her to her limits sometimes, but we did it with loving hearts. Because we did push, Jenny managed to add new accomplishments and became more aware of the lives around her. I think the pushing, prodding, and pulling has been worth it.

When we returned from one ski outing our conversation turned to vacation plans. Being cooped up in a car often prompted such discussions.

One of the boys asked, "Where are we going on our summer trip?"

Dad replied, "I don't think we'll go anywhere this summer."

"Ahh, Dad!" voices wailed, "Why not?"

"Because we don't want you to assume you can always go on a trip each summer. Lots of kids never get to go on trips."

They knew that. There was an understanding silence.

Then Dad said, "If we do, where would you want to go?"

Over the seat went the ragged Rand McNally road atlas. Our children were vividly aware of their country and its states. They knew the terrain of states and had their favorites. Their car games included naming states, capitals, cities, and countries. They learned how to navigate, and even Jenny eventually learned. They associated friends and relatives with states and couldn't understand why some of their schoolmates had no idea where their own relatives lived. Geography was alive for our young ones.

Planning a trip included planning how the children could earn some extra money. They received an allowance, but it was minimal, especially compared to what some of their friends were given. Besides personal spending, it had to be budgeted to include gift-buying and charity. On birthdays it was raised by nickel-and-dime increments. That year Jenny received seventy-five cents a week. By age eighteen it would be three dollars. There would be none after graduation if she were able to work for income. The limited amount allowed them to want, and need, to earn extra money. I think it also kept them interested in simple pleasures of life that didn't cost money. We never threatened to take away their allowance. It wasn't enough so that we felt we were paying them to do their chores. Chores were merely expected of them. For instance, they could not leave for school until their beds were made, rooms reasonably picked up, and any requested chores finished. Meal preparations, cleanup, lawn care were teamwork. They did such jobs because they were part of our family and our family worked together.

The actual value of money meant little to Jenny, but she enjoyed sorting her coins. She knew she had to have money to buy something from a store, but a gift was a gift — simple as that. In her mind, pricetags were incomprehensible. Jenny needed guidance in using her money; she probably will always need it.

We chose our own ways to pass on values; what is right for us might not be right for another. Some of our methods were chosen because of what Ken's and my childhood was like and how we reacted to it. It behooved us to look at ourselves critically once in a while to see just what it was we were passing on to our children, and if it was in their best interests.

Sometimes we passed on values by unexpected actions. I wonder how many times our children hear me say, "If God has given you a talent, you should be willing to share it." Whether they were to perform in a skit, a play, at a band performance, in sports, or whatever, I spoke of sharing talents. It's easy to preach, but what to do when a child turns the tables? It was tempting to say, "Let the other guy do it." Another method, though, allows credibility. And that's what Ken and I did when a ridiculous basketball game was scheduled involving the medical community to earn money for the hospital. Our kids loved it when Dad or I shot baskets with them, so when they heard about the upcoming game they automatically assumed we should play. We vacillated but finally agreed. Our sons' eager encouraging turned to disbelief when they saw our uniforms — Dad looked really fetching in a green curly wig and tennis shorts topped with a supportive orthopedic corset. I hid behind a frumpy housedress, high-top tennis shoes and wig. Our laughing consent to be part of that charity project turned to disbelief when we saw the spectator-packed gym! At least we had put our actions where our words were.

Days proceeded toward spring without incident, until we noticed Jenny was beginning to do exaggerated blinking. What had caused that? We discouraged it, we discussed it, we got her hair cut in case it was irritating, and finally impatiently tried to accept it. That often was the course we followed through the years when we frustratingly dealt with her adverse reactions. We looked at ourselves, wondering if in some way we were to blame — maybe we weren't giving her the time or attention that she needed?

Never could she tell us how she felt about anything. We could only guess. She talked only of things, never ideas or feelings. There was so much we needed to know.

I suppose we could have had more parent-teacher conferences, and yet when we had them the same topics were discussed repeatedly. With caring, certainly, but Jenny did not make strides like the normal child, so of course there was repetition in discussing her. Her advancements were labored and time-consuming.

Her teacher made a home visit, which we readily agreed to. It gave her the opportunity to see Jenny's home environment, as important for the teacher as it was for us to see Jenny's classroom.

We discussed Jenny's eye-blinking and came to no conclusions.

However, a few weeks later her teacher determined that Jenny, for some reason unknown to all, no longer tolerated going to the first-grade social-studies class. Mrs. Webb knew that we would respect her decision to withdraw Jenny from that class. She knew we cared a great deal about Jenny and so gave us support. We in turn trusted her.

Out of that kind of respect comes cooperation that can result in success.

We still didn't associate the eye blinking to the social-studies class. Maybe it's just as well. Had we recognized the correlation, perhaps we wouldn't have taken a critical look at ourselves. On the other hand, we might have prevented Jenny some agonizing moments, and she might have been able to learn something else more effectively.

It was not easy to see patterns while we lived out our lives. Only when I did research about Jenny's life did I see the correlation between the blinking and the social-studies class.

Jenny blinked into spring as the seasonal fever hit us. We went for hikes along the creek and purchased gardening seeds. With the blossoming of spring I looked at Jenny with new awareness. She might not have the mentality to grasp all that was around her, but her body was progressing in its growth no matter what. Oh! To have been able to keep her a child.

I made half-hearted attempts to prepare her for eventual body changes. It was not easy. Since I still helped her with bath preparations and hair washes, some of our conversations about personal things took place in the bathroom.

Sexuality was not taught in one day nor in one way. Sexuality was not a graphic description of the marital act. Sexuality was an understanding and respect for self and a respect for others.

We had tried to teach Jenny to sit like a lady and to act like a lady. Isn't that the age-old admonition? There is much more that constitutes a morally sexual character. Yet, perhaps an understanding for it all stems back to that simple admonition that can be understood by a child.

Jenny needed to learn to be responsible for her own actions; that she must respect her own and other peoples' needs; that her body would undergo changes. She could not understand that in one quick lesson. It had to be taught whenever a chance presented itself.

We tried to teach her that good behavior is a compliment to herself, to others, and to God. We pointed out other peoples' behavior and Jenny answered simple questions about why it is easier to like some people more than others.

Through a repetitive process we hoped Jenny would become familiar with herself and with her relationship to the rest of mankind.

What wasn't so easy was to prepare her for her body changes. With a normal child the foundation is that each body function has a purpose and some of them lead to the procreation of mankind.

With Jenny it wasn't that simple, because at that point in her life it seemed highly unlikely that she would ever be capable of being a mother. Mothering begs for an intelligent response to children's needs. Since I believe that the marital act should be receptive to creation, I wanted to help Jenny attain an aesthetic level beyond just the acceptance of physical change only for the purpose of conjugal love.

I *want* to let children be like children for as long as possible, but that is becoming virtually impossible when the media constantly and irresponsibly wave their banner of temptations. Children must be knowledgeable, certainly, but they need not be tempered into accepting sexuality as only sex.

I feel that spiritual tempering is necessary for an unselfish understanding of sexuality. For that reason, I wonder if schools are able to offer attitudes for moral development. Without a responsible approach, we can only expect animal reactions.

I told Jenny about her internal physical makeup and how it would grow and change just as her external image would. I drew pictures for her. Together we shopped for her sanitary supplies to have on hand for the eventual day when menstruation would start and her body would want it to be known that maturity had set in. Together we practiced the application. I could not, however, emphasize that those changes would come about to prepare her body for motherhood. Instead I spoke in terms of her body becoming complete, as it needs to be when she is a woman.

Instead of using married friends for examples, I talked to her about our single friends who were leading beautiful, caring, fulfilled lives. I told her that their bodies, too, had changed at some time in their lives.

Each year I added depth to the conversations. Later when Jenny was in a high-school physical education class that included information about the characteristics of both the female sexual organs and the male sexual organs I read the chapters with her. I stressed the responsibility that should accompany the use of these organs. I helped her draw pictures and label the body parts.

Jenny's life has remained simplistic, and I'm not sure she imagines marital oneness in the physical sense. It is especially satisfying that she has an aesthetic value of sexuality.

I read an article in *Exceptional Parent* magazine written by a woman with spina bifida who had undergone repeated operations.

Her philosophy was beautiful. She gained satisfaction, not from the physical sexual world that most people understand, but rather from the aesthetically sexual world of fine arts. That same sense of life is possible for Jenny.

Also in *Exceptional Parent* magazine I read pros and cons concerning sterilization of the handicapped. Rather than reduce Jenny to that reactionary level, I wanted her to learn responsibility for her actions, and to learn that a human being can say no. Jenny was taught that with pleasure of any kind comes responsibility.

She has been told what abortion is. I believe there is a terrible loss of human dignity for everybody involved in that selfish situation. Jenny has been presented with the idea that a human being who learns self-discipline does not have to be subjected to humiliating herself, her child, society, or God in such a way. She also has been told that if anything happens in her life that falls astray of these moral teachings, she can come to her mother, father, sisters, or brothers first. From us comes deep caring and an interest in her that recognizes that her relationship with God supersedes any other interest.

Physical self-stimulation was another puzzle to deal with. I see it as a selfish act that, if allowed to become routine, could lead to the exclusion of others. Of itself it cannot lead to procreation, so therefore it can satisfy only our own emotional needs, which, I believe, can be satisfied by the aesthetics. I therefore believe that self-manipulation is unnecessary. However, it would be unfair of me to judge Jenny's actions in the same way I judge my own. Nor is Jenny's ability to understand moral teachings the same as our other children's; but if I want them to understand certain philosophies, then I should want those same values for Jenny, even if she is retarded.

I did not openly discuss self-stimulation with Jenny because some facets of life might be foreign to her and I saw no good reason to expose her questionably comprehending mind to the idea. Instead, positive actions were substituted. She learned cleanliness and wore well-fitted underclothes. She took a soft animal or doll to bed — perhaps she would cuddle it rather than be interested only in herself. We rocked her with her legs together. Her hands were guided to proper uses.

I had to remember that besides living with Jenny, and she with herself, I also had to live comfortably with myself. I could do that since, in language that she understood, I had tried to present my philosophy in a way that might possibly be effective.

Jenny needed supervision, and it demanded cooperation of one kind and another from all of us who shared her home. As Jenny prepared for her bodily changes, so did the other children. Because our sons learned to be ready for Jenny's needs, they also learned about the girl world that surrounds them. We encouraged them to be protective of their sisters, and of all girls. Though boys' physical characteristics differ from girls,' their understanding can be similar. Ours learned that they have an important role in playing out the game plan for humanity. They learned that love is based on respect — respect for self and respect for others.

Though each of our children was taught essentially the same, they nonetheless developed individual attitudes.

Ken and I don't have all the answers, and obviously Jenny can't possibly have all the answers. But she does have loving. And that loving has been constant through the years, just as the teaching has been constant through the years. There was no instant understanding. It has been a long and continuing process, and it was important that it start when she was a little child. Morality training had to fit into life along with speech therapy, reading, writing, and arithmetic.

Jenny's school year was a good one. Her teacher thought her most progress was in social studies and science, so regardless of the blinking eyes, Jenny did learn. She had participated in discussions and sometimes knew answers when no one else did.

Jenny's 138 sessions of individual speech therapy, 20 minutes each, still did not reap questions from her. She could answer size, shape, color, location, and function. Mrs. Van, as Jenny called her therapist, worked with Jenny to increase her vocabulary to describe people, places, and things. Recall, retention, and sentence structure were in all of the therapy sessions. Jenny still substituted sounds and omitted letters. However, if words were sounded out for her, and written in syllables, she was then able to say most of them correctly.

Language was definitely part of that barrier that we were all trying to penetrate.

Her teachers suggested we let Jenny have a fun summer with no formal classes. They even suggested we do only a minimum correcting of speech mistakes.

eleven and blossoming • 119

"Okay, kids, hang in there!" Dad teased. "School's out in a few days, and then it's trip time!"

And I urged, "Get your toy items packed. Don't forget your diary books."

Finally the day arrived. We fit everything into the station wagon, grabbed the atlas and headed southwest.

"Where was that we ate breakfast?" a young voice asked.

"How do you spell Kewaunee?"

"How do you spell breakfast?"

"How'd you say you spell Kewaunee?"

Breakfast in Kewaunee. Every family has favorite sayings. One of ours is "Breakfast in Kewaunee." I don't know what we ate that morning, but it was the day Jenny started trying to write a diary. That sounds simple enough, doesn't it? But keep in mind that it was Jenny, and no matter what this story sounds like, nothing was simple with Jenny.

We must have spelled Kewaunee at least 137 times before we started spelling Albuquerque and Nogales. First we spelled it for Mark. Then for Paul. Then for Katie. And finally Jenny was ready to attempt it, but she'd get all confused because by then we were spelling other words. Jenny's diary did not have any completed entries, but she definitely had tried.

Among the grand sights and memories of that trip was the Santa Clara Pueblo in New Mexico. When we drove its narrow dirt streets between the adobe dwellings, a little old Indian lady stopped us and asked if we wanted to buy some pottery.

While our eager youngsters pressed noses against the windows, Dad said, "I don't think so, but we'll look at some if you'd like."

She told us to wait, then scurried to a humble dwelling and came back with a tea-towel-lined wicker basket filled with black pottery. She laid pleasing pieces in the hot sand, and of course we knew we must have one.

Later we climbed ladders to uninhabited multi-storied Puye Indian cliff dwellings and imagined what life must have been like in earlier lifetimes. We helped Jenny climb up and down the ladders. I wonder how many Indian children with mental handicaps climbed to their homes in that former era. Some societies are protective of their handicapped members. Some are not. Just as some American families are protective of their handicapped children and some are not. Some schools are and some aren't. I think those who are protective build up a strength in themselves as well as in the handicapped member.

We continued to wend our way through the southwestern states.

I have not mentioned Dad's affinity to shortcuts through the countryside. Any tiny blue line on a map is fair game as far as he is concerned — no matter what the season. We have run out of road in the icy, snowy, isolated reaches of Quebec. We have run into a dusky marsh of Mobile. We have seen where the cattle roam in the back-roads desolation of eastern Montana. And I can assure you, there is a blue line road somewhere around Dinnehotso, Arizona. I know because we spent hours on it. It looked as if rain hadn't fallen in twenty-five years, but I was sure if it did we would be washed away in an arroyo. The children were limited with beverages from the cooler "because we might need them before we ever find civilization again!"

It was comforting to have a doctor in the car. If only he had been a mechanic besides!

We did get back to our familiar Wisconsin civilization and resumed the summer activities.

Before that summer ended there was one special activity. Ken made reservations for dinner for the six of us at Queen's Court in Janesville.

"Here, Jenny, you sit by me," I invited. "Katie, you can sit by Dad." The boys settled in and we placed our orders.

Finally Dad said, "Mom and I have some news for you."

Eager voices questioned, "What? What?"

Dad couldn't resist the temptation to make them guess. He gave the clue that someone new was coming to live with us. They couldn't think of any relatives or friends. Maybe an AFS student? How about a pet? Well, then, were we going to adopt a baby? That let me know how old they must have thought I was!

Finally Dad revealed, "Mom's going to *have* a baby!"

What a delight to watch their reactions! It took them a moment to absorb the news.

We had been so busy pursuing our six-peopled activities for the past six years that perhaps it hadn't occurred to the boys to think it should be any other way. But not so Katie. Katie had been storming heaven. There wasn't a night she didn't put in a petition for a little baby. That was all right with Ken and me if it should be God's will, though Daddy teased her that he'd have to set his alarm clock to get in counteracting praying time.

We had wondered early in the summer trip if there would be this special news to tell. A terrible day in New Mexico, filled with detours to higher elevations, rain, hail, and car trouble, had also been accented by my having abdominal cramps every twenty minutes. Several hours later our car finally limped into Silver City, where we stopped at the first pharmacy we could find. Then we stopped at a car-repair shop. It was to close in a few moments, but they consented to fix the car. Dad called a cab to take the children and me to a motel.

The cabbie warned, "You'd better stay close to your motel room tonight because there's trouble in the town. It has to do with the union and the hospital."

"Oh great!" I thought. "Nothing like a bit of excitement to end an already unusual day."

I thought of that day as we answered questions from around the restaurant table. We asked for prayers for the good health of our new child. We explained to Jenny all that we were talking about and that she would have to wait five more months. After that we didn't care who learned our news. It had been important to us that our children be the first to hear it.

§§ 13 §§

... new chance to learn ...

Jenny gained new knowledge when she placed her little hands on my enlarging tummy to follow the growth of the baby. The children begged to be invited to feel when there was fetal movement. As the months progressed and the movement became more frequent and pronounced, they could hardly contain their excitement.

Ken and I prayed for the well-being of our next child and joined the children in their similar prayers. We also prayed that if anything was wrong we be granted the graces we would need to deal with it. We believe that if we put our trust in Him all things are possible, even accepting disappointment. We didn't, however, hesitate to ask for a healthy child.

I think parents of handicapped children who accept those handicaps and meet the challenges have the potential of becoming stronger persons. Heartaches and fears strew the years of rearing such children, but if we try, we find within us strengths that we had no idea existed.

I shared some of my thoughts with a friend whose second child has cystic fibrosis. She and I faced different challenges, and yet we were committed to creating for our children the best quality of life possible. Barb and her family had to live constantly with the knowledge that they might not have their child tomorrow, but they knew their child could learn and progress. We lived knowing our child would likely be with us for many years, but we had no idea what amount of knowledge she would be able to gain. Neither of us was justified in thinking her own cross was heavier. We watched with interest the research and experiments in medical and educational fields, never giving up hope that our own children might be benefited in time to make a difference.

Barb and I cared about each other, and we appreciated the concern that others showed for us — our support system. And yet we didn't expect or want maudlin sympathy, rather just an acceptance of our children. I loved it when people recognized that Jenny was an important and able person in her own right and accepted her for what she was, not for what she might have been or only for how they could protect her.

After talking to Barb I was always thankful our child was blessed with a healthy body; and perhaps Barb said a prayer of thanksgiving that their child could learn. It is good for parents to compare notes sometimes.

In the fall Jenny resumed school in the same room. Some parents resent that aspect of special ed. They think it offers no incentive to the child for looking forward to a new teacher and a new room. But for Jenny it was good that she could return to familiar surroundings and Mrs. Webb. She was comfortable being with known classmates and readily resumed the routine imposed on her.

She finally had her very own friend — one she hadn't inherited through sister Katie. With happy anticipation Jenny accepted an invitation to Tammy Crawford's birthday party, knowing she would go alone. Katie was genuinely happy for Jenny.

Jenny's progress in school was slow, but we took pleasure in even her smallest accomplishments. At open house we looked at her books and study aids and saw where she would sit. She still couldn't explain the day's activities to us, so it was important that we know her surroundings.

She put forth concentrated effort to learn. She liked to sound out new words and took pride in her workbook, though she needed help with it. Arithmetic perplexed her and demanded memorization since she could not grasp the concepts. She tried to learn to borrow and carry two-digit numbers.

Jenny's actions at home took on a maturity. She became conscious of the days and hours of the week. She remembered the day she and Paul should be at religion class, which day Mark attended, and when Katie should be at Brownies. She was concerned about having gifts for her family's birthdays. She knew which days I would help at the hospital snack bar and was tuned in to Dad's whereabouts. On a daily basis she reminded the boys not to forget to feed Snowball the rabbit. Often she fed Hodel, the mini-dachshund.

Her presence in the family now seemed more normal. What a tremendous difference it made being able to communicate! Even though her speech lacked spontaneity of sentence structure and ideas, we could understand her enough. Jenny was on a new level of learning. She would soon be twelve years old.

While we prepared for Christmas, the conversation often turned to the expected baby. Would it be a boy or a girl? What would we name it? Would it have hair? How long until it would walk? How long before it could play?

Jenny giggled when questioned about getting a new brother or sister. Could she imagine what it would be like to have a baby in the house? She and Katie helped to find good baby clothes among their doll items, and we washed them and replenished what we needed.

"How much longer till the baby comes?" Katie begged.

I reassured, "You only have about a month to wait after Christmas."

After the holidays, with their traditional joys, Jenny wrote thank-you letters. We helped by asking her questions and she tried to make her own answers into sentences. She sounded out and spelled what words she could, then after a copy was drafted she worked hard to print it neatly enough to send. How enlightening that Gramma saved many of those letters!

Jenny's letter that year said: "Dear Gramma. I like Christmas. Did you have snow. We made a Christmas folder. We made pictures at school. We watched Santa Claus is Coming to Town. I worked hard at school. I take my toy rabbit to bed. Hodel jump on my bed. Love, Jenny."

It was fortuitous that we prepared for the baby early, because the final month of pregnancy was a whirl of activities. I can't believe that Jenny, or any of the children, received their rightful parcel of individual attention, though the memory box proves there were parties, hikes, ice skating, and family game times.

It's good we don't know what lies ahead for us. So much better that we are allowed to meet it one day at a time.

The happenings of the next months had little to do with Jenny, though they very much affected her life.

One week before the baby's birth, a friend came to our home and asked, "Do you think that new doctor in town might be interested in buying our house?"

Ken said, "I don't know about him, but we might. Are you going to be home this noon? We'll come out and look at it."

We looked and we liked. We had respect for the carpenter who built it. In fact, we could hardly wait for the children to arrive from school to show them and get their reaction.

They loved it. The plain two-story house with basement and attached garage sat in the middle of four acres of beautiful tall oak and hickory trees. There was finishing work to be done on the house and grounds, so it could allow us to incorporate our own ideas. The children were especially intrigued by the open staircase, and bedrooms that looked out into trees. They thought it far from town, but it measured a mere mile and a half from the middle of town.

By the next day we made the decision to move.

In the midst of all the emotions of the house, we received a disturbing call that Ken's mother was seriously ill and hospitalized. Too much was happening all at once. I thought of Gramma often, and of the wives tales she handed on, especially the one she touted at delivery time — "Now Girl, you know you'll never have that baby unless you get all your little jobs done first."

The biggest activity that was still hanging over my head was Jenny's birthday. In one more day, on February 1, she would be twelve years old. We hadn't planned the traditional twelfth party because of the expected birth. I made an angel food cake and decorated it after Jenny went to bed so she could run to the kitchen in the morning to see what kind she had.

Positioning twelve candles, I thought, "Can it be possible that Jenny is this old already!"

Ken and I knelt in prayer that night and suspected our night might be interrupted with labor pains. We hoped the night wouldn't also include worse news about his mother. About midnight Ken called our neighbor to accept her offer. "Hello, Phoebe? Sorry to awaken you. Can you come and spend the rest of the night with the kids?"

Phoebe had raised a family, so she understood when I said, "You can let the kids have birthday cake for breakfast, but be sure Jenny gets to blow out the candles first."

After several hours of labor it seemed the baby would have a different birth date than Jenny's, so Ken went to give the scheduled immunization shots at school. However, when he returned to the hospital mid-morning he heard, "Hurry to the delivery room!"

He arrived just in time to see his third daughter, Sarah, make her entrance into the world, and he greeted her with, "Thank God, it's not a Cub Scout!"

That night, in the quiet, I wrote a letter to our baby. Parts of that letter read:

> Dear little Sarah Christine,
>
> Today you were born at 10:21 AM and promptly greeted the world with a wail...
>
> It is a clear winter day; snow on the ground, icicles hanging from the roofs, ice on the sidewalk. Paul was excited that he was able to slide *all* the way down the ice covered school hill standing up.
>
> Jenny is happy today; you are her birthday present at 12 years old. She will be happy to share her day with you. I hope you are always good to Jenny and always willing to share with her and all your family.
>
> ... Your Daddy and I truly feel that children are a gift of God. You are born at a time when thousands and thousands of innocent lives are being taken by abortion. We can't accept this. From the very moment we knew you existed you were a real human being and we prayed for your every well-being. We dreamed about you, made dreams for you, and all your brothers and sisters joined in asking God that you be strong and healthy. Your name was selected with loving attention, and we hope you will like it. Christina is the name of your Gramma Pavlik. She is very very sick these days in a hospital.... We had decided to call you Sarah Christine before she got sick, so it is doubly good under the circumstances. We hope she will recover enough to know and enjoy you. If she doesn't, you can be sure that you are bearing the name of a very dear and loved person.
>
> I held you after your birth and now again tonight. It was easy to love you, because we have since we knew you existed. I fed you some glucose water and you knew right away how to suck. It was a quiet and most enjoyable 45 minutes getting acquainted with you. You were stronger than I had remembered babies being. It's been seven years since we had a little one. We are eagerly anticipating the many fun hours to be spent with you....
>
> Sarah, Daddy and I wish you every good blessing from God in your life. We hope you will live a life to be deserving of His care. We have accepted you eagerly and happily... We have placed our

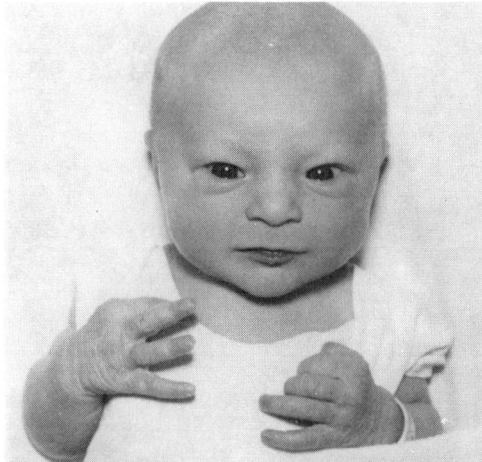

Jenny at birth, February 1, 1960: "Breathing nicely," with "ten fingers and ten toes" — no abnormalities except unusually dry, flaky hands.

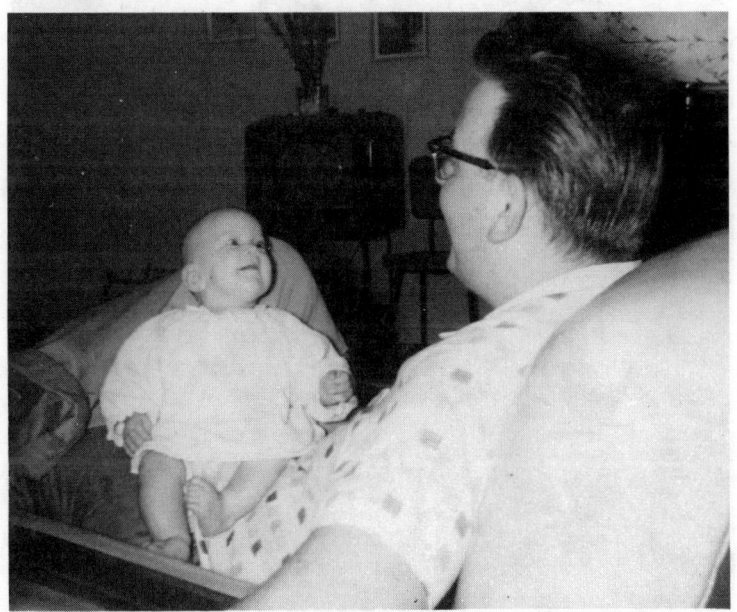

Jenny, at three months of age, scores better than a standoff in a long-drawn-out slow-smiling contest with Daddy Ken.

California in 1961: one-year-old Jenny being taught how to play by brother Mark, who tempts her with colorful wrapping paper.

By Christmas in 1962, Mark and Jenny, still in their robes, flank one of Santa's most pint-sized elves — one-year-old Paul (center).

Protector Mark guides two-year-old Jenny's halting steps in the tiny enclosed backyard of the Pavlik family's billet during the Navy hitch in San Pablo, California

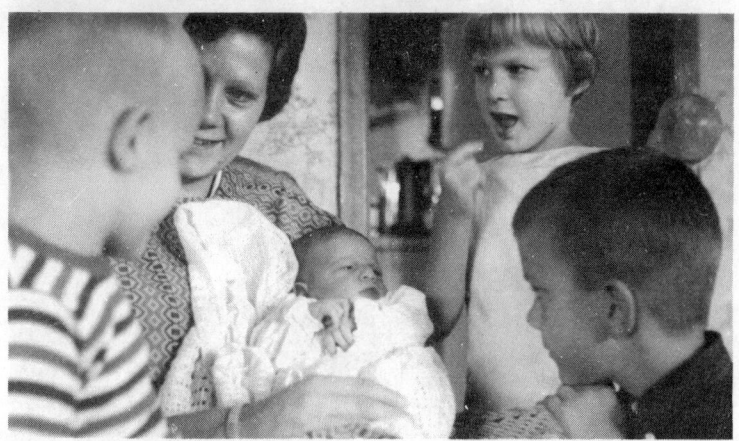

In 1964, new baby Katie, held by mother Norene, seems to elicit reactions of wonder and delight from Mark, Jenny, and Paul.

Dr. Pavlik spent hours in informal home speech therapy, as shown here in 1964, getting Jennifer to imitate the sounds of words.

On Jenny's fifth birthday, Mark shows Paul, Jen, and Katie the scrapbook he assembled for his nearest sister's new words.

Jennifer in 1966, with her steadfast friends — and sometime surrogate grandparents — Edgerton's Mr. and Mrs. Walter Welch.

Daddy Ken took as much leisure time as he could for pastimes like reading bedtime stories to daughters Jen and Katie in 1967.

The third house in Edgerton, in four acres of woods; here Dr. Pavlik carpentered his barn.

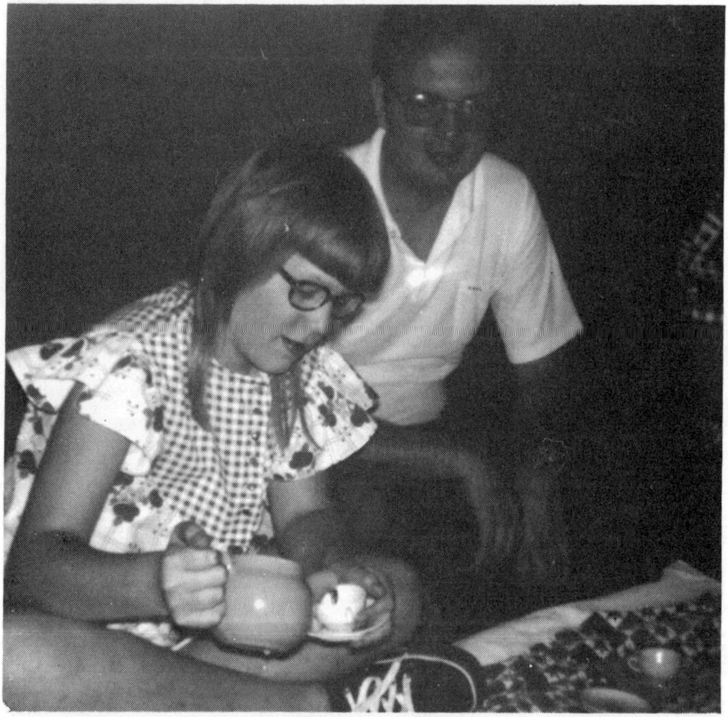

Katie pours for Uncle Keith Pavlik at the long-distance tea party catered in the tent for Gramma's birthday in 1973.

Jenny and family • 133

Even before the Air Force years in Maine and Colorado, Mark was backpacking through streams and climbing mountains in the western states. Photo was taken by cousin Doug Vakoc in 1976.

Photo below by Tom Bowditch, *Janesville Gazette*, Janesville, Wis.

Mark also led his tennis team to the 1976 Wisconsin state finals.

The Pavlik women — Mom Norene, Sarah, Jenny, and Katie — in front of the four-plex, Loring AFB, Maine, in winter 1977-78.

The school year in Maine had to be extended to accommodate the absence of children working on the potato harvest. The younger kids picked potatoes while Mark was running a machine.

Jenny and family • 135

Jenny receives the Sacrament of Confirmation from Archbishop Joseph T. Ryan in 1978; Mom is proxy sponsor for Aunt Lee.

At Confirmation (from left): Fr. Carrier, Limestone; Katie, Archbp. Ryan, Jenny; Fr. John Mahoney, Loring Chaplain; and Paul.

Katie exhibits her prizewinning science-fair entry in 1979.

The Pavliks in Colorado Springs (clockwise from upper left): Mark Paul, Dr. Ken, Jenny, Sarah, Norene, Katie; photo by Alice Bontz.

Paul, who had biked from Maine to Wisconsin, leads "big brother" Mark after the first 600 miles of the 2,200-mile Appalachian Trail.

On Location Photo

Triumphant Jenny in a sylvan setting just before 1980 graduation.

life in God's hand and He saw fit to give us you. So you, our dear child, are a Gift from God.

The day Sarah and I went home from the hospital, we bade goodbye to Daddy as he left, with pictures of the newborn, on the first of several flights to see his mother.

With the sadness, I also remember the joy of relaxation while holding our new daughter during those trying times. There were considerate gifts of food and caring. My favorite gift was a walk in the woods of the ravine behind our house. Jane Nelson made that possible when she brought her daughter to watch the sleeping baby.

Jenny helped get the white baptismal dress from the cedar chest and learned that she had worn the same dress at Baptism.

Mark and Mrs. Welch served as proxy for the godparents, Uncle Danny and Aunt Glenna. While Mark proudly held his baby sister, the children gathered close when Father Turner bestowed the sacrament.

At Sarah's fifth week, we packed everyone into the station wagon and drove six hundred miles to see Gramma. While we were there, Uncle Keith arrived with his young family from Tucson. The little cousins got reacquainted. A happy time. A sad time.

We wished we lived closer. We wished Uncle Keith lived closer. We wished Auntie Lee didn't have to return to her temporary home in Alaska. We wished Gramma weren't so ill. We wished we could stay and not have to get back to school, work, and duties. But that's not what life is about.

Moving day was approaching rapidly, and there was still much sorting and packing to do. The children looked through their belongings, and packaged toys. There wasn't much any of them wanted to throw away or give away. I added more cherished items to the cedar chest and saw the little shoes. Jenny's tiny white three-quarter-top shoes brought back poignant memories. Ken and I had chosen those thinking they might give Jenny more support for walking. How long ago that seemed!

There were items I was tempted to discard, but I'm glad now they survived, especially the reminders of Jenny's successful struggle. Samples of printing and drawing, newspaper articles, school reports, and pictures. Amid packing I sent thank-you notes for the baby gifts Sarah received. In rechecking her presents, I realized the money gifts were missing.

"Hey, you guys, where's the money from Sarah's cards?"

Katie said, "Oh! I made a bank for Sarah. It's all in there."

Indeed, Katie had assumed banker's duties. She could hardly wait to take Sarah to the big bank downtown for a savings passbook. The children made periodic visits to the bank and took pride in their savings accounts. The first time Jenny had gone, she gathered her coins together as the others were doing and carried her little jar carefully. She watched as the boys and Katie did their business at the teller's cage. Then it was her turn.

Mr. Strasburg greeted her: "Hello, Jenny! Do you have some money you want to put in the bank?"

She nodded her head and handed him the jar. He counted her coins and entered the amount on a deposit form. When the transaction was finished we thought we were ready to leave. Jenny knew we weren't. She had gone in with money and now had none. Something was wrong. We thought she had understood about "putting money in the bank." Mr. Strasburg suggested she keep a couple coins for seed. That made her happy.

During those hectic days Ken found time to help his sons enter a hand-baked creation in the annual Cub Scout father-son decorated-cake contest. I call it a creation because their nine-by-thirteen-inch cake fell dismally in the middle. With scant remorse, they merely frosted it to look like a lake. Then from one of the girls' tiny dolls they amputated an arm, stuck it in the center of the lake, and wrote with frosting, "Help! An aquanaut I'm not!"

We moved to our new home, and any questions about the rightness of doing so were dispelled immediately. The quietness! The peace! From the windows we saw trees everywhere. Small animal life was entertainment for the looking. We were ecstatic over the setting of nature and were drawn to it constantly. Oblivious to the dictates of *House Beautiful*, we placed our worn furniture facing the windows.

As for getting the children on the school bus instead of just sending them out the door to walk, it was in fact easier. And a bonus was the sense of safety I felt in putting Jenny in the capable hands of the bus driver. No more wondering how she was faring on her walk to the schoolground. Jenny liked the social atmosphere of her fellow riders — not that she talked to them, but she watched and listened, as evidenced by her affirmations of whatever was told at the supper table.

Changes came not only because the children were getting older, but also because they now lived in a bigger house.

Mark, now in junior high, was the recipient of people's judgments. For the first time he felt a sense of frustration in being the child of a doctor. No qualms about being Dad's son, but rather about how some people reacted to the fact that his dad was a doctor. Mark felt no different from his friends. He wasn't concerned with what kinds of occupations their parents had. He had less money to spend than most of his peers and shared more responsibility at home than some of them. He had a paper route. He was interested in academics and sports, practiced piano and trombone, and entered music contests. He was willing to forego fleeting commercial pleasures in lieu of traveling. But in no way did he feel superior. "Why," he asked, "do people say the things they do?" It hurt especially when a teacher made a snide remark. So again we were reminded how important it is for a child to feel good about himself and to have something beyond the pettiness of this world to hang onto and look forward to.

Our other children would eventually live through such trying circumstances, but not Jenny.

Jenny's experiences joyed her now. She loved to fold the freshly laundered baby clothes and diapers. She stood for hours at cribside watching Sarah, winding the music box on the crib mobile again and again. She did everything to entertain the baby except talk to her. We tried to teach Jenny how she could talk to the baby, but she simply would not try.

Katie, though only seven years old, voluntarily changed wet diapers. Jenny tried, but couldn't latch the safety pin. During nursing she snuggled next to us with a book that I helped her read. Those were happy hours.

Our happiness was shattered by news that Gramma had died. I took Ken and ten-year-old Paul to the Madison airport for their heartbreaking journey, rushing off then to a Madison hospital to be with Mark and bid him good luck as he was wheeled to surgery.

Mark's hearing had become increasingly impaired by fluid behind the eardrums. The surgeon incised the drum and implanted very tiny tubes that allowed the accumulation of fluid to drain from behind the drum. He also removed tonsil tags and adenoids.

When Mark was returned to his room he groggily announced, "I can hear good." I wish every child with hearing disabilities could have the benefit of a medical evaluation. Not all hearing losses can be alleviated, but for some there is a cure.

When Mark and I got home from the hospital, we saw how Katie felt about her disrupted life. An eight-inch circle of gray acrylic fake fur with red felt eyes and a large red exaggerated frowning mouth hung on the refrigerator. Our sentiments exactly! What was life to be without one of our favorite people? Through the adjustments that were necessary, we discussed our feelings, consoled, prayed. I was glad we had not protected our children from the realities of death. It was hard enough as it was.

There was yet another hurdle. After discussing how love and care can come from all sorts of people and how homemaking can be done in different ways, we re-stressed how satisfying it is to help others. Then Dad said, "You know, Mom's been having back problems again. She has to go to the hospital. Since Gramma can no longer be with us, we've asked a lady from town to take care of you kids until Mom's home again."

After that surgery, I changed. Receiving a little baby when Gramma left us, moving to a quiet woods with animal life, and needing recuperation time was bound to have an effect. I spent hours doing nothing except enjoying nature and our baby, and I felt no guilt whatsoever. Storing up memories, I watched the children skip and run to meet their bus every morning, then waited for their return each afternoon; did the necessary housework at a leisurely pace; let the dog out often, then watched her excitedly chase squirrels; strolled with the baby in a buggy, besides walks with Jenny and Katie; watched for the sunset shimmering off the marsh watewrs barely visible through the trees, and took starlight walks with my husband. Sometimes I wrote letters about my thoughts and our actions. I was thirty-eight, and life had a new feel.

In our bedroom Ken created a broad desk for me out of plywood that fit over two file cabinets. A reading chair and lamp soon replaced the bassinet when Sarah was moved to another room. Our room became a gathering place. Sometimes we even had picnics there and pretended we were in a motel on a trip.

My hobby of keeping a family record proved easier now that I could keep memorabilia at hand. I wondered how I had managed without my own desk all those years. Surely every mother needs a desk!

Suddenly, it seemed, the school year ended. We had hardly been tuned into the academics that second semester.

Looking at Jenny's final report card, we readily congratulated her. She showed steady improvements in all areas. For the next school term her teachers recommended she be enrolled in intermediate special ed and again in speech therapy.

With school ended, there was no time for boredom. The boys were expected to help with the large amount of yard work. The girls helped with housework and eagerly took care of Sarah.

Of course, Ken kept at his daily routine, always aware of his family's needs. One morning he called from the hospital and said, "There's been a cancellation in the surgery schedule this morning. I know the car's not working, but if you can get Katie in here she could have her adenoids taken care of and be ready for the trip next week."

"I'll see what I can do," I answered, turning to Katie.

"Listen, Katie, you know how we've been talking about you getting your adenoids taken care of? Would you like to have it done today so you can be ready for traveling next week?"

But where to get a car? Should I call a friend or a neighbor? The pounding of a hammer reminded me the carpenter was working on the deck.

"Hey, John, can I borrow your car to take Katie to the hospital to have surgery?"

"No, you can't," he drawled, "But I'll be glad to take you. You wouldn't be able to drive that thing. It's temperamental."

I didn't tell John about some of the strange temperamental equipment years past on the farm. But John was right, that car was a real clunker. It got us to the hospital only with encouragement. Katie handled the morning's unexpected event very well while her brothers planned the route we'd take to deliver Ken's godson to the Naval Academy in Maryland.

Randy arrived from Oregon State and hesitantly added his suitcases to the pile in the foyer, declaring, "You can't possibly fit all that stuff in the wagon and still have room for us all!"

"Oh, Randy, you of little faith. You just haven't seen this family in action," Ken assured him.

Our system was two kids to a suitcase, while Ken and I shared one. That was the simple part. Then there were jackets, caps, mittens, maps, motel books, and traveling library; toys, games, or craft supplies depending on the ages; diaries, skillet, coffee pot, food box, ice chest, thermos, camera, binoculars, small medical bag, sleeping bags, and pillows with thin car blankets tucked inside each. All those items had been routine for several years. This year we added baby gear, a folding stroller, and Randy's suitcases. No wonder Randy wondered!

On travel mornings we awakened, ate breakfast, got everyone through the bathroom, dressed, got packed into the car, and were on our way in less than one and a half hours. It took cooperation, of course. We all carried gear to the car, and the boys and Ken packed the trunk and car top carrier while the girls and I arranged the inside of the car.

Our first stop was Milwaukee, where the menfolk sailed Lake Michigan with Morgan Jackson. His wife, Anne, asked, "Where do you get your courage to travel with all these kids?"

I see courage as a relative quality. We were so used to our family's way of doing things that it seemed a common occurrence. Whereas I really did wonder where Morgan and Anne got the courage to eventually navigate their forty-five-foot sailboat all the way from Milwaukee to the Caribbean by way of the Mississippi River. I guess we are comfortable with what happens to appeal to us and what we are used to doing.

It was always a pleasure to get off by ourselves with no playmates, no work, no phones to interrupt us. An added bonus was the store of knowledge accumulated. On that trip, more emphasis was put on colleges. Since education is important to us, we fostered the idea of further education by driving around campuses that were conveniently located on our route through Canada, New England and New York City.

When we returned home there wasn't the usual push to join organized sports and playmates. The boys created paths in the woods, chopped wood, and helped prepare a hard-surfaced driveway. They took pride in grooming a neat lawn.

Jenny copied the cursive writing that Katie did. They played kitchen in the basement under the stairs, until one day they found that Paul had rearranged it into an office. They simply set up house in another nook. Hours were spent mooning over catalogs, and Jenny spotted clothes she liked for herself and Sarah, none of which we bought. It was merely a form of play. Jenny responded to having a baby sister in ways that we had not anticipated.

Jenny's speech left much to be desired, and she continued to frustrate us with adverse reactions. Despite these imperfections we loved her. We had loved her as a little girl and we would soon love her as a teenager.

Could Jenny really be on the threshold of her teenage years? She wasn't ready in the way that most girls are. But ready or not, the teenage years were right around the corner.

§§ 14 §§

... besides teenager, what? ...

In August we reluctantly pursued the pre-school clothes-trying-on session that prompted the reshuffling, passing on, reserving, washing, ironing, mending, and buying routine that occurred yearly.

Jenny returned to special ed, still at the elementary school, but now in the intermediate class with Mrs. Anderson.

It didn't bother us to say that Jenny was in special ed, or that she was retarded, because we had every indication that she was. But it bothered some people when they heard us say it.

When I told others that Jenny was retarded, it was so they could immediately know why her actions might be different, and so they could have the understanding to relate to her right away. I wanted no sympathy. I have been questioned about my choice of terminology by those who think it is an injustice to our child.

We react to terminology. And terminology changes with the years.

Some terms did bother me, such as when I heard our children or their friends call each other stupid or dumb. Or worse, to hear someone chide a normal child by saying, "You're a retard." That hurt to the quick. I felt affected because of the children who couldn't help being what they are.

After the homecoming parade, the girls and I joined a friend and her daughter Kathy at the Dairy Queen. Do I say that Kathy is retarded? Is mentally handicapped? Has a learning disability? Is an exceptional child? Is braindamaged? Just how can I describe her other than to say she is our friend? Not that there is anything wrong with that simple description. If I heard her mother tell someone that Kathy is retarded, I wouldn't think a thing of it other than to know it served as a helpful description. But experience tells me that not all people react positively to the term. Reactions vary. Ultimately we say and respond to what feels right for ourselves, but in so doing we must try to respect the needs of those we interact with. That is difficult.

Teachers told us that Jenny was a happy child but that it was not always the case with handicapped children, and they wondered why Jenny was different. We didn't know. Perhaps Jenny was her own type of person despite what we were like or what we said or did. I don't remember sitting Jenny down at any time and saying to her, "You're retarded. Do you know what that means?"

What we did say to her, and often, were such things as, "You did well on your paper," or "Such neat work!" or "You can be proud of how you acted," or "Do you understand what I mean?" And we included her in most of our activities.

We're not saints, Ken and I. Our patience can carry a short fuse, though his is much longer than mine. We weren't always diplomatic with Jenny. She had to learn to handle harsh statements just as the others did. When she behaved poorly we let her know our disapproval. There was consistent discipline through the years, otherwise how could she have learned a sense of right and wrong?

Jenny was a follower, and we were glad she had good examples to imitate.

Mark gave an excellent example for all his siblings. He studied hard, played hard, and had a sense of self-discipline. He compared his abilities to Jenny's and felt fortunate, never seeming to take his competencies for granted. He told me, "Jenny and I came from the same parents, but I can do lots of things she can't. I feel very lucky."

Each child fit well into our family and unconsciously assumed distinctive roles.

That autumn of 1972 Katie turned eight and had her first birthday party. We made chef aprons for Barbie dolls and printed the invitation on them with a felt marker. Katie helped make pink-and-white-striped gingham adjustable chef aprons for each guest, and the scraps of cloth were shaped into place mats. Katie herself chose to set a lace covered table with china dishes and pretty glasses. We baked red Waldorf-Astoria cakes, and her guests especially enjoyed competing to see who could best frost her miniature cake. After games and burgers and chips, each guest created her own ice-cream sundae. Like the other guests, Jenny was pleased to 'take home' her apron, placemat, and self-decorated cake.

Turning eight also meant finally being accepted by Mrs. Downie for piano lessons. Katie was eager to join Mark and Paul at the eighty-eight keys. We questioned the possibility of Jenny taking lessons. Mrs. Downie said, "I've never worked with a handicapped child. I don't know any special teaching procedures, but if you're willing to let me try, I'm receptive."

For never having worked with a learning-disabled child, Ruth Downie had an unerring insight. She suggested, "Since Katie will likely be able to grasp music concepts quickly, perhaps we should wait a couple weeks to start Jenny so she won't feel frustrated when she can't keep up."

Her teacher soon dispelled Jenny's initial concerns. While Katie took her lesson, Jenny listened from the rubber matted stairsteps in the foyer and gained understanding and confidence. She never needed to be reminded to practice because Katie was an avid practicer and Jenny was her constant imitator. Besides that, Jenny was extremely proud of her new achievement.

Rereading letters I wrote during those weeks, it becomes apparent that Jenny showed unexpected progress academically. I am left to wonder whether piano lessons that forced her to coordinate mind and hands were beneficial. Or was progress going to happen anyway?

Or could it have been related to Sarah's crawling, which Jenny enjoyed doing with her? I am reminded of the cross-pattern crawling done with Jenny in earlier years, when we'd heard about the Doman-Delacato theory suggesting a relationship between creeping, crawling, and mental development. Because of that theory, we seldom put Sarah in a playpen, nor had we put Katie in one when she was an infant. They were given every chance to crawl, though Sarah was attracted to the foyer's open stairs and defied all repeated attempts to keep her off them. That meant teaching her, at a very tender age, how to crawl backwards back down them. She crawled often and throughout the house. Whenever Jenny was around she crawled with the baby, acting just as stimulated at the tidbits of treasure happened upon at floor level. This definitely let Jenny recapture a chance to crawl in an uninhibited manner and to experience the curiosity of an infant.

So much was involved in Jenny's learning; perhaps it is unfair to put too much emphasis on the possibility that any one activity played more of a role than another. Nonetheless, in retrospect I recognize a pattern of increased development at that time.

Jenny's frequent nearness permeated Katie's life. Sometimes Katie wavered in patience — which was in sharp contrast to her usual placid personality. No doubt there were times Katie would rather have followed instead of always being the leader for her older sister. That impatient phase was short-lived, but it reminded us that Katie was a mere child of eight with her own needs. That was easy to forget because she seemed so mature. Being a close companion of Jenny's may have helped Katie hone certain traits. Despite language problems, Jenny was a constant chatterbox at home — not of ideas, just things — and Katie learned to live with that roommate by tuning her out, yet provided companionship that was invaluable to Jenny's development. Katie cultivated a fine-tuned concentration that we all envy. She can be engrossed in a book or activity, oblivious to pandemonium around her, and yet respond if required.

Jenny never learned that kind of concentration. When she read she wanted to be by herself with no distractions, not even music. Though Jenny desired privacy and quiet for herself, she seemed to have no idea that she distracted others.

Distractions, frustrations, comprehension, and accomplishments were all part of Jenny's days, but it was up to the rest of us to accept them in the quantities she meted out.

When Jenny got older we were better able to predict her actions, but during those developing years our patience was sorely tested. Jenny needed frequent assurances, but we had to be careful because she did not always follow a predictable course and sometimes resented our assistance. For instance, when ordering at restaurants.

Jenny learned how to read menus, and that aggravated her lack-of-decision process — she simply couldn't make decisions. It was frightful helping her choose what she wanted to eat. Sometimes she went to the restroom and we grabbed that chance to place her order while she was gone. Our best recourse, though it was time-consuming, was to offer her a choice between two items, encourage her to speak her own order, and hope the waitress would be patient in interpreting Jenny's stuttering. With much persistence, Jenny did overcome most restaurant situations.

Somehow Jenny made a definite decision what she wanted for

Christmas that year. Other students had brought statues of saints to religion class, and Jenny indicated to us that she wanted one of her own. She also wanted pretty stationary like what Katie got for her birthday, *and* she wanted a Baby Tender Love doll. That was one of the few years Jenny really had definite desires, and we made certain her wishes were granted.

It was a Christmas with a new tradition added. When buying our tree, Mark eyed a scraggly branch on a trimmings pile and declared, "Hey, look! A Charlie Brown tree!"

With permission, we retrieved it, took it home, set it up in the dining room, and hung it full of handmade ornaments. Katie wrapped the base in pink terry cloth and she and Jenny surrounded it with stuffed animals.

Also we had learned about luminarias, which the boys made to line our porch and front walk. They used brown grocery bags, folded down the top to give upright firmness, poured in a bedding of sand and seated a candle in the sand. When lit after dark, the bags cast a beautiful soft glow. Candles that season in the luminarias and in the house created a sense of fairyland.

One evening during quiet Christmas music by candlelight, Paul wandered off to sit on the landing halfway up the stairs. Later I chose the same spot, watched the intriguing flickering shadows, and wondered what our son had been thinking. Whereas he talked like a chattering magpie when he was little, Paul now seldom volunteered his thoughts. Mark and Katie freely shared their feelings. Jenny couldn't, and of course Sarah was too young. Each child needed to be received on individual terms.

There was much that our family did together that I could tell about, but any family can do likewise. Our children sometimes looked enviously at what other families were doing, and no doubt other children looked at us with similar feelings. I think it is good for children to invite their friends to share some of their life.

Jenny invited friends to share her thirteenth birthday that year. We had been to the annual International Folkfest in Milwaukee, where we sampled ethnic foods, watched dancing, singing, and skits that represented other cultures, and looked at commercial displays of heritage merchandise. It gave me an idea for Jenny's birthday party.

"How about an international party, Jenny?"

Jenny watched with interest while I created hula skirts for her *besides teenager?* • 151

guests' Barbie dolls — to be used with invitations sent to eight girls. Then we made crepe-paper hula skirts for each guest. Game ideas were chosen from the books that had come in Mark's *Around-the-World* subscription. We filled a homemade piñata with candy.

Jenny, trembling with anticipation, could hardly wait!

When celebration day arrived, she welcomed her friends. They donned their hula skirts and pretended they were in Hawaii. Foreign games, similar to ours but with different names, were played. With squeals from the onlookers, each tried to break the piñata while blindfolded. And they ate tostados, which Jenny chose, along with a dish of Japanese noodles which the girls strove, through giggles, to eat with chopsticks. After they opened fortune cookies to learn their destinies, traditional cake, ice cream, and opening of gifts climaxed a birthday pary that was worth waiting an extra year for.

It was fun to plan such a party that was a bit out of the ordinary, but our children liked getting invitations to any party, no matter what kind. The camaraderie in social settings other than school was what was most important.

Other newly-turned-thirteen-year-old girls had adolescent desires, but we had to remind ourselves not to compare Jenny to them. Jenny was a little child. While others learned to dance, Jenny finally learned to ice skate without holding onto a chair. While others discussed the latest adolescent romance they had heard about or lived through, Jenny practiced her piano. While others began baby-sitting, Jenny crawled with her baby sister.

A real dividend for her leisure time was learning to knit. Since I don't know how to knit, it was with special appreciation that we learned Mrs. Carley, Jenny's teacher's aide, had taught her a new skill. Jenny took pride in making slippers for gifts, hiding them carefully in her room until the special day.

Jenny's very favorite activity was cooking. I collected simple recipes that she could make, and no matter how they turned out we ate her culinary offerings and complimented her. She copied the recipes in her very own recipe book and shared them with anyone who showed an interest.

I copy now from that very full book whose entries are in her handwriting, each dated with the first time she used the recipe.

ONE EYED SAILORS — 1973

Cut 3 inch hole in slice of bread. Butter one side. Put in skillet butter side down. Break egg in hole. Fry at 300 until egg starts to set. Turn egg with bread. Fry to desired doneness.

COCKEYED CAKE — CHOCOLATE — 1973

1-1/2 cup sifted flour	5 Tablespoon cooking oil
3 Tablespoon cocoa	1 teaspoon vanilla
1 Tablespoon soda	1 teaspoon vinegar
1/2 teaspoon salt	1 cup cold water
1 cup sugar	

Put sifted flour in sifter and add to it cocoa, soda, sugar, salt and sift this right into greased 9x9 pan. Now make three grooves or holes in this dry mixture. Into one pour the oil. Into the next the vinegar. Into the next the vanilla. Now pour cold water over it all. You'll feel like you're making mud pies. Beat it with a spoon until is is nearly smooth and you can't see the flour. Bake 30 minutes at 350

PEANUT BUTTER LOGS — 1971

1 cup chunk style peanut butter	1-1/4 cup powdered sugar
2 Tablespoon butter or oleo	2 cups rice krispies

In bowl mix together peanut butter and oleo. Stir in powdered sugar. Add cereal, mixing well. Shape into logs. Wrap in foil or plastic wrap. Chill. Slice.

Jenny was proud of her cooking. It took constant supervision, but we would not know until years later that good groundwork was being laid for food preparation and comprehension. She has enjoyed many new people, locales, and situations because of her interest in all kinds of food.

Jenny learned about Southern foods that spring. I am tempted to go on at great lengths about the trips we took because they afforded Jenny such a fantastic classroom. That was the first time we traveled in the spring, incorporating the week of school vacation with a few extra days — with permission from school officials who recognized the unique opportunity for learning.

Springtime in the Southeast was tonic to our senses! The flowers! There were bushes and trees of flowers throughout! Okefenokee Swamp in Georgia was a favorite — its peace and quiet was incredible. We wondered if we would ever be lucky enough to return to historical, lovely Charleston, South Carolina, with its moss-bedecked live-oak trees. Or to Mobile, Jackson, or Montgomery. We talked about the racial marches and spoke to our children about social justice. History came alive for them.

We ate oysters, shrimp, crab, jambalaya, po'boys, grits, red-eye gravy, country ham, she-crab soup, gumbo, and shrimp creole.

After Easter church services in Montgomery, Alabama, brightly dressed black people invited us for cookies and beverage in the church hall. It was the first personal social exposure with black people for our young ones.

In New Orleans we watched the French Quarter transform as if by magic from a daytime shopper's town to a nighttime reveler's paradise. While we boated on the Mississippi bayou waters, the boys dreamed Huckleberry Finn fantasies. And that was a year of devastating floods all through the Mississippi Valley. We looked out over huge valleys of water with islands of buildings.

Seeing the real enhanced what textbooks tried to tell. Oh, that every child could be so fortunate to see what Jenny saw. Of course she wouldn't remember it all, but there was much that she did recall in subsequent classes.

Always there was something that brought reality back to us. While we laid out a picnic in a park at Greenwood, Mississippi, a boy who we suspected might be retarded joined us. He asked for food. He said he was thirteen and in second grade, his parents drank a lot, and he was hungry. We shared our food with him.

Seeing that child reminded us how lucky we were that Jenny had a school that offered special-education classrooms. We were thankful that Jenny's teacher was specially trained to know how to work with children with special needs, and that each child was individually challenged because special-ed classes allow that possibility. We also felt fortunate that we were capable parents who could take care of Jenny, and that Jenny could stay in our family without detrimental effects. In fact, we were finding that because of her our entire family was developing certain positive attitudes and abilities. We were continuing to learn that a family can gain benefits by having a retarded member.

§§ 15 §§

... speaking in sentences! ...

Our home was set back in the woods. We could have isolated Jenny at home to do routine chores instead of encouraging her to participate in challenging experiences. The other children could have gone to school, come home with their tales, and included Jenny only in ways that allowed for her abilities. She could have been left with sitters while the rest of us played and worked. There were enough of us to accomplish the work of house and lawn care; we could have declared Jenny too delicate for such physical labor. We could have accepted her tendency to creep off alone to the solitude of her room, to busy herself with dolls, toys, coloring, and other satisfying pastimes. I'm glad we didn't.

The course we chose was not always easy. Sometimes in public we succumbed to embarrassment, though we knew many people recognized Jenny's ways and understood. We prodded her to keep up with us, to join our play and work when she didn't always want to. We sent her to special-education school, knowing that some taxpayers rebelled against the latest government-edicted education priorities. She joined us on our travels, although her disrupting influence could send us to the brink of despair.

Jenny became a young girl who went into the community where she benefited from instruction and caring and where she touched people's lives. We know from experience that a child like Jenny can be like a metallic thread running through a tapestry — in the wrong light harsh to the eye, but otherwise blending into the whole to create a smoothly finished result.

Sometimes we erred — we didn't always recognize when it was best to let her be alone. It was not easy to know until sometimes it was too late and her behavior proved her negative feelings. She could not seem to say, "I don't want to do this or that." Instead she showed her frustrations by fussing at her clothes, talking louder, biting her already mutilated fingernails, antagonizing her siblings, or just pouting.

We could have taken the easy way out and not tried to keep Jenny immersed in our family, but Ken and I, like all other parents, had no guarantee of how long we would live, and we were concerned for Jenny's future. We hoped to create a bond between our children that would include Jenny. We assumed that college, employment, and independence would become the world of our other children, but we also wanted Jenny to approach some kind of independence as much as possible. Or at least not become a burden to anyone she might live with.

To accomplish such goals, we continued to discipline her as we did the others, taught her right from wrong, gave her encouragement, and exposed her to new things for pleasure and knowledge.

Jenny was now thirteen and unaware of the traditional world of her teenage peers. Her pleasure was in playing hopscotch and top-dog, pushing dolls in the stroller, jumping rope, riding bikes, and drawing colored chalk pictures on the blacktopped driveway. Her summer was carefree except for swimming lessons and piano lessons.

I taught Jenny and Katie how to embroider, and we tried batiking. We baked and cooked, canned and froze what food we grew in the garden or was given us by friends and patients of Ken's. And tea parties abounded.

The girls repeatedly reminded, "Don't forget, we're having a tea party at 2:00 on June 30th for Gramma's birthday."

Jenny and Katie had sent Gramma a tea bag so she could have a cup of tea at that same hour. Uncle Keith and his family were visiting from Tucson, and our children ran between the tent and the house in eager preparation for the tea party. They made brownies, filled the fanciest trays with tiny cups, saucers, flowers and dainty goodies. Then they gathered us moms and dads and older brothers and assigned places around the pretty cloth laid on the floor of the tent. Strains of the happy birthday song soon filled the woods. Gramma would surely have loved her party, but a little one asked, "How could Gramma sit on the ground?"

It was a fun summer. Nine-year-old Katie compiled the memories in a family newspaper — complete with advertisements, social news, chuckles, and weather.

The boys took bike trips and canoed the Yahara River. A treat for the girls and me was to help haul their canoe to a putting-in spot near the Stebbinsville dam. Then we drove downstream and sat under the highway bridge and awaited their arrival. Swallows gracefully swooping into the cool shaded recesses of the bridge pilings entertained us while we pretended the cars passing overhead surely must be Billy Goat Gruff.

We were not fishermen or hunters but loved taking hikes to see nature for the sheer beauty. Sheepskin Marsh, near our home, covered forty acres and harbored animal and bird life. Sunsets beckoned us there with golden rays that silhouetted yellow-headed blackbirds perched on reeds and cattails. Ducks lazed in the evening reflections. Had we been camera buffs, we could have captured nature's presentation. Instead we invited friends and relatives to hike with us, so at least it was shared. We remembered to give credit where it was due by saying a family rosary in that lovely setting.

With such lingering memories of a country summer, is it any wonder we were reluctant to return to the routine of school?

Jenny greeted thirteen classmates for her ninth year of formal schooling. Mrs. Anderson used second-and third-level books for teaching Jenny reading, mathematics, spelling, phonics, language, handwriting, and social studies. Picture dictionaries gave a better understanding of vocabulary words, and Jenny took pride in improving her cursive writing, using it for correspondence.

We never heard a complaint from Jenny about going to school, except for eating breakfast — which continued to be a constant thorn. It had always been my custom, indeed my accepted motherly responsibility, to prepare breakfast; but I took a careful look at the morning scene of our household and decided there must be a better way. Invariably whatever I fixed didn't suit someone's fancy, even though for sure the next morning they would want just that same food. Jenny gagged through it all, no matter what was served. Paul didn't accept morning conversation from anyone. Katie buried her nose in a book and Mark the morning newspaper. Ken escaped most of this kitchen fiasco since he left early for the hospital. Finally I declared, "You kids are on your own for breakfast. Fix what you want. If you need anything you'll find me in the front room."

Mark, a freshman, liked to cook and soon adopted a culinary variation of toast, cold cereal, hot cereal, pancakes, french toast, waffles, omelettes, fried eggs, one-eyed sailors, soft-boiled eggs, poached eggs, Norwegian pancakes, Belgian pancakes, and Dutch babies. He took his chef's choice to a quiet spot with the newspaper. Sometimes the others spoke for extra of his ingredients to cook the same thing, but their true preference at that age was cereal, toast, and juice.

Peace reigned, and I gradually got over my guilt feelings. Thus did our family work into a routine that was right for itself but might have caused visitors to ponder our ways.

Sunday breakfast, however, was as sacred as Tuesday days off. We attended 8:00 church services and sometimes went out to eat, especially if a club was sponsoring a pancake breakfast. But usually I cooked a big breakfast or Dad made his specialty, pancakes. All this after first consideration being Dad's rounds at the hospital.

Sunday's day of rest was seldom uninterrupted for the doctor. I looked forward to a day when he might be able to lead a less rushed existence. That temporary time came when he underwent back surgery. Until then I could not remember him missing a day of work for sickness or for hooky, yet there were days he didn't feel like working. Children learn from example, and ours had an excellent example from their father, just as he had had from his father. As Ken went to work each day, so did his children go to school; unless they were sick with a communicable disease, fever, or nausea.

Jenny had learning problems, but her general health was excellent. Except for occasional tonsillitis, headache, and seasonal hay fever, she had no need for medications. Actually, Jenny might have had days when she didn't feel well. We didn't know her pain threshold, but were sure she felt pain and merely accepted it. The winter before, when she'd sprained her knee while skiing at Devil's Head, we could only guess how much pain she had. It was strange to raise a child and know so little about her inner feelings.

We did understand Jenny's excitement one day after the harsh days of winter when she came home from school chattering about patrol. She had successfully been mainstreaming social studies and science, and now her teachers encouraged her to take on patrol responsibility, even though she still required much reassurance and direction.

We wondered how effective she could be patrolling, and took consolation in knowing she worked with another student. Some days Katie happily announced, "I saw Jenny on patrol duty this noon." It gave Jenny a sense of worth and let her be eligible for the incentive outing to the Wisconsin Dells.

Jenny still learned best by seeing. She expressed gladness over another spring trip to the Southland. School break was long enough for us to go to Texas without missing additional classes. In the land of flowers and leafed-out trees we learned about presidents — Eisenhower's birthplace in Denison, Texas; LBJ's ranch in the lovely Pedernales River Valley west of Austin; and sadly, John Kennedy's memorial in Dallas.

We stepped back in time at the Alamo in San Antonio and glimpsed the future with NASA in Houston. The world of the astronauts, our world, seemed incredible. Of course, our sons were amazed at the immensity of the Houston Astrodome with its restaurants and suites and intricate communications system that complement the sports arena.

In Galveston we heard on the radio that Hank Aaron hit his 615th home run. We took it for granted that we could keep abreast of the latest news when we were traveling in the United States. (We feel at home in the Canadian provinces and easily forget it is a foreign country — until we are reminded by the lack of United States news in their papers and television. Likewise, there is relatively little Canadian news in our media.) In Texas we could get all the news we were accustomed to.

Historical places complemented textbooks, but it was often people who made the biggest impression. On Palm Sunday in Corpus Christi we attended a church whose black people welcomed us with heartwarming hospitality. A lively, beautiful service! Vibrant spring colors! And hearty singing! A noisy, small church it was, with old wooden floors. We waited, along with mostly adult members, wondering why Mass wasn't starting. Finally the reason for the delay became apparent. Children of all sizes, gaily dressed in Easter finery, paraded into church singing and carrying crudely made little crosses decorated in child fashion with greenery, flowers and balloons, and with words declaring that Christ died and was risen to redeem us from our sins. Then they passed out palms to everyone. During the service handsome parents and grandparents bedecked in bright spring colors presented their white-attired black infant for baptism into God's loving care. One hour and thirty-seven minutes later we contentedly walked back to our car and were surprised when we heard. "Dr. Pavlik! We'd like your children to join us for the Easter egg hunt."

How did he know our name?

It sounded like a good idea to the children, so we went to a yard behind the church, where we were served refreshments while little ones cavorted in Easter activity. Afterwards each child was given a decorated basket made from a brown lunch sack and filled with candies. Returning to our car, Katie explained how the man knew our name. "He asked me what my Dad's name was, and I didn't know what else to tell him, so I said it was Dr. Pavlik." Katie took a lot of teasing about that!

Again our children had reason to question racial inequality. They had been shown genuine hospitality by people of another color. Sometimes we learned what we weren't planning to learn.

During our trek home Katie reminded me about the mini-courses her fourth grade classmates were looking forward to. I remembered, but very reluctantly. I remembered how inadequate I had felt when she came with request from school asking mothers to share their talents. Even though I exhorted our children to share, I asked, "But what talents do I have to share with students?"

"Oh, Mom, you've got lots of them!"

"Gee, thanks, Katie." It was bolstering to have my own cheering squad.

"Well, surely, there are things I can do," I consented, "but not professionally enough to teach to someone else."

Katie and I had looked over the list together — at least fifty topics. Some of them I could do, but, "Really, Katie, I can't *teach* any of these!"

She was disappointed and did not want no for an answer. To satisfy her I said, "Okay, I'll give it thought, but don't get your hope up too high."

There must be *something* I could share. But what, oh what? After considerable procrastination and repeated queries from our parent-idolizer, I finally chose the blank space after the word Others and wrote in: Foreign Cooking. Then fingers were crossed that I wouldn't get called.

No such luck. A teacher called to set up a schedule. My theme was encouraging the children to accept and become familiar with the broader world around them; to become aware of other people through the food they eat; to learn what other countries are like by learning what foods are available for them to eat. Some of the foods were unusual to my students' tastes, and we talked about how foreigners probably feel the same way about our foods. Each week the children watched with interest to see what would be extracted from the cloth-lined basket: electric portable appliances, utensils for cooking and eating, and common and not so common food items. If the students were willing to try new foods, they could bring the world to their home.

Such activities created a school year that joined parents and other community members in concert with students and teachers.

Jenny's year in school was slowly but surely productive. She retained her reading vocabulary and seemed to have a good understanding of the words. She learned some multiplication and division. She participated in group activities but still required reassurance. Her attitudes showed signs of maturing — and that was good because she was assigned to enter junior high school.

But the biggest news was that Jenny was now *speaking in sentences*!!!

It had taken Jenny ten years of speech therapy and nine years of formal schooling to learn to speak in sentences! Always I will remember the chilling words that had forecast the possibility that Jenny might not learn the alphabet. Perhaps it was well we had been so warned. It had prevented us from presuming normal accomplishments, and instead had made us receptive, with grateful hearts, for each achievement that Jenny mastered. We had complimented her instead of chiding her for not learning. She had not been put in a position of handling academics that were beyond her capabilities, though the challenge was presented — without a challenge she might not have progressed. Mentally handicapped persons need mental mountains to climb just as all of us do.

There were always reminders to count our blessings, and we were handed another that summer. We were preparing a family picnic in the park at Watertown. An obviously retarded older boy (or man? age is difficult to judge in these childlike individuals) approached us with a crooked stick about eight inches long. He handed the stick to me and spoke some incomprehensible sounds. Then he sauntered toward companions who were like him. I kept that stick and put it in a macramé hanger near our kitchen sink. It has graced every home we have lived in. This stick reminds me to thank God that Jenny can learn and we can accept her, and that she can live in our home.

Jenny's summer days were offered new understandings when we heard over the telephone, "We're going to have a surprise birthday party for Gramma on her seventy-fifth. Can you come? We know it's short notice." Gramma lived four hundred miles from us.

Only the girls were home. Mark was on a bike hike with a friend. Paul, twelve, was on a solo adventure to Grampa's. And Daddy couldn't leave at this time. Jenny, Katie, Sarah, and I packed handmade gifts and set out for our first all-girl adventure. I had a special treat to look forward to. When my brother had married, my widowed mother left the farm to live in town, and I had never returned to my girlhood home to sleep the night. There were invitations to do so, but it seemed I should stay with my mother. Now, finally, since the party was to be held at the home place, I accepted the invitation to surprise my mother. I was going home!

While I drove west, childhood memories permeated my thoughts. I lay on the double bed in my northwest room, cool sheets offering comfort from the hot, corn-tinged air that wafted the curtains. I heard sounds of dirty clothes going down the metal clothes chute. I shivered in a bath of four inches of cold water. I played on the neck of the big moose head on the upstairs hall floor. I sneaked to the attic to read under the rafters, and climbed the apple tree to sit on a limb and read a book. I played behind the juniper bush, and stood behind the old-fashioned cookstove to feel its comforting warmth.

As the miles passed I told my daughters that I wished I could again slide down the banister or down the stairs on my belly; put puzzles together in the cool sunroom; gather a panful of potatoes from the cellar, and a basket of cobs or wood from the fuel room; throw a scoop of coal or a log in the furnace; ride the machinery to cultivate corn rows or tie hay-baling wires. Just once more I yearned to sit on the top stairstep and spy down through the French doors at the grownups in the living room. To have fresh cream on fresh strawberries from the garden, and to pick mulberries and cherries. I wanted to smell my dad's bay rum shaving lotion and the leather razor strop. And hear my mom at the sewing machine stitching aprons and patching overalls.

I carried all such memories and thousands more — like every

adult. But there is no going back. While I drove Interstate 80 to western Iowa I knew there was no going back to the way it was. My childhood home had changed. Now there is no wood cookstove or wringer washing machine. The moose head and other Alaskan trophies made their way to the Union Pacific Museum in Omaha, and finally to the museum in Harlan, Iowa. A modern heating system altered many aspects of my youth, and even the juniper bush is gone.

I suppose there is no necessary solution to the passing of time with its changes except to recall in memories and conversation. Perhaps change is necessary. Otherwise, how would we ever progress beyond Start?

I was returning now as a mother, creating new memories that would allow my daughters happy recollections in future years. While I settled them into my girlhood home, I felt no corn-tinged breezes wafting the curtains — only cool air-conditioned flow from the register. In the ado of busy preparations for Gramma's surprise party, Uncle Don had to climb his twenty-foot ladder to the upstairs bathroom window to retrieve little Sarah, who locked herself in the bathroom with the old fashioned lock that cannot be undone from outside the door.

Jenny, Katie, and Sarah thought it all terribly exciting, especially when they watched Uncle Lud, Uncle Don, and their cousins hide the guests' cars behind the barns. Finally someone screamed, "Here comes Uncle Ray's with Gramma! Quick! Everyone get in the other rooms!"

Standing by Aunt Mary and Aunt Alice, Jenny giggled with tingling anticipation, clamping her hand over her mouth to keep from making too much noise.

Gramma was just enjoying a pleasant country drive, stopping here and there to see sons and daughters and their crops. Or so she thought. Then she heard a burst of song. "Happy birthday to you, Happy birthday to you, Happy birthday dear Gramma — dear Mom — dear Aunt Sidonia — Happy birthday to you."

I felt momentarily sorry for my mother as she quickly regained her composure upon seeing all the dozens of dear relatives who had come from many miles away. Then she spotted us in the crowd. "Norene! What are *you* doing here? And Jenny! And Katie! And you, Sarah!"

It was a glorious day, and though it was impossible, I wanted *speaking in sentences* • 163

ever so much to erase the years, gather my cousins, and play moonlight-starlight-hope-to-see-no-ghost-tonight. Instead we chattered about families, things, places, events. I was sure my cousins remembered the ball games with trees for bases; waiting for the older folks to be served first at family dinners; and washing dishes with much teasing nonsense and snapping of wet dishtowels.

After the party we packed our bags and went to town to Gramma's house to spend the remaining night — I felt I belonged with her. Did I want to? I'm not sure. What I really wanted was a slice of life from the past. That is impossible.

I thank God for the memories.

We also visited a friend of mine and her daughter who has spina bifida. Several of our friends have children with handicaps of one kind or another, such as learning disabilities, cancer, Down's syndrome, cystic fibrosis, blindnesss, cerebral palsy, deafness, and muscular dystrophy. No one is immune. We parents need to share, compare, and encourage, but we do not have to assure society of never having afflicted people inhabiting its good earth. From the afflicted ones we gain strength, if we relate to them unselfishly and try to improve their quality of life.

I did not shield our girls from the fact of spina bifida. What would have been the use? It didn't hurt them to recognize that other people suffer, some of them miserably; that people do what they must to survive, and that much satisfaction lies in accepting and meeting the challenges, often heartrending ones.

In that summer of 1974, when destinies were being molded by the Watergate happenings, Mark had his first taste of mountain hiking that enkindled a lasting fascination in him. Jenny wrote Mark at his cousin's place and told him about sleeping overnight in the tent and about Dad clearing the woods. It was to be a most unusual summer because of the shed in the woods.

How many of us plod along in life, going to work day in and day out, never seizing an opportunity to see what other talents we might have? Well, I watched with interest as my man hurried home from the hospital every evening, quickly donned jeans, gathered his axe, shovel, or level, and proceeded to grub, trench, and smooth. With land prepared, he built forms for a twenty-by-twenty-eight-foot cement foundation. Three times he redid the forms. Then he called for a cement contractor. Before those men poured the concrete, they surveyed Ken's forms and complimented, "You're only one-eighth inch off! Not bad for a doctor!"

With renewed confidence, he reread how-to manuals and made innumerable trips to our garage and basement to scrutinize construction techniques. The children and I hung around our carpenter and watched while he progressed to each next step, hoping to be assigned a job.

With basic plan in mind, he ordered lumber, to be replenished when the need arose. His weekly free hours were limited, but by Friday night he'd figured out needs for the weekend, and Saturday morning, from the hospital, called the lumberyard to place his order.

"When do you need this, Doc?"

"Oh, there's no hurry. Just so I get it today." The lumberyard closed at noon.

People call their doctor wanting instant cures, emergency care, or house calls. None of us wants to wait. Now it was Ken's turn to need some coddling — something that rarely happened. Lumberman Dave obliged. "Doc Pavlik just called in his order. See that he gets it today."

We pounded nails while Richard Nixon resigned from the presidency of the United States. We cared about Mr. Nixon and all those who were affected by the Watergate scandal. With an ear to the political proceedings, we were reminded that it is so very important to do everything right the first time around because we can't be sure life is going to give a second chance.

That is why we knew we must make time for our children. We don't get second chances in raising a child. We tried to do what was right the first time around.

When school started with a half day on August 27, a Tuesday, we took the children out to lunch and listened to their excited voices relate first-day activities and their impressions of teachers and fellow students.

Such things are important to a child.

§§ 16 §§

... mountains and restless ...

Jenny, fourteen years old and wearing her first pair of eyeglasses, started a new school experience at the junior-high building. Math, social studies, spelling, English, and reading were learned in Mrs. Ward's special-ed room. She mainstreamed in music, art, home economics, physical education, and science.

During the summer Jenny had stuttered a lot, so the speech therapist reevaluated her. In testing, Jenny did not stutter. It was recommended we not schedule her for regular speech therapy. Indeed, after school started the stuttering decreased. The therapist emphasized the importance of keeping pressure away from Jenny and suggested that perhaps Jenny was making her own pressure by comparing herself to the other members of the family.

Jenny might have felt inferior to the rest of us, especially when we pounded nails. Though daytime activities had been unaffected, as soon as Dad got home from work, our attention turned to the carpentry. Jenny tried pounding nails but didn't like it, so we tried to create jobs for her. She wasn't interested. Instead, the only chore she really wanted was her self-appointed one of sweeping the circular driveway.

The rest of us worked closely with our carpenter. We offered the position of chief dishwasher and baby-watcher to Jenny. That caught her fancy. She took orders for snacks and beverages and especially liked it when we asked her and Katie to make super nachos. She spread refried beans on tostado shells, topped it with hot sauce and grated cheese, placed them under the broiler until the cheese melted, and proudly delivered them to the building crew. When Jenny wasn't doing those jobs, she went off to her room. We encouraged her to join us, but after many invitations we finally left her alone, always wondering what new phase that might lead to. Apparently it led to stuttering.

It seems contradictory to say so, but Jenny was a sociable child. She spent hours studying the phone book and eventually started making lists of families, their addresses, and phone numbers. Any new clue she heard about people got jotted down on scraps of paper. She studied pictures in the weekly local newspaper, wrote similar names together, and when she matched people to a particular family she created a new listing. Jenny listened at the supper table for tidbits about schoolchildren in other levels of the school system. After church she busied herself compiling lists of family members she had seen in church. She looked up pictures in the church directory and in school yearbooks. If she could have expressed herself better we might have been surprised to learn what all Jenny had gathered about the people of Edgerton.

Jenny helped serve autumn suppers on the deck and called Dad from his carpentering at the last minute. He couldn't squander the limited daylight minutes after doctoring hours. One evening Dad pondered, "You know, kids could sure have fun playing in the upstairs of the shed if we put a barn-style roof on instead of the A shape like is on the house and garage. I think I'll take the measurements to Bob Stricker and ask how to make gambrel rafters."

I went with him to see the carpenter who had built our house. Bob offered to construct a sample rafter to use as a pattern, but then thought a moment and said, "No, I'll just sketch a diagram on this piece of cardboard. If you're smart enough to figure out those cement forms, you're smart enough to figure this out. Half the fun of construction is mastering the problems."

Considerate reasoning.

Ken grappled with the angles, measured, remeasured, and finally got the proportions that he needed. He was justifiably proud of the rafters that fit into place perfectly.

Every so often I looked out the window during the quiet of day and saw Bob drive in and stop near the building, then slowly drive away. Like Bob, we had tried to challenge our children through the years — lead them to knowledge but let them derive the pleasure from analysis. Not always, of course. We're not that patient! That type of guidance takes a great deal of patience. Too often we implied, "You'll do it this way because I *said* so!"

We allowed our children to make their own decisions when feasible. We listened while they juggled decisions. Of course, we wished that Jenny were more capable of making choices. That fall Paul opted for football and Katie chose patrol — they had their own reasons for doing so. Mark declined football, not because he didn't want it but because "when I was hiking mountains, all those other guys got out to practice in that awful heat before school started, and I don't think it's fair if I barge in now when it's cooler" — even though his former teammates encouraged him to join them.

The bonus was that it left time to help his dad with the carpentering. We could no longer call it a shed — with gambrel rafters, it was definitely a barn. Dad even created a balcony on the south side overlooking the house and woods. Also, he tested his ability to figure out how to add a hay hood and to make geometrically-designed Dutch doors for upstairs. He hung a garage-style overhead door and two small doors, then installed windows. Then, after having climbed ladder steps all those weeks, he experimented and constructed stairsteps.

As soon as the last step was complete, Jenny and Katie were waiting with their tray of dainties to host their first tea party in the barn loft. That was a Tuesday, and Ken, with tiny tea cup in hand, declared, "Let's have an open barn Sunday for the clinic and hospital personnel who have so patiently listened to my barn talk all these weeks. How about if we get a keg of beer and serve chili? And pop for the kids?"

Youngsters ran through fallen autumn leaves in the woods playing hide-and-seek games and, with the adult guests, signed the inside walls of the barn. Carpenter Bob Stricker gave Ken a grade of A-plus for his first major effort.

At Thanksgiving, Grampa came from Nebraska and taught his son how to wire the barn for electricity. He also shared our annual Thanksgiving-eve meal of plain rice that emphasized our blessings.

At Christmastime the barn took on special meaning. Ken, with Sarah close at hand, created a three-foot-long Nativity crib out of little tree limbs tied together with twine. As he worked, he told again the story of Baby Jesus. They positioned the manger in the barn, filled it with hay, spread hay around it, and set a twenty-four-inch starched-sheet kneeling Madonna by it.

Some evenings we walked through the snowy cold to make a visit to the manger. On Christmas morning Sarah found a new dolly lying in the manger. She was able to sort out the meaning.

That semester Jenny also learned a type of construction. In

home-ec she sewed basic seams, buttonholes, buttons, darts, and gathering, and at school open house proudly displayed her finished apron and procedure sample book.

Jenny was now fifteen years old. She wrestled with basic concepts of mathematics: multiplications of sevens, eights, and nines; telling time; money concepts. Hour upon hour she bent over papers, resting her head in left hand and clutching her pencil in right hand — writing and erasing, writing and erasing. Over and over she repeated the process in her efforts to learn.

Jenny liked spelling and took pride in doing her workbook alone, but it was difficult for her to express herself orally, artistically, or in spontaneous writing. She could do assignments that required looking up information and filling in the blanks, and always rated an A or Excellent on those papers.

We had to remember to keep our perspective when we saw the A's on Jenny's report card. Though she was unable to grasp concepts, she earned those A's by working hard to look up information and transfer it to her papers. It was heartbreaking sometimes to see the lack of conceptual abilities compared to the amount of effort she expended.

Jenny's interest in spelling was aided by Katie's studying for the spelling bee. For many weeks the spelling of words accompanied us everywhere — in the house, on walks, in the car. Jenny pronounced words syllable by syllable, for Katie to spell, and asked the rest of us for help with the ones she couldn't pronounce. When she asked Paul, we learned an awful truth that dismayed us considerably — Paul sounded out words with difficulty, and he was already in seventh grade! How could we have remained ignorant of that fact through the years? He cared little for reading compared to our other children. Yet in his primary grades he had been an avid reader and in fact had won a high prize for reading. So what had happened since then? A trial method that stressed word recognition rather than phonics had been used in his class. Whether that was the basis for his problem, or whether it was just Paul, we will never know.

Once we recognized his weak spot, we didn't waste time blaming the school, him, or ourselves. There was no time to waste. Paul was on the threshold of high school with its heavier demands of reading, and he needed to know how to pronounce words. We encouraged him to give the spelling words to Katie, and sometimes it was Jenny who helped him pronounce the words. When there was a letter or an article to be read to the family, he did it. I talked to his English teacher, and although she didn't think there was much to be concerned about, she did concur that Paul be given remedial-reading instruction. It bothered me that her concern was not as sharp as ours. She compared him to his classmates. We didn't want him compared to his classmates. We wanted him to challenge his own potential.

Paul achieved, but it was a harder task than it should have been. (During his eleventh grade he finally became interested in literature; he carried a full curriculum in college and earned some remarkably good credits.)

Katie won that spelling bee and competed in the regional bee. Her participation was a bonus for all of us: it certainly helped Jenny become more proficient, and it made us aware of Paul's deficiency.

Jenny was maturing physically whether we wanted her to or not. Her body had no intention of waiting for her mind. Many times I wondered if she was prepared enough for when menstruation started. When her big day arrived, Dad and I treated it with pleasure and congratulated her on becoming like other girls her age. It wasn't easy. Not much was, but it could have been worse.

Jenny learned to take care of her needs. I insisted upon that from the very beginning. She learned personal cleanliness for herself and her clothes. She fought it at first, but persistence paid off and she became solely responsible. There is one thing, though: I am glad I talked to her brothers about the changes that take place in the body of a girl as she matures. They needed to know that, because Jenny's proprieties were sometimes startling to say the very least. We could not allow ourselves a low threshold of embarrassment. It was difficult to teach Jenny that some things are a private situation. But Jenny did learn, although it seemed she would always need to learn more.

As Jenny's body burst into bloom, so did spring in Wisconsin. The hills called us, and we drove leisurely along the Mississippi River to Winona to visit cousin Janie at college. That late-April Sunday evening on the way home in a darkening car, Mark leaned up to the front seat and casually announced, "I invited Ellen to the spring prom."

Driver Dad managed to maintain an amazingly calm composure. Mark, a sophomore, had not dated. He did not have a driver's license, nor did the boy he would double date with, so we discussed various possibilities for an enjoyable evening. The cost would be covered by his paper route and lawn care incomes, and he would order and pay for the corsage — if Mark joined the dating game he had to assume those responsibilities.

The couples hoped to precede the formal dance with a dinner. We offered the possibility of a formal home dinner, assuring that we would not be offended if they chose against it. Otherwise we would drive them to a restaurant.

After a few days Mark asked, "Mom, are you sure you wouldn't mind putting on a dinner for us?"

"I'd love to! *If* it's what you would like."

Together we planned, taking into consideration the simple tastes of teenagers but also the elegance of the evening. His sisters could serve as waitresses. Jenny and Katie then excitedly joined the plannings and when the day arrived they could hardly contain their enthusiasm. Paul escaped the whole affair by going on a twenty-two-mile hunger hike to raise funds for starving people.

We set two tables, one in the dining room for the two prom couples and one in the family room for Ken and me, who were celebrating our anniversary. Jenny, Katie, and I donned long dresses, prettied up Sarah, and turned dinner music on. Ken chauffeured the two couples to our home.

The girls watched at the windows and finally the car came in the driveway to excited squeals and exclamations of, "They're here! They're here!" Nobody could have been more elated than Jenny!

"Lookit! They're in long dresses! Looky, Mom, Ellen's got a shawl on! Oh! Look at Trudy's dress!" Mark had remembered the wrist corsage Jenny received for First Communion, so he ordered one, but was disappointed when it turned out to be one that Ellen had to pin on.

"Shhhhh. They do look nice, don't they? Now, girls, remember what you're supposed to do. You make it a very special evening for them."

Mark had requested beef fondue so the meal could last longer while they cooked their own meat in the hot oil. Their young waitresses served salads and cola, then arranged the beef cubes, sauces, vegetables and hot rolls and scurried between the guest table and anniversary table checking every detail, refilling glasses, and giggling in delight. All too soon it was time to clear the tables and offer Mexican wedding cakes and a pedestal plate mounded with tiny creampuffs drizzled with chocolate sauce — two of Mark's favorites. After pictures and goodbyes, Dad drove them to the dance at school and turned chauffering duties over to Tim's dad.

A cherished memory. But how had the years gone so quickly? Those girls were Jenny's age. It seemed remote that Jenny could ever be in a similar dating situation.

We could not let ourselves dwell on such comparisons, but they did creep in.

While her peers entered the dating realm, Jenny finished her first year at junior high school. Her biggest accomplishments were in spelling, phonics, and home ec, where she proved her patience and understanding by sewing a strawberry-printed cotton slacks-and-tunic outfit. She took great pride in that outfit and wore it often.

Math presented insurmountable problems, and Jenny still couldn't comprehend telling time. We worked with her at home on measurements and time, especially when making recipes.

Welcoming summer, we waited impatiently for June 21. Our yard had shaped up nicely through the steady cooperation of each family member, so we felt justified in rewarding ourselves.

On that awaited day we were on the road by 5:30 A.M.. The children listened carefully at the Canadian border when Dad explained to the customs agent that we planned to go to Winnepeg and then travel all the way west to Edmonton and Victoria and re-enter the United States in western Washington.

It is interesting to reread some of the diary entries. After driving around a Mennonite community in Manitoba, Mark wrote, "No external differences." That could be said about most of Canada. Canadian and American people present a unified image although we are two separate countries. We live in similar dwellings, attend similar churches, shop in stores and till the land in the same ways. Even in poverty there is not much distinction — except that in some of our southern states there is an unwieldy display of litter. The land in Canada is an extension of ours, or is ours an extension of theirs? Driving west, we passed from trees to rolling farms to plains that stretched hundreds of miles with waving fields of grain. Then we felt the same awesome intrigue when we caught first sight of the Canadian Rocky mountains as we do when we see our own Rockies.

At Hinton, Alberta, at an overnight cabin, the girls gathered wild flowers, pressed them in books, and put tiny fragrant pine boughs by the beds. Ken and I sat outside the cabin and sensed an excitement in our boys as they looked toward the mountains. We should have guessed that our family would never again be the same.

It wasn't just the mountains. It wasn't just that we were in Canada. It was the maturing of the family. Our eldest son had gotten his driver's license the day before we left on the trip, and we entrusted our car, heavy with the weight of packed gear and precious lives, to his abilities. In subtle ways we would continue to use him as a trusted example for the other children. He had earned our respect. We knew we could allow him to satisfy his desire for new adventures, but in allowing that, we would automatically open those same doors to his brothers and sisters if they, too, continued to earn our respect for their judgments.

Mark was sixteen, Jenny fifteen, Paul thirteen, Katie ten, and Sarah three. We had no intentions of keeping them shackled to us. They deserved to be allowed to test their wings gradually so that when it came time to fly the nest they would be ready. Sometimes that meant letting them pull us along to show us their abilities.

Mark had been in Colorado the summer before and climbed Capitol Peak, a 14,000-foot mountain, with his cousin. It became apparent that he yearned for more such adventure. As soon as we settled into a cabin in Jasper at the Takara Lodge, he urged us all to climb a beginners' mountain which he'd read about.

"Are you sure the girls can do it?"

"Of course they can! It's recommended for families or novices. That fits us perfectly!"

"How about Dad and me?" out-of-shape Mom asked. We would soon see.

The boys breezed along the trail, through trees, and into clearings. They called back encouraging words to help us gain new heights: "C'mon, Mom, you can do it!"

"C'mon, Jenny, here, take my hand."

"Here, Dad, let me carry Sarah now."

The boys were in the prime of youth and teased the rest of us.

"It's not much farther now!"

"Oh! It's so *pretty!* Come on!"

With a preparatory squad like that, how could we not continue? Katie scampered on ahead with the boys and Sarah. Between rests Ken and I pulled and prodded and encouraged Jenny along. At times she was sure she couldn't go any farther. Finally we reached the top. It was magnificent! It could have been the opening scene in the meadow for the movie *Sound of Music*. Mountains everywhere, and we were a part of it. It was absolutely beautiful! We sat for long moments and soaked in the beauty. If we had been singers we would have burst into song, but we are quiet people. We look, and we think, and we thank God that we can enjoy this world. He has been good to us.

The next morning we arose early and went to Maligne Lake for a boat trip deep into the land of glaciers that rise from water's edge. The grandeur was spectacular! The icy-cold reflective lake was surrounded by majestic peaks, one of them named Mount Paul — a fitting find for our young son in his first teenage year.

Back toward town by way of Edith Lake, our next point of interest was Whistler's Mountain. Since we had joined our sons on a mini-mountain trek, we now trusted them with a bigger challenge of hiking to the top of Whistler. Dad called after them, "Good luck! If we never see you again, it's been nice knowing you!"

During their two-hour-and-ten-minute climb, the rest of us rode a tram to the top, where Jenny, Katie, and Sarah threw peanuts to entice the marmots, small squirrel-like animals. The boys arrived, weary but exhilarated, and Mark continued another 1,500 feet to the summit, where he placed a small stone at the very top.

Jasper and its environs captured our hearts. It was jeans country, where people looked as if they were there to physically partake of the beauty. Reluctantly we left to continue westward.

In a snowstorm we rode a monster snowmobile onto the Columbia icefield, land of active glaciers. We hiked miles to see waterfalls. And the men (when does a family start lumping its sons in with Dad and calling them men?) climbed another mountain in Banff. We skipped stones on water, and threw stones clear across the Columbia River — to be remembered later in Astoria, Oregon, when the odometer showed 3.8 miles from shore to shore of that same river.

In Vancouver we changed out of our jeans for the first time for a restaurant, from which Mt. Baker in the distance looked like the pictures of Mt. Fuji in Japan. While Jenny ate her shrimp, the conversation flowed extensively about places, activities, restlessness, hopes, and wishes. Sarah's eyes closed and we slipped her to the floor to sleep among happy feet. She couldn't care that our conversation would someday affect her life.

The next day seagulls escorted our car ferry across the Strait of Georgia to Vancouver Island, where we visited the most intriguing city of Victoria. Near there, years earlier, we had walked the Butchart Gardens, so we knew the thirty-five-acre former quarry, filled with flowers and fountains, would transport the children into a fairyland as the mountains had done. We timed our tour for late afternoon to see the lights come on. It was breathtakingly beautiful! There happened to be an open-air concert that evening, so we ignored any semblance of schedule and stretched out on the lawn to settle into individual reveries. With still unresolved thoughts, we retraced our steps through the gardens and were among the last to leave at 11:00 P.M.

We felt something special in Canada. We have seen similar sights in our United States, but there seemed to be a soft caress from the breezes off Juan de Fuca Strait as we rode a horse-drawn surrey through Old English neighborhoods of Victoria. Where is there a parliament or capitol building quite like Victoria's, dressed in necklaces of light at sundown? Even the flowers showed a brilliance.

With reluctance we headed on, this time to leave Canada via ferry to the Olympic Peninsula of Washington state. Now that we had our own baby sitters, Ken and I sometimes lingered to talk over wine in a restaurant or sit under the stars. We spoke of the past. We spoke of the future. Did we have what we wanted? We weren't too sure. We reminded ourselves that when we'd started out years before, we had wanted to remember that if ever the day came when we wondered what was around the next bend in the road, we hoped we would be strong enough to answer that call together. Somehow we felt sure we could find happiness in just about any setting. Were we content to stay where we were for the rest of our lives? We needed to give that more thought.

We did think about it. We discussed it often. We talked with the children when the restless feelings arose. We questioned our reasons for feeling restless. We discussed what it would mean to each member of our family if we should decide to uproot, especially what it would do to Jenny. We didn't understand why we couldn't feel completely satisfied with life as it was, because it did seem so good.

Down-coast we played on tumbled driftwood at Kaloloch Beach. We cavorted on hundred-foot-high sand dunes that stretched for forty miles near Winchester, Oregon. We toured a wood-products factory and wondered why myrtle wood is so dense it won't float in water — supposedly it grows only there in Oregon and in the Holy Land.

Finally we arrived at our relatives' in the Rogue River valley of southern Oregon and were dismayed to learn that brother-in-law Russell was in the hospital clinging to threads of life. "But why? He's always been such a strong person, almost indestructible! He's not old. Why this?"

We stayed longer than anticipated, unwilling to tear ourselves away when it looked as if eternity were calling a loved one. But we are of this world, and time pressed on. We had many miles to cover and responsibilities to meet. As we traveled east, we called west. Each call was increasingly bad news. It made us continue to ask ourselves if we were satisfied with the way in which we were living out our lives. Often the topic arose.

Always when we traveled, in every part of the country, from relatives, friends, and even strangers, we heard, "We could surely use a doctor in town!"

What lay ahead for us? Unceasingly, when we asked ourselves if we should change our lifestyle, we also asked, "How would it affect Jenny?"

Jenny, Jenny. How she permeated our lives. And our plans. There was no way we could know the answers. All we could do was to make whatever plans felt comfortable to us and hope she could keep in step. If Jenny couldn't keep up with us, we would simply have to deal with that problem when it came.

In the meantime we kept saying "C'mon Jenny!"

And kept feeling, "What if she can't?"

§§ 17 §§

...uprooting...

The rest of the summer of '75 had a different feel to it. While the girls lived domestically, the boys craved adventure. Besides playing, Jenny learned how to scrub kitchen cupboards, to cook, and to bake. During berry season she daily checked the bushes in the woods and served her treasured pickings with cream. She gathered tame and wild flowers for bouquets.

Mark and two friends, Tim Murphy and Eric Bostwick, bicycled six hundred miles via Door County. Jenny helped carry canoe gear for Paul and his friends so they could ply the local waterways. And she dunked in the Kickapoo River with Dad and me when we beached our own canoe. Such giggling!

As we played and worked our way through summer, we had many searching conversations. We chide ourselves for not being able to make decisions easily, and for drifting into final decisions. In reality, though, we present pros and cons to be used in making the really big decisions. The decision now concerned our restless feelings. We were dealing with seven different personalities, and Jenny's special needs, and it was important to us that we live in a manner that could potentially stimulate each of us.

Ken drew a line down the center of a paper. At the top of one column he wrote: "Reasons for continuing our present lifestyle." At the top of the other column he wrote: "Reasons for changing our lifestyle." That process was only one we used, but it was the one we could look at and study. We prayed together often as a family, asking for guidance. We did not, however, ask opinions from friends and relatives. If we chose to change our lifestyle, it had to be our own decision.

On August 26 the children boarded the big yellow bus for their first day back in school. That night at the dinner table each child gave his impressions of the return to the new year of academics. Then Dad said, "Now it's Mom's and my turn."

Three pairs of eyes focused on their Dad. Jenny's and Sarah's would, eventually.

Dad said, "The recruiters from the Air Force had lunch here today. I gave them my application."

So there, it was done. It had been a most difficult decision that had spanned the months. There wasn't a local person who would have suggested that Ken leave. He was a well-liked physician, and sorely needed. After we decided to make a change in our life, it was inconceivable to us that we simply move to another town. That would be like telling the people of Edgerton we didn't like them. Nothing could be further from the truth. We had interrelated in so many ways, developing strong bonds, and our children had benefited in countless ways through school, church, and community. Ken liked his partner, we certainly were fond of our home in the woods, and the children were doing exceptionally well in school. No wonder it was difficult to explain our leaving to people who had their roots so firmly planted.

But the persistent nagging to move on could not be ignored; it stayed with us daily. We blindly answered that feeling, because it somehow seemed the right thing to do.

Making the decision to uproot and move on put an entirely different outlook on our last months in Edgerton. We savored every activity and every nature offering, knowing it would be the last in that setting. Nature played into our hands: the hickory nuts dropped by the thousands; the flowers bloomed in profuse glory; the oaks displayed breathtaking autumn colors; the winds murmured thruogh the trees to whip the flagpole lanyard, giving sounds to remember; and we even had a devastating ice storm that felled branches from our trees, ripped out power lines, and left us with four days of winter solitude filled with old-fashioned living that created new memories.

School, church, community, and social functions were the last of their kind for us. And always we had to answer questions. We had offered to wait until Mark graduated from high school in one more year, but he said, "Oh no! If you're going to move, let's do it while I'm still at home, so I can have the experience too."

Little did Mark know what consequences that statement would hold for him. Perhaps he lived the most bittersweet year of us all. In eleventh grade and sixteen, he lived a life that proved he wasn't just living for one day but rather in preparation for a full, wonderful lifetime. He was not interested in the drinking or drug scene that some of his peers experimented with. He was a thinker; he cared about others; he held respect for his elders and for the less fortunate; he understood that not all his teachers had great abilities, but that he could still learn from them if he applied his own talents.

His philosophy concerning Jenny was reiterated through the years: "I have to try to do my best. Look at Jenny. She was given so much less than what I have, and yet she's always trying to learn. I would feel like a fool if I didn't use what God gave me."

Sports were important to Mark, but he didn't let them be all-consuming. He learned the hard way why it was wise he had developed other talents. During that basketball season his years of persistent practicing finally bore fruit and he was becoming a good, accurate team player. But then, during Christmas break while playing ice hockey on the marsh, he tore ligaments in his knee. Cast and crutches ended basketball for that season. It didn't affect him adversely. Instead, he brushed off his trombone, rejoined the pep band, and faithfully did exercises to get his knee back in shape for tennis.

That, or the fact that we were leaving, didn't deter him from keeping involved with school, church, and community activities. While he was forced out of basketball because of injury, he couldn't understand why Paul willfully chose to quit basketball.

Each to his own reasons! We listened to Paul, and he wrote out for us his reasons for wanting to quit. We left the final decision to him and his coach. Whereas his brother was seemingly willing to have his last months structured with activities, it was more important to Paul to have hours to call his own. He would be leaving the only hometown he remembered. In fact, all of our children considered Edgerton their hometown, and despite their willingness to reach out to a new life, there were plenty of harsh emotions.

We attended many events that year that included music and one or more of our children. Music was important to us, but we weren't into classical music. Before band concerts, Ken teased his kids, "How many Sousa marches are you playing tonight?"

"None."

"None! Then I'm not coming. Who ever heard of a band not playing Sousa!" But of course he went.

When I listened to Mark on trombone, Paul on cornet, and Katie on clarinet, I wondered if Jenny might be capable of learning an instrument. Besides piano, we wished she could understand band language. The junior-high instructor offered to try Jenny on a school clarinet, not knowing whether Jenny would take to it well enough to warrant buying or renting a horn.

The instructor knew she could withdraw her teaching at any time and we would respect her decision to do so. She chose, however, to continue teaching Jenny, and even wondered if other of the special-education students might benefit from the band program. Some mentally handicapped persons have unusual propensities for music.

Daily Jenny struggled with blowing and with fingering; her left hand seeming more agile than her right. Jenny never became very proficient, but she liked being able to practice an instrument along with Katie and the boys. She exhibited some impatience with the process, which brought threats from us to curtail her lessons; but the benefits seemed to outweigh the agonies — Jenny gained new knowledge, took added interest in band concerts, and wore her red Tider band jacket with pleasure.

Life's unplanned processes entertained us, and this time Jenny lucked out. We asked widowed Auntie Lee to visit us to get new thoughts. We certainly didn't expect those new thoughts to involve bypass surgery for her. While she recuperated, Jenny thrived from this aunt's ever-present patience. They read together, did needlework, listened to music, took many walks, gathered nuts, and picked out hickory nutmeats by the hours to give as gifts.

When Auntie stitched Christmas gifts, Jenny covered clothes hangers with chenille. She proudly gave them to her teachers and friends; since they were usable items, she received genuinely-pleased thank-you notes. Correspondence was cherished by Jenny. She kept every letter and note she received and entered the addresses in her own address book.

We continued to wonder what a move would do to Jenny. Some days we were scared. She had steadily made progress and had gained confidence in social situations. She was better able to handle her emotions, but in stressful situations could quickly resort to frustrations and tears. Would a move away from people she had learned to depend on be detrimental?

Katie, now in junior high, offered a mother-hen role over Jenny. "I'll watch out for Jen at the skating rink if you let her go on the school trip to Janesville."

Jenny needed supervision, but she also needed companionship. She got along okay with normal students at school, but social outings asked more of her. Katie was a willing companion, but it was only natural that she didn't *always* want to be involved. Her brothers were helpful, but couldn't be saddled with Jenny at school social functions. And chaperons could not be expected to give all that was needed. We would have felt better about letting Jenny attend extracurricular activities had a volunteer buddy system been offered. A school is never all that we wish.

Jenny turned sixteen, oblivious to some of the peer world around her. Despite her age, she was still a little child. Perhaps her social life was best left uncomplicated? I don't know, but that's the way it had to be. Her performance age was now calculated at approximately a ten-to-eleven age level. The Wechsler Intelligence Scale for Children showed her Verbal IQ to be sixty-two: Performance IQ, seventy-four; Full Scale IQ, sixty-seven. This indicated that she had varying functional abilities, and was in a mentally deficient range along with about one percent of individuals with her same chronological age.

Let's recall that after Jenny finished four sessions of kindergarten and started special ed her WISC scores were: Verbal IQ, fifty-three; Performance IQ, sixty-one; Full Scale IQ, fifty-three.

To show a comparison, children with intelligence quotients below twenty are profoundly retarded and usually lack verbal expressions. Often they have gross physical handicaps. Severely retarded children range in IQ's from about twenty to thirty-five and can barely speak or take care of their personal needs. Those with IQ's of about thirty-six to forty-nine are considered moderatley retarded and might attend classes and learn to do routine tasks. Mildly retarded children have IQ's ranging from about fifty to sixty-nine; and borderline have IQ's of about seventy to eighty-three. This is based on an IQ of one hundred for an average developing person.

Just because Jenny preferred certain actions and social situations didn't necessarily mean the other one percent of Americans in her category had the same preferences. Even within their own limited category, children like Jenny are individuals and should be treated as such. For that reason it is wise not to put too much emphasis on IQ ratings. However, for us the IQ was a convenient tool to use in anticipating Jenny's needs in her next school.

We contacted Jenny's principal to discuss our move, and he set up a conference to include her teacher, the school psychologist, and the counselor, so we could discuss Jenny's future and get recommendations. Of course, none of us could be certain about Jenny's future. We could offer her next school a report of what Jenny had already achieved, but beyond that we could only hope that Jenny would maintain her positive attitude toward schooling and that her next school would be able to stimulate her toward more learning.

Instead of sterile report cards with only letter grades, Jenny's teachers had written comments that gave a clue to how she reacted as a student. That would make it easier for her next teachers to understand her working potential. They could know that Jenny was a good student, worked hard to get all her assignments in when they were due, was prepared for class, attentive, and responsible, respected her teachers and classmates, and was well liked, participated in group activities, had an excellent attitude toward her work whether she worked alone or with others, and was courteous.

Jenny liked all of her classes, and sometimes reading and spelling were favorites, but just as often phy ed or home ec were the favorites, especially when cooking was included. She proudly brought recipes home and made them for us. During the second semester she sewed a skirt with zipper and waistband.

Jenny's reading comprehension improved, and a new world opened when she met Nancy Drew, Trixie Belden, Cherry Ames, and the Bobbsey Twins. She read what books we owned, and since the library didn't carry Nancy Drew, she borrowed them from friends and saved her precious coins to buy more, asking us when she had enough money to buy another. It seemed she would never fully understand money and its value.

As winter waned, word came that Dad would be assigned to northern Maine. The opportunity to learn more about Canada's Maritime provinces led us to literature concerning them. We also subscribed to the Caribou, Maine, weekly newspaper, and the children pored over school news and sports news trying to glimpse their future. There was one thing certain: tennis was not a common sport to the schools in that snow belt.

New schools beckoned while the current school year passed with lightning speed. It seemed there were a zillion and one things that had to be done besides what we wanted to enjoy one more time. Mark had to update his immunizations for a passport, and Ken and I drove one of the carloads of classmates to Minneapolis to meet their chartered flight to Spain for a two-week learning experience.

There were dental appointments, orthodontist appointments, and eye exams for the six of us who wore glasses. Sarah had tubes put in her ears. And of course there was constant sorting out of belongings that had accumulated over the past thirteen years, some to be sold at auction or rummage sale, others to be passed on or given to Goodwill.

Real-estate people and potential buyers had to be cordially welcomed. And no sooner did we get our place shaped up to sell than the severe ice storm devastated the trees and knocked out power for four days. We were grateful to teenage friends who rallied to assist in the cleanup, but it still took many days of family cooperation to complete the task.

Always and everywhere there were questions to answer about why we were moving away from Edgerton and where we were going and how we could possibly have the courage to uproot all these kids.

Ken's final weeks were so full I wondered how he lasted under the pressure. His patients dreaded to see him leave. Over and over he heard, "Who will take care of me? When are you coming back? Did you find someone to take your place?"

In the late days of winter we had the overwhelming need for a brief respite. We didn't care where we went as long as we could escape the ever-pressing duties and questions, though unfailingly we were offered best wishes in our ventures and were often told, "I surely do envy you. I wish we could do that."

Where could we get away to? We couldn't be gone longer than the spring school break. What about Mark's tennis? We didn't want to go to relatives for more questions, and we wished for sun and warmth.

Finally Dad suggested, "How about if we head south?"
"Where to?"

"Oh, anyplace. No particular place. Or maybe Kentucky or Atlanta. Just pack and we'll see what happens." Now that was our kind of adventure!

As soon as Mark finished playing and winning a quadrangle tennis tournament, we left on our escape jaunt. By the time we decided to get a motel, we were in Purdue country of Indiana and were told, "There's not a place to be had within forty miles of here because the college is having some sort of music festival."

Dad said, "Well, we've never driven all night, but it looks like tonight's the night. How about if we head on to Atlanta?"

In flower-bedecked Atlanta we played tennis, swam, climbed Stone Mountain, walked, relaxed, and greatly enjoyed the quietness without a care in the world. When time ran out we went home.

At home Mark continued to win his school team tennis matches, and I declared, "Tomorrow is the rummage sale! If you kids want to sell any more stuff you've got to get it in the garage and get it priced. *Now!*"

Jenny didn't earn much personal money at the sale because she couldn't part with any of her treasures, but the other kids put their wares out. Paul earned forty-five dollars from empty beer cans he salvaged from vacation trashcans. He was disappointed that some of his collection was stolen — we were leaving with memories of all kinds of friends and acquaintances.

Farewell functions were held in our honor, but I don't think anyone was more pleased than Mark when he received an unexpected invitation to the Lions club sports banquet for seniors. Mark was deep into tennis season, and we attended as many of his matches as our busy hours allowed. His conference tournament happened on the Saturday Jenny invited Tammy to play. We had to allow for Jenny's rights, also.

That afternoon the phone rang. Friend Jane announced, "Mark won the conference title!"

Two days later nothing could have kept me from attending the sub-sectional tournament. I could hardly wait to get home to announce, "Mark won again!"

Three days later friends went with me to Janesville for the sectional tournament. Dad joined us as soon as he could get away from his medical duties. This time, "Congratulations, Mark! How does it feel to win the sectional tourney?"

Now there was a new dimension to the questions: How can you take him away now? He can live with us if you let him stay here to play tennis next year. You mean there might not even be a tennis team at his school in Maine? Are you sure you have to leave Edgerton? Keep our college in mind.

Most pleasant of all comments was, "You must be proud of him."

Yes, we were proud of him. Mark had worked for years to excel in sports. He had been a husky, slow youngster whose Little League coach teased that he had to hit a home run just to get to first base. Mark learned that accuracy could pay off. We were proud not only that he won a berth at the state tournament for himself and his teammates for the first time in the school's history, but that he accepted it in a mature manner. A newspaper reporter questioned him about his move to Maine, where he might not be able to play tennis. Mark answered, "I can explore the Allagash wilderness, play basketball, and if I can't attend a school that plays tennis I'll just have to play in the band or something. Tennis isn't my only ability." Mark was also keenly interested in academics.

He won his first match at the Wisconsin state tournament but lost his second. None of us minded. It had been a tremendous thrill for him, his team and coach Cronick, his brothers and sisters, and his parents. Yes, we were proud of him.

Final countdown to moving day followed in earnest. Those last two weeks in Edgerton were unreal. The calendar looked like a battle plan, and Sarah and I had all we could do to keep track of where everyone was.

There was band marching on Memorial Day, bike rides, canoeing on Saunders Creek, Rock River, Lake Koshkonong, and the Kickapoo; overnights with friends, and the girls lunched one last time with their special friend, Anna Olson. There were dinners, parties, houseguests, orthodontist appointments, the Air Force swearing-in, and our auction. Ken soothed patients, and I took time to write letters.

School ended and the auction was held. Then the packers came. Time and again we had explained to Jenny what would happen next and how she could help and what was ahead for her and us. If she had any deep or questioning thoughts, she was unwilling or unable to share them.

The packers filled boxes while the girls helped Mark and Paul pack the lime-green Pinto with camping gear and the overflow of belongings that we wanted for an interim visit to Grandparents' homes, where Ken and I would do home repairs for them. The boys would travel on to recapture the adventure of mountaineering in Colorado with cousin Doug Vakoc, who had first exposed Mark to it. Then alone they would spend days camping, hiking mountains, making decisions, and no doubt surviving wrong decisions.

That incited more questions: How can you let those kids do that alone? They're so young! Doesn't that frighten you to death? What if they have troubles? What if they get sick or hurt?

The boys had earned our trust. No, they didn't always make perfect judgments, but neither did Dad and I. They had learned to budget their incomes, accept responsibility for their own actions, and treat people the way they themselves wanted to be treated. They did not really know how to take care of themselves if they got sick, because they had seldom been sick. If that happened they would have to deal with it as needed at the time. When we trusted them, they responded to that trust.

We bade goodbye to our adventuresome sons and then allowed Jenny, Katie, and Sarah to spend their last hours with friends. That night Dave and Jane brought a pot of barbecue to share with the truckers and us. We all sat on the now-empty deck lit by tiki torches. The trucker exclaimed, "How can you leave all this!"

The next day the white-and-silver Wheaton Van Lines truck filled with our belongings pulled out of the drive with Mike O'Shea at the helm. Ken and I, with reined-in emotions, burned the last bits of trash, did one final vacuuming of the carpets, checked the windows and doors, signed the inside wall of the barn, and then stood in the front yard under the tall trees. For long moments we did nothing but look. The house, the barn, the woods, the tree swing, the basketball hoops, the circular driveway and shrubbery, the berry bushes, fruit and nut trees, and off through the trees the marsh. So much of it was a part of us. We were burning a bridge behind us. Quietly we got into our station wagon. We stopped at the bank to retrieve the safe-deposit belongings, then picked up the girls, and slowly drove out of town.

Somehow it seemed right, but we didn't understand why. We may never understand.

§§ 18 §§

...out of the cocoon...

During orientation to the Air Force in Wichita Falls, Texas, Ken knew he was back in the military when he got his uniform and wore it for the first time. Until then, in civilian dress, the new recruits had exchanged words freely. That evening in our efficiency motel room Ken said, "No one talked to me today." He was playfully exaggerating, but not much. His uniform showed a higher rank than most of the other recruits. There would be much to get used to.

After our family regrouped in Wisconsin and exchanged tales of the several weeks apart, we repacked the cars with suitcases full of newly laundered clothes; secured two bikes on front of the station wagon, and two on the back; tightened the car-top carriers; positioned a box of houseplants; added ice to the food chests; decided which car Hodel the dog should ride in, reminded each other, "Don't forget her and don't lose her!" and finally figured out who should ride where, and that if we got separated in Chicago we would meet at the first oasis after the Indiana border.

We drove across Michigan, Ontario, and Quebec wondering what lay ahead for us.

At a shoreside overnight cabin near Beaumont, Quebec, four-year-old Sarah played with a little girl from the next cabin whom we invited along for a walk by the St. Lawrence River. She and Sarah communicated adequately, which caused Paul to exclaim, "That little kid's talking French! How can they understand each other?"

The simplicity of childhood! Young children often don't know there is a problem until bigger people point it out to them. In earlier years, Katie had similarly interpreted Jenny's incomprehensible jargon.

I am reminded of the short book *Joey*, credited to Joseph John Deacon and published by Charles Scribner and Sons. The writing of that book was possible only because four institutionalized, handicapped men had an uncanny way of understanding one another. Joey, with limiting cerebral palsy, communicated with another resident who somehow understood though the employees could not. That non-writing friend related Joey's personal story to another handicapped friend who printed it enough so a fourth friend could laboriously peck it out on a typewriter. Because those handicapped people somehow comprehended one another, we are admitted to Joey's world.

We wished we could be admitted further into Jenny's mind. We shared common experiences but didn't know what she was thinking. How did she feel about moving away from Edgerton? Was she scared or happy or excited? Was there more she had wanted to do before leaving her friends? Did she fully understand what we were doing? Did we?

Neither Ken nor I had scouted out Loring Air Force Base, so we knew little of what to expect. We had decided there would be negative aspects to any place we might be assigned to, so had taken our chances. Our curiosity increased with the miles.

From Edmundston, New Brunswick, the highway followed lush green fields and low mountains that lined the St. John River; thence southeast through potato fields and woods to Limestone, Maine. It was beautiful country! Mountains in the distance, rolling hills, farms and streams, pine trees, and hardwoods.

In Limestone, curious voices chorused, "Can we drive by the school and stop to see the church?"

"Jenny, this might be your school. They wrote us that they have the kind of classes you need.

"It's neat-looking."

"Oh, look, there's a greenhouse."

"There's no tennis courts."

"What're we, about seven miles from Base?"

We'd timed our arrival at the Air Force base for midday so daylight hours could aid a possible good first impression. Loring gave that, except for housing.

"Those are homes?"

After settling into temporary quarters on base, we got identification cards (I.D.'s) for the children and then snooped the neighboring towns of Caribou and Ft. Fairfield to see their schools, homes, churches, and shopping. Back on base we checked locations of the BX, Commissary, bowling alley, golf course, youth center, tennis courts, and library. Each time we passed the housing it seemed worse. There were ten single dwellings, a few duplexes and the remainder were long rows of connected units that looked like something out of a ghetto.

On the fourth day the housing department gave us a key to a living quarters we could have.

"Is *this* where we're going to live?"
"Our stuff won't all fit in here, will it?"
"It surely is clean."
"It sure is tiny."
"There sure isn't any privacy."
"It's got three-quarters of a basement."
"How come there's no garage?"
"Looks like a fair number of kitchen cabinets."
"Well, at least there's four bedrooms, but they're not very big."
"The porch is sure scroungy, and we have to share it with someone."
"It's got two bathrooms, but they're both upstairs."
"It's a good thing we're flexible. We are, aren't we?"

It was a four-plex, one of two that sat back from the street. We wouldn't recognize that bonus until winter. There was absolutely no privacy. Landscaping was almost nonexistent. What on earth were we doing to our family? Ken was quiet and so was I. I'm certain we were both praying — hard! I would be lying if I said we had a positive feeling those first days. We had come from four acres of privacy, lots of room in the house, and a life we called our own. All we could say was that we had answered a call in us to uproot and had chosen to face any and all consequences that went with that decision. Now we must face reality. Buying a home was out of the question, since there was a possibility the base might close. Perhaps we should look for a place to rent off base? We discussed it, but after much consideration we decided to stay on base and live in the four-plex that was offered. There were many people who would consider these same accommodations akin to a palace.

My desolation was short-lived. The celebrant at Sunday's Mass happened to be a visiting missionary. He spoke of living conditions in some of the areas he had served. The clincher came when he told of a family with three little children whose only home was one of those magazine-newspaper stands we see on city street corners.

Well! I decided we had the world in our hands! We had each other; our children were healthy and happy, capable and talented, each in his own way; Ken had a job, and he and I had our own bank of talents; we had chanced onto a beautiful section of the country; and God willing, we would learn lots during the next four years of our commitment.

It wasn't long before we were certain we had the best living unit on base — small and nonprivate to be sure, but it had a basement, and four small bedrooms on the second floor, so it was possible to get away from one another when we needed to. Only the four-plexes had basements. We carpeted and hung curtains, arranged and rearranged until the essentials and decorative items turned our little square quarters into a comfortable home. One lilac bush out the front window, a small pine tree by the front sidewalk, and a little tree in the back, fighting for its life against swarms of children, were the only landscaping.

Wooden buildings, connecting living quarters with all caliber of sometimes careless homemakers, and very cold winters that required constant home heating kept the safety department fearful of fires. We laughed when they advised, "If a fire breaks out in the winter, just step out your second story window." Everyone kidded about the expected snow but held sincere respect for the cold, the wind chill, and the psychological hazards of a long winter confinement.

What we had to face seemed awesome. But as in all of life, events came one at a time, and instead of being awesome, they proved stimulating.

Immediately Dad had to assume the duties of hospital commander for a few weeks and quickly learned that orientation hadn't taught him everything he needed to know. His fellow workers guessed as much when a disaster drill was called and he had to ask, "What's a flight line?" Being a quick learner, he soon settled comfortably into his new life.

My pertinent duties were to get the children enrolled in school at Limestone. Time was at a premium.

"August 17th!" they wailed. "That's only a week away! Why does school have to start so soon?"

"Because they close for three weeks during potato harvest so kids can help in the fields. And they have to allow for snow-days — they get 150-200 inches of snow here."

Hurricane Belle dropped residual rains on us when we drove to school to register and were warmly welcomed. Jenny's counselor made her transition especially easy. Jenny felt totally comfortable in Mrs. Barker's cheerful office with its yellow beanbag chair. We discussed Jenny's previous school year and the progression of her life, signed forms to allow the Edgerton administration to forward scholastic records, and toured the building.

The first morning of school Jenny was ready and waiting, with time to spare, to catch the 7:35 bus. Within a week we received an explanatory note from Mrs. Barker stating that Jenny had been given an achievement test required of all new transfer students. She added a personal note. There were many students new to the school system because of military transfers, so we had dared not hope for personal attention those first hectic days. The fact that Mrs. Barker found time and cared enough to send a note was a heartwarming gesture of reassurance.

Limestone School received Jenny's reports from Edgerton, and Mrs. Barker and special-ed teacher Mrs. Reynolds concurred, "Not often do we get such a complete worthwhile folder as Jenny's." It included testing results, conference sheets, pictures of Jenny, consultation reports we had submitted, teachers' comments and lists of the books Jenny had studied. It made Jenny's transition smoother since she was able to be placed into the right levels of classwork immediately.

Teachers told us they liked teaching at Limestone because the children of the military had varied backgrounds and interests garnered from having lived in other sections of the U.S.A. and the world. Class discussions were stimulating. It seemed local children had the same feeling.

Paul said, "A kid named Cameron talked to me today. He lives on a potato farm."

And Katie reported, "A couple girls sat with me at lunch. They live in town."

From Mark, "I met Bob Cyr today. He's a native. He says I oughta try out for the golf team. They don't have tennis. And the basketball coach acknowledged my height and asked if I play ball." Mark did try out for golf and made the team.

Always at supper we shared the day's activities, and from

each child came encouraging reports. School was going better than our concerned imaginations had anticipated it might. Repeatedly we heard names of students who befriended ours, and we were reassured that youth has a way of making new friends. Similar personalities seemed to attract, so we felt comfortable with the friends our children chose. Even so, we wished we knew the families.

In that respect we relied a bit on Jenny. She had resumed her practice of compiling family listings using her various means. Gradually individuals became families and families became our friends and acquaintances. The large wooded Air Force base with its security gates and guards began to feel comfortable; however, other mothers warned that we really couldn't let our guard down because crime did exist; so we kept tabs on the whereabouts of our children, especially the girls.

The military world is not primarily family-oriented. First and foremost, the uniformed man or woman must be ever available for protective service to our country. I gained admiring respect for the wives of flyers who were often left alone to meet the demands of their family while their men answered the call for duty at any announced location around the world. I learned about mothers who prepared their families for this cold-weather assignment only to have their husbands receive unexpected change of orders to some subtropical island in the Pacific; and about women who could not make the adjustment to moves and who lived month-to-month hoping their man would go civilian or at least be allowed to remain at one base forever. Others lived in eager anticipation, hoping for new orders so they could have the challenge and stimulation of moving on.

Military wives presented similarities, but they certainly did not fit into one neat mold. I was especially intrigued by the ones who moved onto base, settled into their homes within a couple days, and became involved with church, school, or club work immediately. I soon became one of those, because other wives took me under their wing.

Right away Sarah liked my activities because she could go to story hour at the library and to the nursery, which was almost like nursery school.

Living on base brought the rank system to our door, because names and rank were posted on each home. I was dismayed to learn how conscious wives and families were of rank. An officer,

Why should that be any different from the employee structure within a commercial business, factory, or office? Perhaps it wasn't. It did exist and it did affect. We encouraged our children to regard a person's character rather than a rank, though they were to respect authority.

Our children had a good example in their father, who respected each person as an important individual and as a member of a family. In fact a wife spoke of Ken, "For the first time in all the many years we have been in the military, I feel like we finally have a family doctor." I was glad it could be.

As in times past, we had to answer questions: Why did you quit private practice? What do you think is the answer to all the malpractice suits? Why did you join the Air Force? Where did you come from? How do you like Loring? What do you think of this housing? Have your kids adjusted?

The children adjusted amazingly well. Even Sarah entertained herself for hours with a new concept of play — she cut carpet remnants for the rooms of her Fisher Price dollhouse, hauled her toy furniture in a truck, and repeatedly settled in, rearranging her household furnishings at every whim.

At dinner we exchanged the day's gleanings. Like the teachers, we found it interesting to hear about other people's lives. Jenny listened with interest when conversation was about people, but quickly became distracted when topics became abstract.

We had uprooted ourselves hoping to learn all we possibly could. At every chance we went sightseeing. Jenny often recalls, "Remember when Dad and I went for a newspaper that morning in Machias and Dad had coffee and I had hot chocolate?" There, at the Bluebird Motel, we celebrated Katie's twelfth birthday with cake and candles we had secretly packed along. The highlight of the day was touring Campobello, summer home of Franklin D. Roosevelt. We were glad we'd had her "traditional twelfth birthday party" a year earlier in Edgerton because she hadn't yet established a core of close friends in Maine. For such reasons it was good we'd had several months to plan our move.

Potato harvest and the justifiably famous colorama of New England autumn offered new pleasures. During the school harvest break Jenny roamed the woods with Sarah and me to find dried foliage trimmings to use for crafts. Other of her hours were spent baking cookies and bars to pack into lunch bags for Mark, Paul, and Katie when they worked in the potato fields.

Potato harvest was a cause of unrest for some mothers, who accused, "That's downright child abuse to make those kids work from 6:00 in the morning till 6:00 at night and then only get forty cents a barrel!" There were even letters to the editor.

We looked at it as an opportunity for our children to appreciate the produce they took for granted in the grocery store. Mark was old enough to work on a harvester machine — which wasn't all fun and easy as it sounded to Paul and Katie, who spent their days on hands and knees grubbing potatoes from the dirt.

Jenny anxiously waited for them to trudge home in the evening and tell about how many barrels they got, and if they built a bonfire to keep warm or to cook hot dogs, and whom they worked with.

With winter approaching, we double-checked our supply of mittens, caps, and long johns.

School resumed, and we homebound people were advised to get projects for the long snow months so as to avoid cabin fever. Classes were given by military wives for a very reasonable fee. I signed up for drawing because it was something I'd never done. The day I shaded a circle and it ended up looking like an orange, I felt my whole life had changed!

Then I took tole painting, but where to put the painting clutter? As it was, our quarters were wall-to-wall everything, and when new hobbies were added it meant scrunching belongings in even tighter. None of us really minded, though, because we cared more that our lives be stimulating. Thus the game of acceptance included my clearing painting supplies off the dining table before meals. I teasingly refused to feed the family until they had dutifully oohed and aahed over my latest artistic endeavor.

Sarah was stimulated, too. She learned ballet and taught steps to Jenny and Katie in exchange for gymnastics maneuvers. The boys skied at the base slope, sometimes joined by the rest of us.

Domestically, Jenny kept at her knitting. Someone at school taught her how to knit bells for Christmas ornaments. But mostly she was obsessed with knitting a striped scarf for Paul in school colors of orange and black. Her patience to knit stripes and tie knots seemed endless. Jenny also created homework for herself, filling reams of paper with made-up match problems, sentences, and spelling words.

There was no question that Jenny was still learning. Probably she would have learned no matter where we lived, but there was a wealth of new information she was interested in. Maine and Canadian travels piqued her interests and spurred her on to study the road atlas and advertising brochures. She listened to the radio and wrote lists of songs and singers. She attended religion classes and kept bits of notes about what she learned.

She cared little about the constant verbiage concerning the probable closure of the base. Every day was lived to its fullest. Did it really matter where we lived? Or for how long?

As I rolled bath towels and tucked them around the windows to keep blowing wind and snow from penetrating our rooms, I was grateful for the personal quality of life we led.

By December the snow was beginning to accumulate. Dad teased, "I don't think we can have Christmas this year because there's no room to put up a tree."

"Ahhhh, Dad!"

"We'll make room!"

"It doesn't have to be very big."

"C'mon Dad, we've gotta have a tree!"

Then Dad admitted, "We've got an invitation to go to Killion's farm to cut a tree."

"Really?" chorused youthful voices. "Where's that? When can we go?"

We put on layers of warm clothing and drove west to New Sweden. Trekking through snowy wilds sounded better than the reality of the bitter cold, but that experience is recalled every holiday season. From a field of many, we chose just the right tall tree, sawed its trunk, and carried it back to the car. After we tied the tree to the top, Bonnie called to us, "C'mon in for some stew!" With home-canned applesauce, it was a regal start to the holiday season.

That holiday was accompanied by eight extra little hands that helped decorate our tree and cookies. Porch neighbor Barb was notified of urgent family problems in Florida, and her husband was a flyer. What more need be said? Another trait of military wives: whenever anyone needed help someone was there in an instant to offer it. Likewise I said, "Pack the children's clothes and bring their sleeping bags. We'll take care of them for these couple weeks." Two, four, six, and eight. Lisa, Patrick, Eric, and Mike were with us until four days before Christmas. When they left, our little house seemed larger.

The deep snow propelled us into holiday-spirited contentment. Earlier in the season we went to Portland to shop in a big enclosed mall. After a short while we were eager to return to the quiet remoteness of northern Maine.

"Too many people!"

"Too much commotion!"

"Christmas doesn't have to be that complicated!"

It was nice to realize our satisfaction with the rural style of life.

When Christmas greetings arrived, the children hungrily looked for familiar return addresses, but after reading the letters they admitted, "They're just doing the same old stuff."

Whereas we had snooped the nooks and crannies of new states and provinces, met the challenges of living a totally new life style, met new people, and made new friends; nonetheless, we missed our former home and old friends and felt our loss.

The memories were always there. Moving didn't erase them, and it was surprising to find which memories came forth when least expected.

Many winter evenings were spent at basketball games. Paul and Katie played in the pep band, and Sarah watched the cheerleaders to imitate later. Jenny scanned the crowd for people she knew. She linked school friends to adults who she assumed were their parents, and later at home penciled more entries in her notes. Mark developed into an excellent team player and accurate shooter. In the final game he made 100 percent of his shots for a total of 23 points. His successful season as his team's leading scorer in field goals, free throws, and rebounds almost made up for not being able to play tennis.

Now, if only that boy would decide where to go to college! It was his choice, regardless of location, but we preferred it be Catholic. That allowed many possibilities throughout the nation, and he had his list whittled down to seventeen.

It was strange to think we had a child ready for college. He was only thirteen months older than Jenny, and she seemed hardly ready for high school.

Mrs. Barker, Mrs. Reynolds, and I reviewed Jenny's needs. Since she could stay in public school only four more years, they suggested Jenny be officially considered in ninth grade so that she could perhaps imagine the end of her schooling. Always we had unqualifiedly said Jenny was in special ed. It made a difference to now think of her being in a specific grade in high school.

Jenny was doing very well. To think of the months we had wondered whether she would be able to handle a new environment! Teachers in this school were just as committed to helping her learn as past teachers had been. Even a business teacher volunteered to teach her how to type. It was evident that Jenny's future lay in the vocational field rather than academics, and perhaps typing could be of use.

She mastered the position of the keys and practiced at home. Though she didn't gain speed we felt certain the necessary coordination between hands and brain was beneficial.

Wisely, the Limestone school competed in the national spelling bee. Some schools don't. Again words stimulated Jenny's mind as she helped Katie. Jenny filled pages and pages of a notebook with words. She checked and rechecked spellings and asked for definitions. It tested our creativeness to give definitions that Jenny could understand. For words such as silhouette and prejudice she needed definitions that weren't too abstract. Besides pronouncing words for Katie to spell, we did also for Jenny. Definitely the bee was an aid to Jenny's learning, even though she was not a competitive participant.

While Jenny's academic achievements progressed, her social world remained static. The need for caring adults continued. They existed at school, church, in the community, and among our neighbors and friends. A special one was at the base library. After Jenny's frequent trips there to get books, she was always sure to tell if the lady was on duty.

That librarian friend, Mrs. Kohout, invited Jenny to help at the birthday party for her twins, and Jenny was especially pleased because Sarah was invited to that party. Since it was Sarah's first birthday party, Jenny proceeded to tell her what to expect. Sarah disclosed unleashed excitement by crawling into our bed in the dark of morning and asking, "Will I get to the party on time?" We assured her she had eleven hours to spare.

Jenny was interested in our friends and neighbors. Her interest wasn't an insinuating kind. She accepted people as they seemed. It probably never occurred to her to look further into a personality than what met her eye.

Jenny lingered closely to listen when the women and I talked. By watching my friends and me, she learned how to enter the grown-up world. I hope we set a good example. She was included in conversation, and in recipe exchanges. She always gave the one for delicious fudgelike brownies she had gotten from Jane Nelson. Actually, Jane's recipe called for melted oleo, but substituting oil made it easier for Jenny to make.

JENNY'S BROWNIES

Blend together: 4 eggs
2 cups granulated sugar

Add: 1 cup oil
1 cup sifted flour
4-1/2 Tablespoon cocoa
1/2 teaspoon salt
1 teaspoon vanilla

Bake in greased 9 x 13 pan . . . 25 minutes . . . 350 degrees

It was reasonable that Jenny be brought increasingly into my world, but I felt guilty sometimes expecting her to do more housework; and yet, when I thought about it clearly, I realized she wouldn't want to play all of her life. What is housework? How does a child play? Except for the caliber of equipment, they are essentially the same. Once I accepted that, I could see that Jenny probably enjoyed being included in the adult realm of duties.

Jenny's life was absorbing other characteristics of adulthood, although at times it was difficult for her to understand distinctly. Such was the case with the newest event.

Her piano teacher moved away, and we were never quite sure why, but there were rumors of divorce. That in itself opened new lines of thought for Jenny, now that she was conscious of her lists of families and who belonged where. Her simple knowledges were now put to the task of interpreting more broadly.

We found another teacher who would meet the quickly developing piano talents of Katie; and for the persistent efforts of

Jenny she suggested a pupil of hers. We never took it for granted that someone would want to teach Jenny, because it takes a special patience. Presumably any teacher who chooses to teach in special education has examined that quality in himself; others probably haven't. Therefore we gave high-schooler Pam Keith the option to decline after she had given trial lessons to Jenny. She chose to continue teaching her.

Pam lived farther away than Jenny's first teacher, and it was tempting to drive Jenny to lessons, but I would not have done that for the other children under the same circumstances. So again it meant pushing Jenny. The winter was cold, and in snow months there was no such thing as a sidewalk. In fact, we had learned why we were lucky that our four-plex sat back from the street several yards: the monster snowblower that cleared the streets had to blow the snow somewhere; for many of the dwellings that meant into their limited front yards, so that views from their windows became obliterated and trenches were necessitated to get to front doors.

The path to the area of Pam's house went through woods, and I was reticent to let Jenny go that route. She would have to go by way of the road. We practiced to make sure she knew the way.

When Jenny dressed for her lessons, one or another of us reminded, "Have you got your long johns on?"

"How about your wool sox?"

"If the wind is bad, pull your neck scarf up over your nose and mouth, but be sure to watch for traffic."

Some days I gave her a ride, but most times Jenny managed alone. From the kitchen window I watched her trudge in heavy snowmobile boots up the rise in our backyard, past the dumpster, through the neighboring garage area, to the street beyond, where she turned out of sight and plodded three more blocks on snow-packed streets to Pam's house. It wasn't easy to urge Jenny to self-sufficiency.

The winter intrigued. After the holidays we set our ceiling-tall Christmas tree in the backyard, and over the weeks the snows that fell diminished its height until only a foot remained uncovered. Beyond, cross-country skiers counterbalanced the antagonism of noisy snowmobiles. What a peaceful sight to watch serenely graceful skiers silently glide across the winterscape. The increasingly popular cross-country skiing made us wish we didn't already have downhill equipment, but outfitting a family of seven through the years inadvertently set the pattern. That birthday, Jenny's ski boots were added.

With winter break coming, we scanned ski brochures to see what nearby Quebec offered. But another place beckoned. Dad said, "There's Cape Smoky near the northern tip of Nova Scotia. If we went there, we'd have a chance to see what that country is like in the winter."

"Good idea, Dad!"

A most varied experience! Sarah spiked a fever the second day, so before journeying on to our relatively isolated destination of Ingonish on Cape Breton Island, we stayed overnight in Sydney, Nova Scotia. In the motel room someone flicked on the television. A gentle pleasant voiced man was singing. We listened.

"Who is that guy?" Dad asked.

"Don't know," usually-knowledgeable kids answered. "Never heard him before."

His style and songs captivated. He sang of goodness and family and patriotism. Some of his songs were as though we were hearing about ourselves and our families. At the end of the program we learned it was Roger Whittaker. At our first chance we stopped at a music store to buy his tapes. He quickly became a lasting favorite of our entire family.

Many of Sydney's population of 30,000 were employed in submarine coal mines, coal and steel industries, and seaport operations. Despite a high unemployment rate, there, in that remote ferry departure port to Newfoundland, we saw young people doing the same weekend evening activity they did in other cities of Canada and the United States: cruising. Time and again they drove up and down the streets, honking and waving to their friends — a flirtation dance reminiscent of the animal kingdom.

Our destination, government-owned and -operated Keltic Lodge, was a quiet haven. Jenny was content to play games with Sarah and me while the others repeatedly met the challenge of icy ski slopes. There were no stores near, no recreation areas in the lodge, no TV, no winter weekday restaurant. There weren't even other guests during that week, though we were told it was packed on the weekends. We ate from our plentiful food box, and the children played together, read, wrote, did not get bored, and did not complain. We all were perfectly satisfied to be away from society.

A lady at the ski-area snack bar declared, "No one from the states comes way up here in the winter! Why on earth did you?"

Why did we? For the adventure! To see a country in a new seasonal setting!

Carefully, we drove the partially sanded, snowpacked, and icy mountainous road of the Cabot Trail around the northern Cape Breton Island that forms upper Nova Scotia. Whereas the Atlantic Ocean was open water, we saw that open water gradually change to broken, thick ice in the Gulf of St. Lawrence. The farther we got toward the gulf side, the denser the ice. That dense ice, having heaved and hove with the movement of the tides, created an awesome seascape suggestive of pictures we had seen of the polar ice cap.

Gas stations were closed. Restaurants were closed. Life appeared at a standstill — except that fresh wooden lobster traps stacked dozens high at homes gave other evidence. It was obvious that fishermen had to spend their winter months preparing for the next season of work.

Then wouldn't you know. Jenny begged, "I have to go potty!"

Perhaps one of the local folk wouldn't have minded had we knocked on their door and asked to use their facility. In fact, they might have gladly welcomed travelers at that time of year. But we didn't. We happened onto a shoreside park but the restroom was locked; so Jenny gained the experience of going behind the building.

I have wondered if she carries any memories like mine. I was positively awed by where we were. I looked out on miles and miles of massive hunks of frozen bay piled on top of itself. Jenny, shivering, returned to the car, but I stood there long moments and just looked. I wondered about the submarines that ply the polar cap; about the ships and boats that must escape the St. Lawrence River and Gulf before it ices over for the winter; about those people who carve out a living in a remote region. Thoughts flashed through my mind about modes of living and how, by miracle of birth, we fit into it all.

The memory of that sight and conceptions has penetrated my years. Did Jenny's mind register anything? I doubt it.

What a trip! Though it was February, it rained on the way home. Inching our way to Antigonish, we prayed for care and guidance as we watched heavy layers of ice accumulate on a commercial bus ahead. The same thing was happening to our car. We whiled away those icy hours shopping for a graduation suit for Mark. To no avail. His six-foot-three-inch frame could not be fitted. In St. John, New Brunswick, our ski apparel looked out of place among the fur coats in a downtown church. We understood why those people chose the warmth of fur for that cold climate, especially when we saw that they walked toward their homes after church.

Reality resumed, and Jenny continued to pound out her version of "The Battle Hymn of the Republic" on the piano, and gave cue lines to Katie for learning a play. The snows kept coming. Newspaper headlines affirmed that it was one of the hardest winters that Maine had ever known. The countryside was beautifully peaceful with green pine trees accenting the snowscape. The snowfall amounted to 190 inches in our locale.

"Surely spring is just around the corner, isn't it?" No one person hoped that. Everybody did!

At least we had gotten out instead of staying cooped up in our small, confined dwelling. Those who didn't were deep into cabin fever.

One exciting day the word went around, "The sap is running!" Defying snow, for three weeks the maple trees announced the sure coming of spring. We gathered the children and Mark's girl friend and went searching the backwoods for a sugaring shed. In New Brunswick we found one with a French-speaking family wreathed in aromatic vapors. Pans of simmering maple sap were in varying stages of sweet doneness. Our smattering of conversational French that served us adequately in restaurants had to be enhanced by charades to learn from the friendly farmer the sugaring process.

While spring arrived, and always with the interest of learning how other people live, we considered requesting transfer abroad; but military parents who had been there warned, "If your kids are in high school you might want to reconsider."

Jenny was uppermost in our concerns. If we went to a foreign country, would there be special education available? With her needs, would we have the option of living off base? If we didn't live off base, what would be the value of going? How would she handle linguistic differences? She needed fulfillment as much as the rest of us.

Many of our thoughts and plans took Jenny into consideration. One day I read a short article and felt a stab of hurt. It concerned leaving inheritance for a retarded child. It seemed to say if the handicapped person had too much of an inheritance, he couldn't be eligible for government-sponsored facilities. What was too much? We had made out our will and hoped it would allow each child to have what he needed, depending on his circumstances. We feel ever so grateful for the rewarding government-sponsored programs that Jenny has benefited from. But our parental inclination is to treat each child equally. We certainly hope Jenny will have what she needs. Does one ever really know?

We couldn't be sure of the eventual financial needs of our family, but we were satisfied with their emerging personal characters and talents. We looked carefully at them now and knew they could be left alone for several days if Mrs. Sutherland next door took care of little Sarah until the others arrived home from school.

While Ken and I were gone to the medical seminar, Katie signed up for softball, Paul assumed the managership of a softball team, Mark took care of college applications, Mark and Paul registered for a French-class trip to French-speaking Quebec City, Jenny and Katie baked cookies for the May baskets, and Jenny and Sarah made the May baskets. None of them had relied solely on Dad's or my assurance that life would go on.

Dad scooped snow off the sidewalks, and once again May baskets were delivered, this time in northern Maine.

The first school year of a new life came to an end. We had survived amazingly well! In fact, far better than we had dared to hope. Dad and I proved that we could adapt to a new lifestyle during our middle age. Sarah's childlike needs had been easily met. Mark graduated with academic and sports honors. Paul and Katie did well, and all had made friends. Jenny proved she could hold her own. But even more, Jenny pleased herself, us, and her teachers by proving that she could continue to learn and function in a new environment.

Many of our concerns of the past couple of years could be laid to rest. Jenny's progress had definitely not been reversed. From all appearances, it looked as if Jenny would be able to carve new grooves wherever she lived.

"If that is true, should we still consider going overseas?"

§§ 19 §§

...proving and trusting...

Calendar pages and letters from the summer of 1977 remind that every available free day was spent sightseeing. Not always were we a complete family, because the boys had jobs and events. Nor was Jenny always easy to travel with. She fussed if it was hot, complained if it was cold, itched when things didn't go just right. Too often, it seemed, she jotted down notes on bits of paper. She sometimes was more interested in keeping notes than in seeing, which caused us frequent consternation. The rest of us could not contain our insatiable appetite for traveling and did not want to leave Jenny behind, so we simply had to develop a higher tolerance to her reactions. If only she could respond uncomplainingly to what we saw and did!

It surprised us, therefore, to see her take an interest in the food of the sea. Of course, that was food, and Jenny continued an avid interest in most foods.

Her first exposure to fresh steamed clams was on the shore of Chaleur Bay. A bold advertisement for fresh lobsters and clams called us to a red building on the shore. We found a man outside cooking over an open fire. Despite the drizzly, overcast day, we accepted that Indian's offer to steam us a bucket of clams. He filled a dented black bucket with fresh clams, added just a touch of water and a cover, and hung it over the fire. His wife came from the simple frame house, wiped off a dirty picnic table, and set out five plastic bowls. A daughter, home from college, wandered out and sat at the table to chat with us. She revealed that she'd much rather remain at home in that peaceful spot on the shore of the big bay than go to college. Her father, a man of few words offered gruntingly, changed abruptly when Ken noticed a half-built canoe next to the shed and asked, "Do you build boats?"

The Indian forsook his task of steaming lobsters for market, invited us into his shed, and proudly and wordily explained his process for making canoes, showing us his equipment. He also made snowshoes. Eventually the daughter called that the clams were ready and that the Indian needed to get back to his lobsters. He poured hot clam broth from the bucket into our bowls, then showed the girls how to open the shell, extract the clam, and dip it in the broth to clean off sand particles before eating it.

Jenny proceeded cautiously but determinedly. Soon her discarded shells mounted into a pile. While we ate, the Indian plopped a one-clawed steamed lobster on our table and invited us to eat it. That experience far surpassed the shellfish dining we had done on white linen cloth at Fisherman's Wharf in San Francisco.

Jenny's new knowledge also concerned tides. We knew for sure that Jenny's memory was in operation; she had heard about tides. She was amazed to see the extreme contrast between low and high tide on the Bay of Fundy. She exclaimed as we sat on a cabin porch at Eastport, Maine, and watched a forty-foot-high stilted pier sink to its walkway in the rising tide while seagulls searched for incoming fish.

Such adventures continued to intrigue us but ineffectively camouflaged a subtle change that was happening in our family. It was an inevitable change. Jenny, Katie, and Sarah continued to need our care and concern, but the boys were at an age that harbored independence. I was glad to see that Ken, unlike the way I thought my father had with us, was able to accept the maturing stages in his children.

I don't like having to think back to some of the progressive stages of life, especially those that involved the process of leaving the nest. I am grateful that I had common tales told me by experienced mothers who had struggled successfully through the teenage-to-adult transition syndrome of their children. It isn't as though anyone does anything wrong; it's just that life doesn't seem the same anymore. It becomes important to the child that his values correspond rather closely to those of his peers, and when they don't he questions whether his own are justified. Adolescents want to be accepted, and if that means changing some of their conditioned responses to life, they are sometimes willing to do that.

Thus must parents watch their efforts of disciplinarian struggles waver in the challenging winds of adversity that blow from innocent-looking neighboring houses. Out of values formerly instilled, their child now chooses the ones that feel right with his personality. His peers are perhaps choosing from a different set of values, and not wanting to stray too far from their companionship, he incorporates some of their choices into his own existence. Dating and peer pressures pose new situations, sometimes disputing good sense based on proffered values. While the parent can only watch, the child also sometimes sets aside longtime friendships because he sees that others are emerging more to his liking. From all this, the child molds a style of living and thinking that, for the time, seems to satisfy his searchings.

While the maturing process unfolds, Mamas and Papas sit by apprehensively, wondering if their years of persistent parenting and caring have been worthwhile. Through their children's developing stages, it is important that parents remember that in their own youth they too set aside old friendships to accommodate new ones that fit better into their lives; felt certain of abilities and couldn't understand their parents' questioning of their judgments; temporarily shelved family to test their own wings; and, if lucky, remembered gentle and caring guidance that was based on sound values. The stifling demands that existed just because they'd always existed were rejected. Finally, out of the cocoon emerged the person who met another and jelled into one parenting unit.

Moms and dads hold different good and bad memories that carry the fruits of individual approaches used by their parents. While their own progeny test their wobbly wings, they watch with bated breath and nervously grab for all-but-forgotten guidelines — but it is too late. The children can't listen, as the parents themselves couldn't listen at that age. The parents now suddenly know why it was so terribly important to offer wise guidance consistently through all the years from infancy. It simply can't be given all at once. It had to evolve.

So, while Ken's and my children were choosing their paths to independence, I remembered insights I had gained from other mothers, finding that I had to do some readjusting of my own emotions. Ken's days continued essentially away from home, and he didn't always understand what I went through in the day-to-day vigil of the maturing process. Our children's friends unintentionally vied with us for the position of advisor, entertainer, and confidant. Home was a place to sleep, put on clean clothes that would automatically be available, and grab a bite to eat between sports and music commitments, school and pleasure. I had to understand that youth does not like to mind a clock or do anything that isn't spontaneous.

But understanding the ways of a teenager and living through them were two different things for me.

One afternoon my tolerance level reached its breaking point. I wanted to scream that I was leaving and might never come back; but I couldn't do that to Jenny and Sarah because they could never sort out the meanings. Instead I yelled, "Somebody take care of the household while I'm gone!" I grabbed a notebook and didn't tell them where I was going because I didn't know where I was going. I wouldn't interrupt Ken and his patients. I didn't want to burden my friends or parish priest with my problems, though they certainly would have had receptive ears and hearts. I really didn't want to run away. So I went to a lake and wandered along its shore trying to sort out my feelings. I shed some tears of despair. I sat and watched the calming ripples as I threw occasional small stones into the water. Finally I wrote. For two hours I filled pages with frustrations.

With emotions spent I reread the pages.

Well, surely, life wasn't that bad either. So I wrote thoughts that counterbalanced the bad. I reached a point of relaxation and realized I had been gone quite a while and the kids would probably be wondering about me. I gathered my things and went home.

No one greeted me. No one had shown any concern about supper. Ken was late getting home from work; Katie was reading; Jenny was embroidering; Sarah was playing with friends. And where were those pesky teeners? Why, golfing, of course. Should I be glad that Jenny was incapable of pursuing her rightful course of adolescent behavior?

I did lots more thinking. Days of it. And I finally came to decisions that I adopted. I enjoyed life too much to let it get me down. I knew that Ken and I had conscientiously reared our children with sound moral values. It was time to admit that each child could select his own way of living out the trust we placed in him. Though we might not approve of every situation, we had to trust that our children would prefer the high standards we had taught through the years. It would serve no purpose to blame ourselves if they faltered or failed; we had to let them experience their own will in choosing between right and wrong, and if they made a gross mistake they must be allowed the responsibility to live with it.

And I made other decisions: It remained important to me that the rapport between my husband and me not be altered by unnecessary emotions about our children; that our rapport with each child be based on that child's individual needs. I even had to admit to myself that the deep trust Ken and I had developed for each other through the years must be recognized and not allowed to erode through petty jealousies.

A day arrived when I had my thoughts sorted. I donned my long red-and-white-checked skirt and red blouse, fixed a tall cool drink, went to the webbed lounge chair in our nonprivate back yard, sat back, watched the little children play, and wondered how I could have let even them get under my skin.

I felt good again. I felt ready to get back into the stream of life.

There was plenty to keep us all busy. Local communities took advantage quickly of the short summer to host art fairs, weekly band concerts in the parks, and sports events. We worked at food stands at the Base open house that attracted 20,000. We climbed the tallest mountains in New Brunswick and Quebec: Mt. Carleton and Mt. Jacques Cartier. We ate the unlike-McDonald's food sold at Quebec drive-in stands: loaves of fresh-baked bread, toutier (a meat-filled pie), quarts of baked beans, and freshly made eight-inch berry pies. We walked, at low tide, to massive Percé Rock off the tip of Gaspé Peninsula.

And Jenny bowled for the first time and played tennis with us. She helped fry apple fritters in the backyard for all the neighbor kids. She baked batches of cookies with Katie.

College was often the topic of conversation at our supper table. Jenny was curious about college. She stutteringly asked, "What is it? What will Mark do there?"

We tried to explain what it was like, that he would go to classes, live in a dormitory, eat his meals in a large cafeteria with all the other students, and have a roommate.

Dad pondered, "I have to attend more medical seminars. There's an interesting-sounding one by Colby College in Waterville that families are invited to. How about if you and the girls join me? Would you girls like that?"

Jenny helped pack her own suitcase and told the neighbors, "We're going to college!"

She, Katie, and Sarah shared a dorm room next to Ken's and mine and thought it great fun to use the women's communal washroom, walk to other buildings on campus, eat in the cafeteria, see where Daddy went to lectures, and attend a magic show presented by a chemistry professor. We also participated in other interesting tours and events offered for the families.

Jenny could now tie Mark's future college life into her own imagination.

During all these new experiences, Jenny wrote more often on bits of paper, but she was embarrassed to let us see them. "It's nuthin'," she'd say, and quickly hide the note.

I even had to retrieve her from public restrooms where she would sit on the stool and write. When I sorted the dirty clothes for the laundry, there were always bits of paper in her pockets. They were in her dresser drawers and in her books and under the bed. They included a list of the weekly Top Forty songs she'd gleaned from the radio. It was part of her compulsive behavior, and there seemed to be no way of subduing it.

Potato fields dressed in white-and-pink blossoms warned that school would start all too soon. Sarah, due to enter kindergarten, was determined she should know all sorts of things to be ready. Paul gladly accommodated by giving her problems. He'd ask, "What's half of six; of ten; of thirty; of seventeen? What's one-fourth of sixteen; of twenty-four; of eighteen? How do you spell dog? How do you spell Dad?"

Somehow that little girl came up with correct answers. Then he'd tease, "Saaaaaarrrrrrah, how do you spell college?"

We remembered when Jenny was that age. She couldn't speak but a few brief words, had rejected playmates, and wouldn't go to bed without awful screaming tantrums. Ken and I had been frustrated. I had been scared. And we had prayed. We thank God there were many people who cared about her and helped us teach her.

Now Jenny was seventeen years old and proving her worth. We dared not underestimate her potential. She eagerly boarded the school bus for another academic year. "Tenth-grade special ed," she answered when asked what grade she was in. She seemed at ease with the term.

Enthusiastically she reported that home-room teacher Mrs. Reynolds would teach English and math and tutor; Mrs. Bugbee, home ec; Mrs. Brewer, biology; Mr. James, typing; and Mrs. Plourde, physical education.

With the late summer now taking on a semblance of quiet, Mark's last days before college were spent meeting certain goals he set for himself. He ran nonstop seven miles to the neighboring town of Caribou to win a bet; climbed Mt. Katahdin; biked to Grand Falls, and took Sarah out for lunch. And he entered the Aroostook County clay court tennis tournament at the suggestion of his basketball coach Bill Casavant.

Mark had never played on clay, but at eighteen he was willing to attempt anything. He won the first match, then the second. Coach enthusiastically urged, "You can do it, Mark!" An avid group of tennis devotees had come from miles around to compete in that tournament. During the semifinals match they began to congregate at the private court where Mark and opponent, former champion Gary Bowden, were battling it out.

As the match progressed, murmurings from the spectators arose.

"Who is this guy?"
"He's surely older than eighteen!"
"Is he military!"
"Where'd he come from?"
"Where's he going to college?"

Points were not gained easily. Back and forth. Back and forth. Both Mark and Gary were determined. Then rain interrupted play until the next day.

Returning to the clay, Mark finally won that semifinal match after long minutes of hard work.

While he competed in the final match, we answered questions. "He's eighteen; he didn't start playing until eighth grade; no, he's not going to school in the south; no, he doesn't have a tennis scholarship; no, Gonzaga University is not known for its tennis program; he chose his college for academic reasons and for location; it's in Washington State."

It was like a rerun of a year earlier when we left Edgerton amidst tennis championships. If tennis was to be a part of Mark's future, it would have to be because he really wanted it and not because he happened to get a scholarship.

Mark, 1977 clay court champion of Aroostook County, Maine, couldn't have been prouder. The natives, who had to turn over the honor to an outsider, can be assured that he loved their country. He had not passed through to pluck only what he could and then leave. He left a part of his heart in those potato fields, those hills, those rivers, with those farmers, teachers, and friends. He would be back. Now he was ready for Gonzaga University in Spokane, Washington. He had lived his young years wisely. We had no qualms about letting loose.

When we returned from taking him to the airport in Boston, I cleaned his room top to bottom, set aside his treasures, put books, stuffed animals, and dolls on the shelves, and officially declared it Sarah's room to be used also for guests. It should have been Katie's or Jenny's room, but Jenny benefited from having Katie as her roommate. Jenny watched her study, read, do needlework, keep written records, write letters and a diary, listen to music. Those gentle habits rubbed off on Jenny, and she continued to form improved habits. Good-humored Katie didn't mind being the live-in teacher.

It had been especially hard for Jenny to bid farewell to Mark, though she would see him before long. When school suspended for the three-week potato harvest, we drove to Spokane to take Mark's gear, to see his college, and to visit grandparents. Auntie Lee returned with us to two unexpected surprises. First we learned that potato harvest had been detained because of rains; school had been recalled, and we had missed it; 25,000 acres of potatoes were still in the ground, winter was encroaching, and the farmers were very concerned! School was planned day by day and we listened to radio for directions. On weather-suitable days, Paul and Katie helped in the field, renewing warmth over bonfires.

The other surprise was new porch neighbors. While we were gone, teenagers had replaced the four little children. What a shock! Our own teenagers kept a cautious eye on their new porchmates and formed opinions. Except Jenny. They were her neighbors and treated her kindly, therefore they must be okay. Simple as that. Sarah showed the same philosophy.

Eventually the kids congregated on the porch for gabfests. There were many children in the four-plexes on our street, and it was interesting to watch how friendships developed. They didn't develop just because of proximity. They developed because children felt comfortable with one another. Jenny didn't develop close friendships but was accepted by all as she accepted them.

We weren't sure how to handle the peer situation with Jenny. Or perhaps I should say we didn't know how to handle our own emotions about it. Of course, we wished that our child could have associations, but what could we do? It would take an unusually caring normal child to befriend a handicapped child. We were glad the high-school religious education teacher was receptive to having Jenny attend the evening classes in her home. Though Jenny fought sleepiness, it was an opportunity to be with her peers in a social setting.

Making friends at school, Jenny came home mentioning one or another of them. One girl in particular was spoken of often. One day Jenny told us that friend had invited her to a nighttime Halloween party. As the days passed, the details of the party remained skimpy. We didn't know the girl or the family, but finally making contact with the dad, I learned about the party and that it would be held in a church basement. If only Jenny could communicate better!

Dad was on overnight duty at the hospital the night of the party. While Auntie Lee and I helped Jenny dress in her costume, we admonished her to stay awake at the party and to remember it all so she could tell us about it.

Her friend breezed into our house, quickly greeted Jenny and us, and proceeded to tell Lee and me about how her Dad and Mom had met one night and she was conceived; and then just as quickly, it seemed, she whisked Jenny off to their car.

Well! That brief episode had a straggering effect on me. Jenny's life rushed at me; all her struggles of the past and her uncertain future swirled about my head. I felt completely overwhelmed. I sat down, dropping my head and shoulders on the table, and sobbed and sobbed and sobbed. I don't know how long I cried, but it seemed like years. Thoughts rushed through my mind. So many things about her future I wanted to know. So many things about her past I didn't understand.

Mentally Jenny was just a little child. Physically she was a young lady. Surely we couldn't keep treating her like a little child. But how and when does a parent cross the threshold? When could we trust her totally to society? And if not totally, how could we decide which situations she could handle? Questions, questions, questions! And furthermore, what would become of her if we weren't around anymore? Add that one to the list!

Katie had taken her first steps on Halloween night twelve years before. Perhaps this Halloween I was being forced into taking some more of my steps in allowing Jenny to enter her next phase. I was glad Auntie Lee was with me to lend her support since Ken couldn't be home.

I barely survived that Halloween night, though Jenny recalled it with pleasure. She admitted having been afraid to go through the witch's maze with its scary accouterments. Similarly, I had been frightened of the witch's maze I had allowed in my own mind.

There really wasn't much more we could do to prepare Jenny for the approaching adult years. She was a product of discipline, loving care, education in both temporal and spiritual topics. As we would with the other children, we must trust that somehow Jenny in her own way would be able to choose the path that would be right for her.

Life was kind: It didn't come to a standstill so I could wallow in self-pity or discouragement. The repetition of seasons once again brought the nourishment of snow, basketball games, and celebrations. Friends stimulated us, and letters proved that we were being remembered elsewhere. Mark shared his college experiences with us. And Jenny shared it all, unaware of the recurrent traumatic emotions she sometimes caused in us.

Christmas held new meaning because we welcomed our firstborn home. The collegian settled expectantly into traditions. He had told his new friends exactly what he would eat over the holidays. Eve morning would be quiche; seafood chowder on Christmas Eve. Christmas morning we'd have homemade cinnamon rolls and juice. Then duck, or goose, or turkey with dressing; kraut and potato dumplings and all the trimmings. New Year's Eve would probably be an hors d'oeuvres buffet. Each meal had its place in the holiday week.

"Who made the cranberry bread?" he asked.

'Who do you think?"

"Hey, Jen! Did you do it again?"

"Yes, I did," she happily declared.

That was her third year of being responsible for having a supply of cranberry nut-bread stashed in the freezer.

Skiing. Ice skating. Conversation. Shopping. Secretive gift wrapping. Music. Some of the traditions survived, but new ones entered unexpectedly. That year for the first time, we all attended midnight Mass. Even little Sarah was content to prolong the anticipation by not opening any gifts on Christmas Eve.

Everybody's favorite gift was mine to Dad. I'd sorted through all the years of photos and assembled a book of pictures that depict him and his growing family learning, working, and playing together.

Following the holidays, on January 4, I cooked with mixed emotions and forewarned, "Dad has some news to tell us at supper."

After the commotion of passing food and filling our plates, he said, "I received orders today for Colorado Springs."

"Hey! That's okay! You'll be closer to Spokane!"

Paul added, "I hope we can hike in the mountains!"

Sarah asked, "Where's Colorado?"

Katie ruefully said, "That's a city, isn't it?"

Jenny looked from one to another, listening for the answers. We assured her there would be a school for her and that she could help prepare our belongings for the eventual move in the summer.

Nonmilitary acquaintances asked, "So Ken's going to be at the Air Force Academy?"

"No," we'd correct. "He'll be stationed at Peterson Air Force Base. It's the support command for NORAD and the Academy."

We wondered what winter in Colorado would be like. Would there be lots of snow? Or icing rains and penetrating cold like what we were now having? Would Rocky Mountain winters claim cars as Maine's had claimed the Pinto?

During those cold evenings Jenny, cozy in a red-and-white flannel nightie that Katie had made her for Christmas, listened to Olivia Newton John and other records that Paul had given her, hooking a rug she bought with Gramma's Christmas money. She had been gifted caringly. Even Sarah thoughtfully chose potholder gloves "so Jenny won't burn her hands when she takes cookies from the oven." Mark knew about the profusion of notes she wrote on bits of paper, so he gave her an empty bound book.

Jenny still begged for help to spell words. She wanted to know meanings of words. She wanted her own calendar. She garnered newspapers, sport programs, playbills, matchbooks, and travel brochures to use for spelling words. Little did we know it was the eruption of compulsive diary-keeping.

Her first brief entry in the empty bound book was only a list of the gifts she received for Christmas and for her eighteenth birthday. Also names of her teachers and houseguests.

The passing months brought out new characteristics in Jenny as they did in her brothers and sisters.

Car pooling in our new van was often interesting as I listened to adolescent chatter and teen-chosen music. One day eight girls and four boys discussed girl abuse.

"He hit me."

A boy exclaimed, "You mean he actually hit you?"

"Yes! What was I to do?"

"Guys aren't supposed to hit girls or anyone!"

"What did you do?"

"I didn't know what to do."

"You can't let him get away with that!"

"Yeah, tell everyone he did it. Don't hide the fact. Make him have to feel guilty about it."

"If you don't tell, then he'll do it to someone else."

"Lots of times he doesn't act very nice to girls."

"See ya."

"Hey, yeah, see ya tomorrow."

"Turn at the next corner, Mom, and go another block. She lives on the right. I'll tell you when."

"Thanks, Mrs. Pavlik."

"You goin' to the game tonight?"

"Yeah. See ya there."

"What's for supper?"

Unfinished conversations. Tentative suggestions. Caring. Sharing. Learning through one another.

Later I asked Ken, "How about Jen? How will she keep learning? Have you heard anything about special ed in Colorado?"

"I called the CHAP officer today. They'll look into it and get back to us. CHAP stands for Children Have A Potential."

We also wrote for information from St. Coletta's School for Exceptional Children in Jefferson, Wisconsin. Since Mark was away at college, we increasingly wondered whether Jenny should have a chance to get away from her family. Not that we were looking for a way to get rid of her. We only wished to give her every experience that might benefit her. We'd say, "What if she got away from this family for a while and it opened a door to her mentality? What a shame it would be to miss such an opportunity!"

Discussions usually ended with us deciding that our family life was quite stimulating and we didn't want Jenny to miss any of it. Jenny seemed to learn best from seeing, so maybe we were doing what was right.

Paula Wright next door was another good neighbor. She recognized Jenny's limitations and understood our attempt to help her become independent and productive. She knew we occasionally needed time away for recreation when we didn't have to fawn over Jenny and Sarah. She and I talked about Jenny's age, eighteen, and about Sarah's mature abilities though she was only six. It wasn't easy to ask a young sitter to come in because Jenny stayed up after Sarah went to bed at 7:00. Finally Paula and I devised a plan to allow Jenny the chance to baby-sit — real baby-sitting when the rest of us went out of town to ski. Since the Wrights shared our porch, and since our dog announced arrivals, we felt confident that Jenny could be trusted for an evening with Paula's earful concern. The girls would go to bed at their usual hour.

It was a red-letter evening in Jenny's life. She was proud of her accomplishment and the money she earned, though its actual monetary value eluded her. Even Sarah was pleased about being good for Jenny. Had we not prodded Jenny into this new accomplishment, she would never have asked to be allowed to try it.

That's the way it was with most new activities. Jenny lacked imagination to picture herself in new situations, but if we placed the stepping stones, then she'd try to maneuver them.

In the same way Jenny entered further into her spiritual life. A child like Jenny cannot comprehend the intricacies of belief; however, she proved she was interested by doing what she had to do to worship alongside us. Paul and Katie were going to be confirmed. Was it feasible to think that Jenny could possibly receive the Sacrament of Confirmation — the sacrament that further infuses in us the help of the Holy Spirit? It required restudying the religious truths she had learned all through the years. The teacher understood about Jenny and willingly incorporated her into the class.

Paul and Katie studied, and so did Jenny. When we said our family rosaries, we included new petitions concerning the forthcoming Confirmation. I made sheets of questions and answers, placing them through the house, even hanging one on a clothespin in the bathroom. That one showed evidence of being studied.

When the final test was scored, there was good reason to compliment Jenny. It was apparent that she understood enough about her religion to receive the sacrament.

We practiced the ceremony with Jenny, guessing at the procedure that would likely be used. After Militariate Archbishop Joseph T. Ryan of New York City confirmed Jenny, Paul, Katie, and their classmates, we took pictures of them with His Excellency and chatted at the reception. Thus did Jenny's life follow the traditional paths of not only educational and social progress but also spiritual progress.

It's tempting to think that we must get up on a soapbox to reveal God's working through us. It's tempting to think that after receiving the Sacrament of Confirmation we must walk the streets and knock on doors as the only way to declare the message of salvation. It's tempting to think that only through some kind of verbal contact can we effectively minister to someone. I learned that such thoughts are not valid.

One afternoon an acquaintance offered me a ride home. I gladly accepted. We chatted aimlessly until suddenly she turned to me in seriousness and asked, "Why is it I have trouble with my children and you don't?"

I didn't know her family personally. She and I sat in her car and talked. I cared about her because she, like me, was a mother trying to do the best possible job of raising children. She was right: we were a strong family, and even though we uprooted, we had maintained that strength; our children seemed to have an inner strength individually and weren't tied to our apron strings, nor we to theirs; we could let go of them and trust them to try their wings, knowing they made mistakes but also knowing they were more interested in testing themselves against man, nature, and self instead of against drugs, crime and moral abuses.

This concerned mother didn't like their living accommodations but recognized that our family had to live the same way and so did other families. She compared her children to ours in school situations and found similarities. She compared sports involvement. She compared our actions in the community. In fact, it sounded as if she'd been watching us for several months.

"What is the difference?" she wondered.

I couldn't know because I didn't know what it was like in their home. Then she admitted, "I have noticed only one major difference. You go to church as a family. Otherwise we seem to be doing the same type of living."

Then I remembered a conversation I had walked in on earlier. This lady was telling how Sunday mornings in their household used to be such a hassle because they all wanted to do their own things and some wanted their sports activities, golf being the current season. Each week they fought the same battle. Finally they quit going to church, and she was saying what a sane Sunday morning it had turned into.

Well, what was the answer?

It probably wasn't just that we went to church together, but rather that because our family worked together as a unit we also went to church together. We tried not to pursue selfish activity when it affected someone else's freedom. We truly enjoyed sharing with one another.

Even so, perhaps worshiping together made a bigger difference than I cared to deny.

I have thought about that conversation frequently. I wished she received better cooperation from all her family members. If our family's example had even a slight effect in their life, or in other people's lives, then our two years at Loring was well worth it.

Now that we knew we were leaving Maine, we became acutely aware that our children had formed good friendships and were involved with activities that could hinge onto the next year. They were in various sports, and Paul was doing the high jump in track. Katie was in the All-County band and had won the spelling bee. How fair was it to be uprooted so soon, as seemed to be necessary in the military way of life?

We were still new to the process. We didn't know then that our children would gain as much as or more than what they gave up.

When I tell how Jenny fit into school, church, and family living, it is sometimes easy to forget that she had limitations. It was only fair to her that they be acknowledged and that she not be forced too far beyond her capabilities, or for that matter not far enough. As so often through the years, we wondered if what we were doing was right.

We relied heavily on the recommendations of school personnel, but again we sought the guidance of a psychologist. I suppose what we were seeking was assurance that Jenny would not be adversely affected by another move.

Dr. Singer saw in Jenny a frail, well-groomed, friendly girl who looked smaller than eighteen years old. She had an unsteady gait and a slight lisp. In testing her, he learned that she became angry and frustrated when she could not complete an assigned task that grew gradually more difficult. She had considerable difficulty with non-structured tasks. She showed gross impairments in numerical skills, social judgment, ability to anticipate and plan for future events. She had significant problems with visual-motor coordination and fine motor control. She could not make up stories, and would not expand on the contents of a particular story. And she was uncomfortable with situations that were unfamiliar to her.

He noticed, however, that Jenny commented with pleasure when she faced tests that she recognized from previous testings. Her current scores were higher than in the past, and he felt the reason was probably attributable to the fact that she had been tested frequently and was too familiar with the problems. Perhaps psychological testing had passed its usefulness in determining Jenny's potential. Comparing her scores to her actions, he felt it was reasonable to assume that her true functioning was probably in the 66-72 I.Q. range.

He concurred with previous suggestions and with our own philosophy that we ignore Jenny's IQ and let her pursue life without expecting certain results. As Dr. Klové had opined years before in Madison, Dr. Singer believed Jenny was thriving partly because of her home life, and he suggested we continue to keep her at our side and give her loving concern as we had all through the years.

Though we planned to keep Jenny at our side in the immediate future, we never assumed that any of our children needed us by their side every minute of every difficulty, otherwise how could they learn to be independent? We talked about that with Sarah when we prepared her for her tonsillectomy at the hospital in a neighboring town. She was to report there at noon on the day before surgery. Shortly after I settled her in the sterile white bed, Sarah urged me, "You can go home now. I want to take care of myself."

"Okay," I said. "You're such a nice big girl. Daddy and I are so proud of you. You be good to the nurses and be sure to thank them if they give you a Popsicle."

I didn't go home. Instead I went to a local cafe and read a book for an hour. Then I went back to the hospital. Sarah was very glad to see me and thought I'd been gone an awfully long time. I didn't tell her what a short time it had been, but rather complimented her on getting along without me. We played cards and games until seven that evening, interspersed with conversations about her year in kindergarten, about Jenny, and Mark soon coming home from college, about moving, and even about having babies and what Caesarian sections are. There was never any guarantee what direction a conversation would turn with that child.

There wasn't even any guarantee in what direction a conversation would turn with the big kids. At home our dinner topic led into a fascinating area. Mark would soon arrive from his first year of college. It was suddenly realized that if he flew into Halifax instead of Boston, we could have the chance to still get to the southern coast of Nova Scotia. Then the phone rang. It was my brother from Iowa.

He asked, "Is it possible for a couple of our kids to visit you? They'd like to come next week."

"Sure! That'd be just fine. But there's one thing. They'll have to go to Nova Scotia with us. We've got room in the van. Have them bring sleeping bags and birth certificates. Who's coming?" We'd gladly include Mike and Joanne.

We arrived in Halifax a half hour before Mark's plane. The extended weekend was filled with beautiful seeds for future nostalgia, marred only by motor trouble out in the country, luckily near a lonely gas station. It would take several hours to get supplies and do repairs, so the maintenance man offered to take us back to town.

"How many of you are there?"

"Nine."

"Nine! The only way is to ride in the back of my pickup."

"That's fine with us!"

Memories, memories! And so, too, do the boys have memories of a final canoe trip down the headwaters of the St. John River. Never mind that their canoe got ripped apart by menacing rocks and they lost gear. The mailman saw the damaged canoe and exclaimed, "I hope whoever was in that thing got out alive. They don't always, you know."

Yes, we knew. And we did feel concern for the safety of our lads. I would have been content had they gotten their exercise by jogging, but life was not destined to be so simple for our children. We didn't even want to saddle Jenny with remaining in her own yard. We had to be accepting when she came limping home with a broken toe. She had lost her balance and her bike collided with a school building.

Paul declared, "It's a good thing Jenny's not going with me!" And where was Paul going? To Wisconsin on his bicycle — alone!

I don't know whether Ken had any time for prayers those final days before moving, but I *made* time, even as we said goodbye to Mark when he hitched a ride to southern coastal York Harbor, Maine, for a summer job that would entice him back again and again.

We faced queries from relatives, friends, and neighbors about Paul. How old did you say he is? Has he had experience doing this? How far is it? How on earth can you let him do such a thing? Aren't you scared? How long will it take? And we answered: Sixteen; no, not really; fifteen hundred miles; he has proved our trust in him; yes, we get scared; about three weeks.

The only place he had to prepare his bicycle was in his tiny bedroom where there was barely enough floor space for it. While he made last-day preparations, Father Shorty stopped by with a letter of introduction that Paul could use en route if he needed help.

When Paul finally moved the gear-laden bike outside, a neighbor boy came over and asked, "Where are you going?"

Paul answered, "Wisconsin."

Tony gasped, "Wisconsin! My Mom would never let me do that. Besides, I'd get lost!" I would guess Tony was about thirteen or fourteen.

Paul had confidence, though he later confessed he was more nervous the night before this trip than he'd ever been before or since. He was to head south the same morning the rest of us left for a quick visit to the provincial island of Prince Edward; but heavy rain delayed him a day, so he joined his science teacher, Jim Barden, for supper and last survival suggestions. Mr. Barden had, months earlier, exposed Paul to wilderness canoeing when they'd lashed their canoe under the wing of a small plane and flown into the Allagash to the St. John's headwaters.

That night Ken and I and the girls stayed in a tiny wood-heated cottage in Cocagne, New Brunswick. I lay awake many of the hours thinking about our children and us and our response to life. Neither Ken nor I had felt we should deny Paul permission for this bike hike. It seemed if he harbored that kind of confidence in himself, he probably had the ability. We had assured him it was all right with us if he changed his mind somewhere into his trip; that he wouldn't have to feel ashamed if he couldn't tolerate the challenge. Of course he should have a good reason for quitting. He was physically fit, mentally responsible, respectful of other people and their property.

Those thoughts were all such material reasonings. As the night hours ticked away along the Northumberland Strait, I kept vigil for our son with spiritual thoughts. I gained a peaceful feeling that Paul was doing what he was supposed to be doing, and those thoughts soothed.

After we returned home, laden with L.M. Montgomery books chronicling the tales of Prince Edward Island's Anne of Green Gables, we accepted an invitation for Katie to spend her last week with her transplanted friend Jenifer Kohout in Pleasantville, New York. We would pick her up on our way westward.

At the Presque Isle airport — the only one in northern Maine — we could hear Katie's Delta plane circling above the low-hanging clouds. For reasons unknown to us, it did not land. Katie readily welcomed an alternate plan to ride the little commuter Bar Harbor airline that local folk fondly, or not so fondly, called Tree Top Airlines. "Oh, good! That'll be fun! I'll get to change planes in Boston!"

Good grief! Surely we weren't rearing another adventure seeker! Katie had only just finished eighth grade. Maybe we would *need* Jenny in our future to stabilize it!

Dad had planned a phoning arrangement around all of our traveling and moving disarrangements so Paul, Mark, Katie, and we could keep contact. I was home with the packers when Paul called to report that he was at the Vermont border.

The older packer couldn't believe it. "Well, what d'ya know!" he laughed. "Maybe the young kids up here in the County will hear about this and realize there's a way out of this depressed area after all!"

Our home furnishings went into storage, the now empty quarters in the four-plex got cleaned, Ken processed out, and we spent our final hours in temporary quarters where no one knew our phone number. Just minutes before we were to start our journey away from beautiful northern Maine, the phone rang. It was Steve Ray's mother, and heaven only knows how she learned where we were.

Steve had biked with Paul the first twenty miles to bid him farewell for his long bike ride. Now Steve's bade us farewell with the news, "Paul called from Edgerton, Wisconsin. He arrived safely at his destination last evening!"

Hooray for Paul!

I called the newspaper and gave them the follow-up. They had wanted to know if this sixteen-year-old kid could really accomplish his dream. Paul indeed had — in twenty days.

Though there was much more we wanted to see and do in the northeast section of America, we wondered now how so much could have happened in just two years. It couldn't have, certainly, had we stayed in Edgerton. Ken received the Air Force commendation medal. I learned to paint pictures. Mark, Paul, and Katie were well launched into self-confidence. Little One had excelled in kindergarten.

And what about Jenny? Despite our initial fears concerning what uprooting might do to her, it was evident that she, too, had benefited.

I sit here, now, with her first diary — the bound book that Mark gave her for Christmas. It is full. There are some early tidbits of entries, but when is her first lengthy entry? July 21, 1978. That was the day we left Maine.

Let me copy from it word for word:

> We left Loring at 9:30. 2904C (Loring Drive). Cloudy. Mom drove the van. Dad drove the station wagon. Paul biked to Wisconsin he arrived there Thursday. Katie is visiting Jennifer Kohout in Pleasantville, New York. Mark is working at York Harbor tennis Golf club. On the van there is two car carriers, the canoe, and three bikes. Got donuts at Presque Isle 10:30. Talk to Mr. Casavant. Jenny rode with Mom. Sarah rode with Dad. 12:30 stopped at Medway

rest stop. Gased up at Old town Exit and gave Hodel a drink of water. We got to York Harbor tennis Golf club to see Mark. We transferred our stuff from the Station wagon to the van. We stopped at a rest stop. Stayed o'nite at Gills had stew, salad, milk, pie, rolls, for supper. it was very good. Mark and Cathy made blueberry pancakes for Breakfast. They were very good.

Jenny, Jenny. Who would have dreamed in years past that inarticulate Jenny could possibly someday become proficient at keeping a diary!

Her diary entry is a fitting testimony to her ability and desire to learn. While her brothers and sisters reached for higher achievements, Jenny was also conquering new heights that in their own way were just as exhilarating.

§§ 20 §§

...culture shock...

Some weeks later, we all congregated in temporary quarters at Peterson Air Force Base to await the availability of a newly purchased home. Even the miniature dachshund had enjoyed a two-week adventure after we lost her in Wisconsin, where we'd forgotten she'd jumped out at a gas station. When Mark drove the station wagon west, he retrieved Hodel and learned that she'd had royal treatment at her remembered foster home on the Burns's farm — sleeping on their bed and snitching T-bone steak off the cupboard.

Paul seemed more mature than the sixteen-year-old we had known in Maine. Emotionally and physically, he'd pedaled into a new life as he dealt with personal emotions, social problems, physical discomforts, road-maneuvering dangers, kind and unkind people, decisions, flat tires, nutrition, and money budgeting. In a residential area in New York, he'd been brushed by a pickup and had crashed. Though unharmed, he felt hurt that the driver had not stopped to assist him. Perhaps the driver wasn't aware of the accident? During those four weeks since we had bidden him good-bye he garnered understandings to carry the rest of his life.

Mark's employment experience on the coast of Maine gave him considerable satisfaction. And so, too, did Katie's experience enrich her life. The Kohout family exposed her to cultural aspects of New York City that helped firm her foundation for a future interest in the humanities. It was good for her to escape Jenny's constant presence, just as it was good for Jenny to fill her own days without relying on Katie's initiatives.

The move to Colorado Springs gave added insights into what it means to uproot. Frankly, some of us experienced culture shock. I suppose part of the reason was that we had let ourselves think we were moving to the mountains. Yes, the mountains were near, but Colorado Springs is a city, and even though we met acculturated people who critically compared its cultural offerings and night life to the big time, for us it was an adjustment. It had been many years since we'd lived in a city, long before we had children to enroll in school. Now there was not just one school, but three.

The day after we moved into our home with its beautiful view of Pike's Peak and the front range of mountains, we attended an orientation meeting at several-hundred-student Mitchell High School. Talk about culture shock! I felt I was in college. Paul remained quiet. Ken took it in stride, and Jenny acted as though she were along for the ride. There seemed no way of letting Jenny understand what it meant to have two thousand students in a three-year high school.

That week was a blur of meeting with guidance counselors, arranging class schedules, enrolling Katie at thousand-student Irving Junior High, and Sarah at Patrick Henry elementary school. The house at 1810 Darley Drive was not in the school districts we had hoped for, nor was it on a school-bus route. We didn't want our children to be totally dependent on my driving them to and from school, so that meant walking. Before we could get serious about unpacking boxed home furnishings, we had to learn the walking routes.

We mapped out the safest route for Jenny to walk the one and two-tenths miles from school and drove it with her several times. Then one or another of us walked with her, teaching her the traffic-light routine and how to safely cross intersections. It was decided I would drive her to school each morning and she would walk home. Sarah would also walk, so we taught her that six-block route and how to master traffic lights.

In the meantime, Paul and Katie considered their own routes and Mark returned to college in Spokane. Among other reasons, I hated to see him, my chief unpacker, leave.

Ken donned his blues and resumed work. I mustered courage and took Jenny for her formal registration. Paul handled his own registration and offered to do what he could for Jenny, but I didn't want to saddle him with the full responsibility of getting her settled. The process was confusing because time and open facilities did not always mesh and lines were long. I wondered how someone like Jenny could be expected to understand. Lunch tickets, picture for the yearbook and I.D., locker; pay for this and pay for that and fill out forms. Jenny trailed along beside, showing interest when I continually explained everything. She had no success getting a locker, so was pleased when Paul announced he'd been able to get one and had signed for her to share it with him.

It was not consistently easy for Paul to tolerate Jenny, because some of her actions embarrassed him at that age. Her proprieties had no comparison to his because her comprehension was not the same. We needed to allow each family member some protection against those embarrassments. The proportion of embarrassment changed with age and experience. Maybe our protecting our son, not making him take care of Jenny's registration, helped him willingly take her on as a locker-mate. The locker could be a meeting place, thus a perfect setup, because sometimes Jenny's books and supplies overtaxed her walking up the grade to our street. Paul acted as her carrier. In turn, she sometimes acted as courier for him.

There was much more to test the emotions before the carrying of books and supplies and messages started. Jenny's counselor had been helpful, but there were flaws in my understanding. I didn't realize that until the night before school. Of course, things are always worse in the dark, and add to that the fact that Dad was on overnight duty at the base emergency room.

After deciding what to wear her first day of eleventh grade, as a first-grader might, Jenny settled into bed. Later I lay in the dark and tried to think through Jenny's school day and I couldn't. Suddenly I felt panic. My thoughts were running all around the schoolrooms but were finding no answers.

"Where is the special-ed department? No one said anything about special ed! Work-study — that's all the counselor mentioned, wasn't it? Where is this work-study? He's got her signed with some regular classes to fulfill her high school graduation requirements, but what one person can she go to for help? Besides him, of course. What particular room can Jenny go to for protection against the masses of humanity who jam the halls? So she shares a locker with Paul, what good does that do her? Who, who, *who* will ever care that a Jenny Pavlik even exists in the large school?"

The more I wondered about it, the more frightened for Jenny I became.

It obviously wasn't only Jenny who had become comfortable with special ed. It was what I had also gotten used to. It spelled a certain degree of protection. Wracked by doubts, I fumbled for a light switch and ran to the other room, remembering another school we'd heard about. I rummaged for literature. What was that special school? Oh, yes, Giles Institute, that's it. A school for special children, not just retarded. But for them also. A small school. With individual attention. A close ratio of teachers to students. Now *that's* what Jenny needs! Maybe they'd have room for Jenny. At least she wouldn't get lost in the shuffle *there*!

Thoughts, thoughts, and more thoughts! I could hardly wait until morning. As soon as time allowed, I dialed Giles Institute. "Please! Can I talk to you about our child?"

After my dialogue with a friendly, concerned gentleman I felt calmer. And I thought, "Now, let's be reasonable about this whole business. Surely I've overlooked something. Have I remembered that terminology differs?"

I grabbed the packet of registration material from school and, with tears still blurring my eyes, searched the pages. Finally! How had I missed it? The phone number was obviously what I needed. I dialed and, trying to hold down the huge lump in my throat, spilled out my dismay to a Mrs. Divers.

I was to learn there were tremendously caring teachers in that huge school, just as there had been in the smaller halls of Edgerton and Limestone. It had just taken longer for me to find the ones associated specifically with Jenny's needs, because in my own little culture shock I had not heard what the equally friendly and helpful counselor had said. Mrs. Divers, with kindness wrapping every word, told me where Jenny and I could meet her. Then she would take us to meet some of Jenny's teachers and show us where Jenny could get special help and individual attention and spend her study time.

"We'll be there within minutes," I answered. I had tried to hide my panic from Jenny because I wanted her adjustment to her new school to be hers and not mine.

Jenny made the transition to her new classes, though it became apparent that despite tutoring she was in over her potential in some of them as far as comprehending the material.

Several days after the beginning of school, we received a letter scheduling a staffing conference to finalize Jenny's curriculum. I'd made it through registration; there was no question that I could handle this. I confidently entered the counselor's department, glad of the kindness he had shown us.

"Hello, Mrs. Pavlik! Come with me. You can wait in this room."

I thought nothing of it when I sat at the large table surrounded by a dozen empty chairs. When people started filing into the room and claimed the chairs I wondered where I should go. I thought I had been put in the wrong room and was an intruder. But there was the counselor and I was being introduced to the attendees. What was this?

I soon learned.

Regulations must be met before a child is accepted into special forms of education. In no way did a school want to be guilty of wrongly categorizing a student. Following a brief presentation suggesting a curriculum, I was handed papers to sign and was asked if there were any questions. Good heavens, I didn't know! I did know one thing, and that was that none of these people knew a thing about Jenny's struggle through life to finally arrive in their hallowed halls. I felt compelled to give them a brief glimpse into her past and to let them know that this child had fought against odds to be there; that she was not just a lone entity but had people who cared with all their hearts what became of her; that we appreciated everything that anyone would do for her; and that she must not be allowed to lose the ground she had worked so hard to attain.

As I looked into the sea of faces I wondered if they could possibly understand. I wondered if they thought I was a doting mother. I wondered if they resented having to be at a conference at that hour of the day when they could have been on their way home after a busy day of teaching. I wondered if they railed against government and school regulations. I wondered if they could possibly care about the light-brown-haired girl who was willing to trust them all unequivocally.

Who were these people attending the conference? They had been introduced, but I hadn't been ready to absorb it all. Well, they were the vice principal, speech therapist, work-study and special ed instructors, teachers, counselors, secretary and who knows who all.

I went home dazed, not knowing whether to feel consoled at what might be a caring structure for our daughter or to feel angered at having been put through a potentially traumatic experience because I'd not had sense enough to suspect what legalities do to the system of education. When a conference was scheduled to discuss Jenny's curriculum, I had presumed it would be a typical conference like those in so many past years. I didn't know there would be a roomful of school personnel. It had been called a staffing conference, but again the different terminology had escaped me.

I preferred private conferences, but I recognized there were limiting factors such as too few hours in a day for teachers and parents. Besides the number of people at that conference intimidating me, I felt it was important that Jenny not become a statistic to be dealt with just so check marks could be made on regulation forms to satisfy legal protection.

My option, though, had been to attend the conference or not to attend and just sign my name. I'm very glad I went to that conference. It set a tone of cooperation for Jenny's final years of schooling. Later I considered all those school personnel as friends.

When Ken and I attended Paul's and Katie's and Sarah's and Jenny's open houses we were pleased to learn that the teachers knew our children. Even though the quantity of students appeared unwieldy, there seemed to be a system whereby students could exist as individuals if they wanted to. We learned that those large schools were as caring as the small schools. However, this was evident: if a teacher was to be willing to expend the energies that were necessary to teach effectively, it meant a student must likewise display a willingness to learn. It wasn't enough that a parent wanted success — the student must also be so inclined.

I gained a better insight into the world of the teacher when I volunteered as an aide for first grade. For the first year in a long time, we had no preschool child to keep me at home. While I watched and listened and worked with those first graders, I knew the cooperation that Ken and I had given the teachers through the years, and the encouragement we'd given our children, had been worthwhile.

There is more to teaching than just working directly with a child. I was glad to re-witness what goes into a school day, rather than only remembering what it was like when I was in school. My memories tended to pick out the highlights and forget the hour-to-hour requirements. The primary teacher I assisted was always busy while I worked with fledgling readers, graded papers, decorated bulletin boards, asked spelling words, took the children to the library, mimeographed, plastic-bonded study guides, showed films, and helped with arts and crafts. Despite my time-consuming assistance, there remained much for the teacher to do during and after regular school hours.

I saw firsthand that a teacher's task is complicated by an undisciplined child. I could not blame the teachers or the school for Johnny's or Susie's behavior — that behavior was obviously first molded at home. A child with poor behavior adversely affected all those he came in contact with. I could pick out the children who had learned discipline, and consequently self-worth. They exhibited a style of behavior that complemented their companions.

One of my favorite assignments was to give Self Image tests. I was surprised how well some of those young children knew themselves. And I was dismayed to learn that some had a depressing self-image. What was in their life that made it so? One little lad reminded me of Jenny in years past, and I hoped his parents would recognize that he desperately needed special education. It's that old problem: a school cannot automatically channel a student into special ed unless parents give an okay. We should know — I had just been through that at Jenny's school.

I will never understand why parents think it is a degrading reflection on them or their family to have a child in special ed, or why grandparents and relatives ever feel that way, either. As I worked with that little child, whose attention I never did get even after fifteen minutes, I felt extremely thankful for all the educators through the years who had worked arduously with Jenny with such positive results.

A small percentage of my students were black. One of the questions on the Self Image Test was, "Would you want to change the color of your skin?" In contrast to another pupil, one black, effervescently happy, pigtailed child emphatically declared, "No way!" It made me feel happy all over. I wished I could meet her parents.

Sarah's teacher must have felt the same way about wanting to meet parents and had a unique way of doing so to see the relationship between students and their parents. She invited one child's parents at a time to join her and the child for the noon lunch period. Ken and I were served from the school cafeteria and joined

Mrs. Wicklund and Sarah in the quietness of her empty classroom. Over the leisurely lunch, the teacher gained insight into our personal world. Sarah thrived under her tutelage.

I was reminded while working with those students that there are ways we parents can help our children attain a good self-image. We can accept them for what they are. We can discipline with loving concern and consistency. We can expect them to use and improve what talents they have to the best of their ability, and we can assist them in this goal by admitting if there are any limiting disabilities without effecting fictitious ones. We can't put off giving help until our child is in high school, it must be given consistently from the very beginning.

Acceptance, discipline, and expectation must be offered through the years. Schools are willing to help us — all they ask is our cooperation.

Some years ago in Wisconsin I helped with a school census. The purpose of it was to project the number of students who would be in school in future years and to find out if any of them had physical or mental disabilities that might require special attention. If a pre-schooler needed special help it behooved the parent to inform the school so they could plan for the child. Schools aren't just buildings. They are people, people who care about our children. Those people can be more effective in helping our child reach his potential if they have uncritical support and cooperation. Early and continued cooperation sets a lifetime stage for accomplishment. Jenny's accomplishments perhaps can serve as an example.

Jenny's present school year progressed with a bang. Literally. The phy-ed department called and asked that I come to school because Jenny had been hit on the nose with a racket. When I arrived, Jenny was lying on the athletic office floor with ice applied to her swollen, bruised nose, and feeling woozy. Thinking about the time I molded her teeth back into her gum when she was just a little tyke, I now placed fingers inside and outside her nose to mold in case it had gotten out of shape. Dear Jenny. Let not an injured nose stop her progress!

After several days of non-athletic school days she returned to normal and started her first work-study assignment in the attendance office. She learned the art of filing in alphabetical order and earned her first small paycheck. That prompted us to help her add a checking account to her already established savings account. Financial lessons for Jenny would be a long, ongoing, frustrating experience because she functions on about a third-grade arithmetic level. Dad worked time and again with her with not much success, but he didn't give up.

Math and checkbooks weren't the only lessons we helped her with. Jenny responded to assignments, and as far as Jenny was concerned, when she had assignments, that meant they were to be finished and handed in whether she understood them or not. Some of the assignments affected me more than they did her, such as when we read *Flowers for Algernon* and John Steinbeck's *Of Mice and Men*. Both reach into the world of the retarded. Perhaps they caused no comparing in Jenny's thoughts, but they startled me into comparison. I wanted to ignore the possibilities those stories spoke of and I wanted to think that only good people would exist in Jenny's world. I preferred remembering Jenny's real accomplishments. From Jenny's life I saw reasons for hope. Of course hope was tempered with reasonable expectations.

While we reined in any unreasonable expectations for Jenny, it seemed unlimited realms were opening for Katie. Katie, in ninth grade, continued to be a strong influence on Jenny's life. Katie's every move was noticed and imitation attempted by Jenny when possible; but in no way did Jenny hamper Katie's progress. We were pleased that Katie showed no hesitation in claiming Jenny as her sister, though adolescence sometimes makes even normal family membership awesomely intolerable. Life was proving to be one vastly interesting stimulation for our second daughter.

When Katie won an award from the regional psychological society for her entry in the district science fair, they invited her, Ken and me to their dinner meeting. One of the psychologists quietly asked me what Katie was like. How does one explain a child like that in just a few words? I could have told her volumes alone on how Katie had affected Jenny's life.

Katie's interests were varied. She played clarinet in all-city honor band and was becoming an accomplished pianist. Active in school sports, she also skied and was entrusted to her brothers to learn mountain hiking and camping; rafted on the wilderness Green River of Utah for several days with classmates and counselors; volunteered at the city library. Activities described her somewhat, but her character was better revealed by her good rapport with siblings and friends; her desire to learn for learning's sake, rather than for grades on a report card; and her desire to improve herself in some way each day so she could have something more to offer her friends and teachers. She resented having to hang on a phone just to chat, but if a friend needed anything she was willing to share.

I didn't tell the psychologist about Katie's excitement at winning a school contest for an ascent in a hot-air balloon. Unfortunately winds cancelled the scheduled event, but memories of something else were joggled. Katie liked to stitch stuffed animals for gifts, and an especially favorite pattern was a bunny with movable legs and ears. One day in Maine, when driving home after purchasing another bag of polyfill, she noticed on the back of the sack some contest rules for making stuffed animals. They would be judged by the Grange and then given to children's homes and hospitals. Promptly she sewed a red print bunny with yellow soles, packaged it neatly and sent it to the contest. In the process of moving to Colorado, we forgot about her entry until a letter arrived announcing that she was first-place winner in her age category for the state of Maine.

The lady who corresponded with her and eventually sent her the prize mentioned that it was from their farm in Aroostook County that the hot-air balloon *The Double Eagle* lifted for its historic flight across the Atlantic Ocean. Colorado Springs hosted balloonists, and when fifty balloons assembled, were filled with hot air, and ascended in colorful pageantry, our whole family paid particular attention to the one designated as Maxie Anderson's and wondered how his feelings that day contrasted to the day he ascended from a farm in northern Maine. (Years later we were distressed to hear of his death in a ballooning accident.)

As Katie enriched our lives, so did we hope to enrich hers in any way we could — hers and all the children's.

A family begets its own particular personality. We learned from one another. We encouraged one another. We usually had confidence in one another, though sometimes that flagged. Sometimes we squabbled and ridiculed and tattled and berated. We are far from perfect, but what does it accomplish to belabor those negative points of our life? Just be assured there were plenty of days that held tensions that had to be worked out. We weren't always patient, though we strove to be. What is important is that we did grasp quiet moments to discuss our feelings and vent our frustrations. Routinely that was at the supper table. Family mealtime remained important to us. It was the one time of day when we respectfully listened to one another and became aware of what transpired in each of our hours. There could never be reason for any of us to deny knowing about the others, and it saddened us that other families failed to care what was happening to each of their members.

We helped one another. When Dad rebuilt the deck, he had willing carpenters. When he gardened, there were those nearby either assisting or just chatting. The kids all helped build a gym bar for Sarah. None of our other children had needed a bar to swing from, but Sarah definitely desired one. It was placed near a window where we could watch her antics.

The "older" children recommended reading books to Jenny, such as the books of Narnia by C.S. Lewis, which she then bought with her own money. The books they'd had as youngsters were what they urged onto Sarah. For that reason Katie made a special walking trip to the store with Sarah to purchase a notebook that could be compiled into Sarah's very own cookbook that would contain only recipes she herself cooked.

At times it seemed we lived a rerun of life. Sarah played and went to school in some of the same clothes the other kids had worn, read the same stories, listened to the same records, tried the same recipes, learned the same things. We built the same kind of love framework that had enveloped our earlier years.

There were other similarities. One evening I was busily preparing supper, trying to beat a deadline, when Sarah came and stood by my side. Solemnly, hesitantly, she said, "Can I talk to you?" It seemed advisable to put down my utensils and invite our first-grader out to sit on the deck steps.

"What is it, Little One?"

"I don't know if I should tell you."

I assured her I had kindly ears to hear her tale of woe or happiness, whichever it might be.

"We-ellll, my friend told me you're stripped. What does that mean?"

My goodness. Stripped. Hmmmm, now what on earth was probably meant by that? We established which friend it was so I might have a chance at interpreting such a statement. We discussed the day's events. Finally it came out — it seemed there had been discussion about a slumber party and Sarah had shown little interest in it, and that's when her friend said I must be that word.

I said, "Stripped. Stripped? Do you think she could possibly have said 'strict'?"

"Oh, yeah, that's the word!"

As we sat side by side on the deck step, we talked about what strict means, and how love is wrapped in the meaning of it. We talked about how some parents allow their children more doings than other parents; and how some children prove their trustworthiness better than other children. We talked about the different kinds of children that make up a classroom and the different kinds of families and homes those children come from and about reciprocating invitations. And then we talked about the fact that I didn't know there had been consideration of a slumber party. It turned out that Sarah really didn't want to go and so hadn't said anything to us. We talked about ways that Sarah proved her worthiness and how she could continue to earn our trust.

What a child! We enjoyed her so much. For weeks before Mark came home from college, she squirreled away coins and planned which restaurant she was going to take him to for lunch. Finally the long-awaited day arrived.

He teased her, "Where are we going for lunch, Bud?"

"The Soda Straw!"

She made sure she had her little doggy coin purse before they went to the ice cream emporium.

When they came home Mark was chiding with loving unmercifulness. "Hey, you guys! Do you know what Bud did? She almost had to wash dishes! You should have seen what all she ordered! No way did she have enough money to pay for all that stuff! It cost *us* $8.40!"

"But Marrrrkkkkeeeeee, don't forget how lucky you were cuz I had a dollar bill for the tip!"

Later Sarah confided some of her excitement to me. She wondered if people who saw them at the restaurant thought maybe they didn't have a father or a mother. It was one of her favorite pleasures when her brothers did something special with her.

Jenny benefited by watching this younger child progress through life. We couldn't have planned Jenny's life better had we tried.

Because we had wanted to allow Katie to finally have a room

of her own, Jenny and Sarah roomed together. Eventually, though, they went through a stage when they feistily picked at each other — Jenny especially tormenting. No matter what Sarah did, Jenny tended to noisily react to it. It was good that Paul had a room downstairs in the raised ranch-style house, because when he was upstairs and the girls were existing in their manner, he'd demand, "When on earth are you going to separate those girls!"

I'd chide, "Whenever you tell us which one you want for your roomie."

With thanks for Katie's typical unselfish acceptance, we let Jenny switch rooms with Katie. What habits would she retain on her own? Restrictions were set as to when she could visit in the other room because Katie did lots of studying.

It worked well. Jenny settled into quiet activities, listened to music whenever she wanted, and seemed very content. Sarah absolutely loved having the chance to room alone with Katie and nestled quietly for sleep while Katie studied with the light on.

Occasionally Jenny showed assertiveness, such as when she clearly wanted to attend a style show at the Cloth World material shop. Her home-ec teacher, Mrs. Magruder, was involved in the show. Jenny watched with interest as the women modeled clothing made from fabrics and trims available at that store.

Subtly, Jenny was growing up.

Over the holidays when Mark visited school, he and Paul witnessed Jenny doing filing in the attendance office. They were surprised to see that she looked and acted like a regular employee. It seemed strange to them to see her in that mature capacity, and it gave them hope for her future employment.

Jenny was eventually assigned to work-study in the cafeteria and again told us about the nice people she worked with. People responded to Jenny in a special way. Perhaps in Jenny's world all people are nice because she allows them to be by needing their help. Maybe too many of us are so busy proving our self-sufficiency that we never allow others the chance to show their potential for caring.

We had to get used to the emerging capable Jenny. No, she would never be as capable as her peers, but her teachers continually proved that niches were available to suit all abilities — such as when Jenny was in the home-ec handsewn-clothes style show. The students, three or four at a time, modeled their clothes while dancing to music. Jenny had tried to explain to us some of the dance steps the students would do, and we wondered how she could possibly handle it. Her teachers proved their resourcefulness. The well-planned style show accommodated all talents. Jenny's proudly sewn rust-colored corduroy slacks and vest were shown off to simple steps which she handled quite adequately.

Telling about Jenny doing steps with other people brings to mind our discussion of whether it was right to allow Jenny to sing in church, since she slurred her words and sang off key. We decided that when it is not choir singing, where an organized effort is expected to produce the best possible effect, of course it's all right for her to sing in her own fashion — just as it's quite permissible to allow her to function at her own level in all areas.

A thread in a tapestry. Isn't that what we all are? Some of the threads might be a bit raveled. Some are rough. Some catch our eye while others recede into the background. But all the threads together create a pleasing picture.

I saw some of the threads that were a little raveled and rough when I was the only parent who accompanied Jenny's group of students on the city bus to Pike's Peak Community College, where we toured its vocational training. Jenny's real peers — whose average age was probably higher than the usual eleventh grader — were as diverse as a normal classroom of students. Their personalities and apparent abilities varied. Some were better able to function in public than Jenny, but in Jenny I saw a gentle nature.

Though I was encouraged to learn of the vocational programs available for those students, it was not an easy field trip for me to make.

I wrote of my reactions to it to my mother:

> I've spent hours since then sorting out my feelings, and I still don't know where they stand. There are many hard decisions ahead yet for us about Jenny. She needs some independence away from us eventually. So consequently we speak to her in terms of someday being away from her parents awhile like Mark is now at college. She, being mildly retarded, presents some unique problems. She will always need supervision if she is to have the quality of life we hoped for her. How I wish she could join in family conversations. Or even listen to them. She's usually in her own orbit. I suppose — I hope — as Sarah grows older she will effect changes in Jenny as

> when the other children advanced past her. I wonder if the disciplining will be more lax? Or less constantly needed? I hope so. I call it discipline; actually it's more just trying to keep her buckled into suitable behavior so as not to be offensive to society. When she is disruptive, I guess she's merely getting attention in the ways easiest to her. Her sense of embarrassment has no comparison to ours because her sense of comprehension is not the same. . . .

No, I didn't have all my feelings sorted out. But at least I had a good feeling about how we were raising Jenny, and how Jenny was responding.

Why do we get embarrassed when someone like Jenny acts in the only way she knows how to act while we accept with only an amused twitter when perfectly normal people make social fools of themselves?

§§ 21 §§

... into the challenging world ...

Jenny's last year of formal schooling started in the summer. The Division of Special Education in Colorado funded an experimental program in Saleable Skills Training for handicapped students. Its purpose was to teach skills that could enable a handicapped person to get along in the work world. Jenny was one of thirty students chosen, and it was our responsibility to drive her to Coronado High School for morning classes. That was many miles away.

We had to have a family summit meeting. Summer jobs and activities were such that we all had to go in different directions at different times, but we only had two cars and the bus system didn't answer all our needs.

It was tempting to throw up our hands and scream, "It can't be done! It's not fair to any of us! Let's deal according to potential!"

But we couldn't do that. We are a family, and it was only right to function in a way that took each person into account. Besides, we weren't sure what Jenny's potential was.

It certainly wasn't the first time we had run into conflicts, and if we discussed the challenges calmly, surely we could arrive at a solution. Dad, a most effective organizer, found a meshing arrangement that allowed Jenny her new experience.

Jenny's area of study was office skills and involved filing, typing, machine copying, and using an adding machine. The month-long experimental course gave her new insights into the work world.

When we saw some of those students, it was not readily apparent that all were handicapped. Not all kinds of debilitations meet the eye. I sometimes witness normal people and mistakenly think they are handicapped. Conversely, I have met supposedly handicapped people and thought they surely must be normal. Why do I judge at all? Jenny wouldn't.

When I listened to one of Jenny's classmates I could not guess his problem. He definitely had opinions, which made me wish Jenny could express her opinions. Comparing again! It did creep in. Anyway, his hobby was ventriloquism, and in my remembering what he told me I wondered whether Jenny experienced some fears. He revealed, "When I'm home alone at night I get scared, so then I get my dummy sidekick out for company and we talk together, but you know what? There's one thing wrong with that, and that's that my dummy gets more scared than I do!"

I tried to remember that Jenny might not be able to express some of her fears, even though she appeared old enough to do so. On the other hand, I recognized that my fears need not be passed on to her. She might even be incapable of understanding fears, especially mine. Nonetheless, I have to allow for the possibility of her having fear.

That summer was affected by gas prices that soared and caused readjustments in our choice of recreation. However, living in "Colorful Colorado" solved the question of what to do, because there were often houseguests. Jenny readily assumed assigned duties for helping make our friends feel welcome.

Often we saw Paul with an atlas in his hands. And Mark would come home from bookstores or the library with hiking guides. Then the boys encouraged us to give Katie her birthday gift early, and suggested it should be hiking boots. Before the summer was over, we heard some or all of them report of hiking Pike's Peak, Long's Peak, Humboldt Peak, and Quandary Peak. They told about Cheyenne Canyon, rock rapelling, and wilderness camping. Since neither Ken nor I were inclined to mountaineering for the purpose of reaching the top, we entrusted Katie to her brothers' instructions and care. When I'd watch Katie teach piano to Sarah, or knot macramé necklaces for gifts, or make candy with Jenny, I could hardly envision her maneuvering her way up past trees and rocks and heights so she could say she had mastered a Fourteener (one of Colorado's several highest mountains that rise over fourteen thousand feet).

A new idea peppered Paul's conversations. Even after a day's hike of twenty-seven miles up and down Pike's Peak, he wasn't too tired to pursue the new topic: "What would you folks say if we hiked the Appalachian Trail?"

"Who?"

"Whoever wants to go."

"What section of it?"

challenging world • 241

"All of it."

"Dreamers!"

The idea smoldered. We did recommend that if there was even the remotest possibility that something like that might exist in the future, then they should take every opportunity to prepare themselves, and to plan any purchases of gear wisely. Soon there were lists appearing on the refrigerator with ideas for birthdays and Christmas. Sarah watched for inexpensive items she might be able to afford and found candles and egg containers. Jenny noted wool sox and plastic containers.

Maybe after summer the dreamers would come to their senses. First of all, Mark was committed to college, and Paul's letters of inquiry indicated that he too was college-minded. He chose physics, trigonometry, English, history, psychology, and business law for his last year of high school. These would fulfill his requirements to apply to any college of his choice.

Katie enrolled for tenth grade at Benet Hill Academy, a Benedictine school. We wished Jenny could have that kind of intimate atmosphere with a spiritual quality.

We understood Jenny's curriculum, so we declined a staffing conference, but of course had to sign the curriculum proposal. If I had it to do over again I would attend any staff conference that was offered — it was unlike us to decline this one. I had felt intimidated by the numbers. I had regretted using the teachers' valuable time. I assumed we would have enough contacts with any and all teachers through the year. All inadequate reasons for declining! A large school and city, unlike small schools and towns, is not conducive to frequent communication with teachers. Formal opportunities need to be accepted!

We did, however, have good communication with Mr. Cotton, her WES coordinator.

Jenny's schedule appeared brief on paper but represented many hours. She had small-group discussion in science with Mrs. Middleton, WES — which we now knew meant "work-experience study" — speech therapy, and American history. She wished she could take pottery again from Mr. Schrock, which she had so thoroughly enjoyed the year before. Her schedule would be subject to change as the year progressed, and she settled into a work-training program.

What a contrast to last year's school beginning!

Jenny again quickly mastered not only her own but also Paul's schedule that changed weekly. She kept me informed as to what hours they would be going to and arriving from school.

Before long Jenny came home from school talking about training at Goodwill.

"Goodwill! What do we know about Goodwill?" I asked.

We knew very little about Goodwill except that we used to shop at those stores in earlier years when we'd had very little money. Jenny's beginner's red tricycle, Mark's first toys, books, kitchenware, the white lamp, the table and two chairs. We were still using the meat grinder I purchased for one dollar. Through the years we had gathered our no-longer-needed-but-still-usable items, put them in bags and deposited them in large metal collection boxes that had a logo of Goodwill identifying them. We understood vaguely that handicapped people were employed at the facility in Milwaukee. And that's all we knew.

Now our daughter was talking about training at Goodwill.

From school Mr. Cotton called to discuss the possibility of Jenny's being incorporated into that program. He set up an appointment for Ken and me to join Jenny for a tour. There we saw men and women assembling products, sorting donated items, packaging merchandise, and reupholstering.

We listened with interest as a young man social worker interviewed Jenny. He quickly put her at ease by treating her as a capable individual. Answers were sought from her, not from Ken or me. Jenny's halting, stuttering speech didn't faze him, nor did he turn to us to receive quicker answers. He patiently listened to Jenny and relied on her ability to tell him about herself.

We learned that Goodwill has a goal of training people toward good work habits, good social habits, and an element of independence. The trainees receive pay according to the amount of work they accomplish for commercial companies who offer contracts to Goodwill. Also, donated items are sorted, cleaned, repaired, and then sold through their stores.

After Jenny's interview, it was offered that she could begin training the second of October.

Oh, dear. Was life always going to be so full of conflicts? Ken and I were scheduled to be out of the state for a week, and the Goodwill center was across the city from where we lived. We had carefully planned how the children could take care of themselves, even allowing for emergencies, but it didn't include getting Jenny to work. To detain Jenny's training even for a week seemed an injustice, because she needed every moment available to her for learning. We were especially conscious of that since this was her last year of formal schooling.

Mr. Cotton assured us we didn't have to be concerned about transportation because part of the training process was to help her become familiar with the city bus system and to become totally independent with getting to and from work. Since Jenny still had courses to take at school, her journey would commence from there.

I must admit I worried for Jenny's safety. She had never ridden city buses where she'd have to ask for transfers or watch for certain bus stops. I wondered what kinds of people inhabited those buses now, as opposed to years ago when I'd ridden them during Duchesne College days and nursing school. But what was it that Maria Egg said in her book *The Different Child Grows Up?*

She urged the necessity of letting handicapped children learn to ride public transportation so they wouldn't have to be dependent on a parent.

Yes! Yes! My life could have been a never-ending taxi service, and our child could be a parasite. Instead, Jenny had walked to school in Wisconsin; she had walked the entry roads in Maine, and now she had learned to cross busy streets and walk many blocks in summer heat or threatening weather. Perhaps she *could* learn to ride the city bus system.

I rode the bus with Jenny to her first workday at Goodwill. I felt a gratifying sense of confidence when I followed her off the bus at the downtown terminal and watched as she made her way across the alleys of bus stalls, boarded another bus and handed the driver the transfer she had remembered to ask for. She was proud of her accomplishment and took it for granted I would be following right behind her. She had understood Mr. Cotton's instructions clearly.

I watched her fellow travelers. There were mothers with little children, students with books, people who looked as if they might be going shopping or to the library or to appointments, men and women who looked tired and were obviously going home from work; there were women dressed in uniforms that indicated nursing and household duties, and there were other kinds of work uniforms. The riders watched for their own corners, where they got off the bus after pulling the signal cord to alert the driver. Most of them looked like people who would help Jenny if she ever needed any kind of help.

Jenny started her Goodwill experience, and I returned home by bus, barely remembering to ask for my transfer. While I walked the remaining blocks home I wondered how much independence was right for Jenny, or for all our children. Or for that matter for Ken and me. Our week away was looming over me like a black cloud. Katie and Paul scoffed, "What do you think we are? Of *course* we can take care of Jen and Sarah! We've gone over it all and practically planned every minute. You go, and please trust us. It's only for a week! We can handle it!" Little Sarah conceded that it was harder to see us go away for a week than for just two or three days, but she told me, "I'll be willing to be happy to let you go away that long if you will be happy to see me do some things." That from a second grader? Children do indeed have an interesting depth.

Leaving them seemed so much more difficult living in a city. But when we returned, everything was running smoothly with each child firmly into his routine. Dad asked, "How did Jenny do at Goodwill?"

"Well," Katie said, "One day Jenny told me a man at work asked if she'd be his girl friend. So I talked to her about how it's okay to have all kinds of friends at school and work but that it doesn't mean she has to do things at night with them. And I talked to her about how to decide if he's a good person."

I think my heart skipped several beats. The years of concerned mothering and fathering had so often proved to be of inestimable value.

Jenny's work projects involved assembling key chains, packaging yarn and hardware items, and packaging Christmas ornaments. The training coordinators stressed the idea of earning an income and taking pride in that income just as elementary teachers had drawn similar response by offering prizes.

Within a month Mr. Cotton called to inform us that an opening was available in a training program at Pike's Peak Community College and that Jenny was eligible.

"Is that what you would recommend?"

"Yes," he answered.

So once again we were off to another new adventure in Jenny's pursuit of knowledge and independence. This time Jenny was in food service, which really appealed to her. Mr. Cotton taught her the city bus route to yet another direction in town — south. And once again I rode the bus on her first day so I could know what to expect. It was important to me that I be able to imagine Jenny's entire day. All too well I remember the day Jenny arrived home late. I wondered where she was as I anxiously watched out the window saying prayers. When she finally arrived, she knew the name of her bus driver. It turned out that Jenny had neglected to get off the bus at her regular stop and she didn't know what to do because no other stops looked familiar. When she was still on the bus at the end of the line at the Air Force Base, the driver came to her assistance. That friendly driver also offered any help that Jenny might need in the future.

We simply had to assume that Jenny would be offered help when and if she needed it.

While the children filled their days with schools, homework, and extracurriculars, Dad fulfilled his medical duties. I chose not to just sit at home to cater to the family. A few days after school started, I dutifully served supper and then announced my own plans for the semester. I would teach a CCD class at church, take painting lessons at the Fine Arts Center, and volunteer at the soup kitchen. And furthermore, I had signed up to volunteer at the police station.

Surprised listeners chorused. "The police station!"

Ken looked at me as though he really didn't know me too well after all.

"Yes, the police station."

"Why there?"

"Oh, I don't know. I guess to find out how that segment of society ticks. I saw a short article in the paper asking for volunteers, so I went for an interview and was offered a position."

I didn't like everything I learned there, but it made me more aware of why it is important not to dwell on only the negative aspects of life. After poring over innumerable accounts of petty crimes, I became distrustful of people and tended to forget that the majority of people are good.

Teaching religion class was a fortuitous contrast.

My Christmas gift to the family was to take them all to the

soup kitchen a couple days before Christmas to help pare vegetables and butter bread. Sarah played cards with one of the men who ate there. I wanted our children to realize how fortunate we are. I wanted to remind them that every one of God's people deserves to be treated with respect. We can't know what goes into people's lives to make them what they are, what lack of discipline they may have grown up under, what kind of hard luck may have disrupted their lives, what mental or physical disabilities they might have, or what temporary needs might be dictating their current day.

It was an especially good Christmas season. Paul did his gift shopping at the Goodwill store. We wrapped our gifts in brown grocery-bag paper, with string and ties cut from remnants of red bandanna-print fabric.

Jenny took pride in doing her own Christmas shopping and paying by check, though she still couldn't handle finances intelligently without help. When she infrequently made a larger purchase, I gave a brief explanation to the clerk and Jenny showed her identification. If permission was granted to pay by check, I encouraged the clerk to keep the register clear for other customers because it took Jenny a long time to write a check and enter the amount in her stub.

Some of Jenny's money problems were comical. Like when she had to reimburse Dad $3.79. She had many coins accumulated besides a five dollar bill.

Dad asked, "Would you like to get rid of some of those coins?"

Jenny shrugged and said, "Go ahead, I've had them a long time."

Coins, bills, checks. What difference? Dad guided the entries into her bank account each time she earned any kind of pay or allowance, and helped her decide how much cash to keep on hand.

Besides her using her own checkbook to buy Christmas presents, Jenny's holiday held another new experience. After the college students started their winter break, Mr. Bissonnette invited his food-service students to stay on and make special holiday foods and decorations, using ordinary cooking ingredients. Jenny chose to create Nativity ornaments by copying some of Mr. B's samples. We could hardly believe what we saw when she carefully unwrapped her finished product. Out of flour and salt dough she had modeled two- or three-inch characters of all the traditional crèche figures and then painted them in tones of brown and white. They have a captivating primitive quality that only children seem to acquire in artwork. Each has a wire hanger baked into it so it can be hung.

Jenny's interest in cooking mushroomed. She liked preparing and serving foods at the college. At home on Saturdays, she learned to make more breakfast items. She added new kinds to her cookie repertoire and sent cookies to Mark in college.

Her Christmas vacation also included recuperation. For good reason we were grateful that Dr. Henry had taught Jenny to accept dental care in her younger years. With mature tolerance, she now calmly settled into a dental chair and let the dentist extract four wisdom teeth. She also tolerated, at another time, two root canals.

Looking like a chipmunk with nut-filled cheeks, Jenny quietly recuperated while practicing popular songs that her piano teacher, neighbor Sharon Stelzner, taught her how to play from Easy-Play books. Jenny never learned to play fast, but so what? She enjoyed reproducing familiar tunes, and we simply accepted what she could do. Acceptance. That's the name of the game.

I was reminded about acceptance by our youngest child. One night when I knelt with Sarah for her bedtime prayers, she said, "I think God tests us. Do you think that's why He gave us Jenny? Maybe He wanted to see how well we'll do."

I thought, "Out of the mouths of babes."

Sarah herself was doing very well, was helpful, played nicely with her sister, was usually tolerant, and didn't get embarrassed. We talked about all that and how difficult it is for some children to pass all those tests. We decided maybe it is difficult for some children to act kindly because their moms and dads might not have taught them how because their own moms and dads didn't teach it, and so they can't know how to pass the knowledge on. But keeping in mind the grains of wisdom that had often emitted from Sarah, I also suggested that some children just seem to know how to handle God's tests.

Yes, perhaps God was testing us.

With the new year commencing, the most important thing we had to think about was getting Sarah prepared for First Communion and Paul and Jenny ready for graduation. That should be easy enough.

Well, there was one more incidental: We had to decide what to do when Dad finished his four-year commitment to the Air Force come July. People knew this physician was going to be available, and Ken received phone calls from around the nation. It was again awesome to have to select one of various possibilities. The Air Force hoped to keep him. With all the children, we considered the options, the pros and cons.

Mid-January, when Mark returned to Gonzaga University, he bid goodbye with, "Be sure to let me know where I could go to find you next!"

On January sixteenth Ken received a call from the Public Health Service. They needed a physician to staff a merchant-marine clinic.

That night at supper Dad said, "I got a call today. They need a doctor in Charleston, South Carolina."

"Charleston!"

"The South? Who'd want to live in the South?"

"On the coast?"

"We've been there. Do you remember? It's an old city."

"There's lots of blacks down there, aren't there?"

"What kind of schools do they have?"

"Hmmmm, Charleston."

"It certainly would be a new experience."

"Well, that's what we're looking for, isn't it?"

"What's the Public Health Service?"

"You mean you'd take care of fishermen? And guys who work on shipping vessels?"

"Yeah, I understand, there's more to Public Health than that."

"Hmmmm. Charleston."

A couple days later we called Mark and said he could set his sails for Charleston, South Carolina.

"Charleston! I didn't even know it was in the running!"

Neither did we. How does one get the feeling that something is right? We didn't know then and we still don't know. But somehow Charleston seemed right.

That put a new light on priorities. It seemed, if we were going to move to the other end of the continent, that we should visit Mark at his campus one more time because it wasn't likely we would all get to attend his graduation next year — considering the new distance.

"How about spring break? Do you kids all have it at the same time?" Dad asked.

Paul's desire to hike the Appalachian Trail had gained momentum. He was hesitant to tell anyone, and yet he hoped for someone to hike it with, preferably his brother. But Mark had decided to work all summer. Paul studied the Trail as described by former hikers, and acknowledged the awesome challenges that were represented. He had no way of knowing if his body or his mind could handle the grueling experience of backpacking twenty-two hundred mostly wilderness miles that followed mountains from Georgia to Maine, but he wanted to try. Ken and I had mixed emotions. In a way we were glad our son had such dreams because it meant he was receptive to challenges. On the other hand, we understood the dangers he would face.

As the weeks passed, his enthusiasm grew. There seemed no denying his need to pursue the task. School, though, must take priority, and he had to prove to us that we wouldn't let any part of it slide. A looming problem was that if he was going to try the Trail at all he wanted to allow enough time to finish the entire route in one summer. Hikers usually started in spring in Georgia and followed its blossoming north, hoping to finish the climb up Mt. Katahdin in Maine before bad weather settled in — often in early autumn. Paul had been accepted to begin college in the fall at St. Michael's in Winooski, Vermont, so must strive to meet that deadline. A calculator accompanied Paul everywhere, as he figured miles, days, pounds, dollars. He finally knew he would have to start the Trail two weeks before he was to graduate.

'Oh, swell!" my heart cried. "Isn't that just jim-dandy! All the time we've been feeling so good that Paul and Jenny would be graduating together and we could plan festivities and have all the family celebrating her accomplishment. Now he's probably not even going to be there!"

But it did seem reasonable that he allow time enough for the complete hike if that much thought and energy were going into it. Perhaps to postpone such an intensely felt experience that had been thought through so carefully could be inadvisable.

Paul's teachers okayed his request to graduate two weeks early but would assign extra reading and written papers that must be handed in.

Paul could hardly wait to pore over maps and plans with his

brother. Mark had hiked the Grand Canyon and mountains in the western United States. Paul held hope for his companionship.

We packed with visions of visiting various relatives en route to Portland, Seattle, and eventually Spokane. We left notes in our house to accommodate friends who were moving to Colorado Springs and would stay in our home until they could find a place to rent. Then we added the ice chest and the dog to our gear, climbed into the van, and headed west. First destination: Uncle Van's and Aunt Jo's in Parma, Idaho.

We arrived there, but not in the style we were accustomed to. From a hospital in Burley, Idaho, Ken called his uncle and said "We've had an accident. Can you come to Burley and get us?"

We had never had an accident before. We hope never to have another one, ever again. We know how lucky we are, and we don't forget to say thanks. Drizzle and gradually rising altitude effected icy conditions, and suddenly, in the early morning dawn when most of us were sleeping, our van spun 180 degrees and rolled completely over. That doesn't sound like much, but it created havoc. Cold air and snow whipped at us through broken windows and jimmied doors. Jenny and Sarah started to cry. Before we did anything we said the Hail Mary, and by the time we'd said three of them everyone was quiet. Ken made cursory diagnoses, and we proceeded with the task of covering the girls with blankets and finding caps and jackets which had been in one container but were now strewn all over as was everything else, including broken pickle jars, picnic gear, and tools. We didn't know where the dog was. She had left a mess behind and disappeared.

Cars and a semitrailer stopped to help us. No use calling for an ambulance, because it and the hospital were fifty miles away. Sarah was laid in the sleeper of the truck complaining of injured elbow and abdominal pains. In the cab I wondered how to communicate with Sarah, because it hurt to turn around and the noise of the motor and the CB radio made it difficult to hear. Roger Whittaker, the singer, supplied an answer. Our entire family loved his song *Squeeze My Little Finger*, so I held Sarah's hand and we squeezed intermittently to reassure that each of us was still okay. In the meanwhile Ken got Jenny and Katie into a car. Paul hunted for the dog, and just when hope was about abandoned someone drove off and saw our miniature dachshund walking along the road.

Needless to say, we didn't get to Portland or Seattle, but recuperated a few days with Aunt Jo's excellent care and cooking. Uncle Van helped Ken and Paul rearrange our needs. Katie lamented that her broken collarbone would cancel team tennis playing. Jenny's main complaint was a sore back. Despite lingering headaches, pains, and sore muscles, we felt extremely fortunate. Especially so after we arrived in Spokane and heard Mark say, "You guys are indeed lucky. Last night my classmate wasn't that fortunate. He was killed in a car accident." Mark went to our hotel window, pointed to a spot a block away, and said, "That's where it happened."

We attended the memorial Mass at the college for his classmate. I prayed for his soul, but I especially prayed for his mother in Hawaii. Her heartache must have been intense.

We all learned from the incident. There was the handling of an emergency, certainly, but more important, it seemed, was another chance to see people helping people. People we will never see again graciously did what they could for us and expected nothing in return. Relatives did much for us because that is what relatives are all about. And we learned that individually we have strengths that we didn't know we had.

Our final weeks in Colorado were full. After selling the house we started May's final countdown to Jenny's graduation. The girls baked delicate flower cookies for their May baskets, and Sarah sneaked around the neighborhood delivering them to doorsteps.

Twenty-seven more days to go.

It seemed crazy. We had spent years and years helping Jenny struggle to learn. Now it came down to the last month, and it seemed so impossible that all those kinds of years had transpired. I had envisioned a celebration to beat all celebrations if a day of graduation should ever arrive for her, but there wasn't going to be an elaborate celebration. Not even would her two brothers be present for her graduation. There were times I thought my heart would break over that state of events. Even Gramma wasn't going to be able to attend. And here I was wanting to scream from the rooftops, "Listen all you people out there! Jenny is going to graduate! Do you hear? She didn't just go to school. To the best of her abilities, she got educated! She reads! She writes! She adds and subtracts and plays the piano! She cooks and she sews! If she can do it, so can others!"

There were moments I cried.

Jenny and Paul had their pictures taken by the On Location studio — interesting outdoor photos taken at Palmer Park. Paul wedged in minutes to address graduation announcements and included notes about his hiking plans. Jenny took pride in addressing all of hers, too. She ordered her cap and gown and eagerly looked forward to getting her yearbook. Paul asked that she get his, too.

While we rushed from one appointment to another, so did Mark in Spokane. He had decided to use his savings and join Paul on the Appalachian Trail hike. During his finals week he had to fly with his college tennis teammates to Malibu to participate in conference play. He would have only two days at home to make final preparations for backpacking; consequently, the hike planning rested on Paul's shoulders.

Paul finished his school assignments and got his diploma from Mitchell High School with best wishes for a successful life. Few knew what he was planning to do.

The night Mark arrived we had our traditional holiday meal. It served as a welcome home for him and a graduation dinner for Jenny and Paul. They chose pork, kraut, and dumplings. Yes, obviously it was a celebration — we often had kraut and dumplings when we celebrated.

Paul was gifted with an electric typewriter to use in college. We had labored over deciding Jenny's graduation gift. She didn't need a typewriter, nor would she make good use of one. Her dearest pleasure in life was music, so we finally chose a stereo system. It proved to be a perfect gift. She was absolutely elated when she opened what she thought was going to be a typewriter.

Jenny gave Paul an atlas that she had decided on all by herself. It, too, was a perfect gift.

Now if Mark's backpack arrived the boys could go on their hike. When he claimed his luggage at the flight terminal, he was dismayed to learn the pack wasn't there. He would definitely need it to hold all the supplies Paul had accumulated. Kid brother had planned carefully, even including the possibilities for getting them and their gear to their respective colleges or to our new home in South Carolina, depending on whether or not they hiked all summer. We faced many unknown variables.

The airline delivered the backpack to our door via taxi the

next day. Half that night was spent packing and rechecking lists. While Dad and I watched and were given jobs to do — like attaching address labels to film mailers — I thought of the two little boys who so happily used to do helpful jobs for us. Their mature confidence and humor were now gratifying to watch. In the morning they would start a major test of their skills.

After they made a final survey of their gear and traveler's checks, the girls and Dad and I bid farewell to six-foot-three-inch Mark and six-foot-seven-inch Paul. We watched with hope and a bit of fear in our hearts as they accordioned into our gray Suburu. They would leave it at the Ranger station at Amicalola Falls, Georgia, where the Appalachian Trail originates, and we would retrieve it when we drove through on our move to Charleston.

Final words of goodbye included, "Congratulations, Paul, for a successful graduation from high school! Have a safe hike and may God watch over you boys. Don't forget Jenny's graduation!"

We could now return our thoughts to the final days of Jenny's formal schooling. Fourteen more days to go.

When I attended a PEP meeting, I learned still more reasons to feel thankful that Jenny had made a satisfing, successful venture through her school years. PEP stands for Parents Encouraging Parents. When I listened to the discouragements, the hopes, the fears, and the frustrations of those parents, I nonetheless recognized how lucky we all were that so much had happened in the past twenty years in the world of the mentally and physically handicapped. During the meeting, ideas were vented, but during lunch frustrations were vented.

Yes, there will always be frustrations and heartaches. And there will be clashes of personalities. We will always want the ultimate in care for our children. Sometimes it will be hard to remember that our type of handicap problem is not acknowledged as being nearly so awful as someone else's. We will always wonder why all people can't recognize our particular heartache. Well, they can't, that's all. An affliction doesn't become real unless it happens to us personally. It is unfair to assume that everyone should unselfishly share our affliction, any more than others should assume that we should share all their woes. We can't feel it all. None of us can. Not one of us can know it all. No teacher or no doctor can know all the answers. No minister can answer all our heartrending searches.

No person should be expected to sympathize in an all-knowing manner if a handicapped child is born to us. We should not expect friends, acquaintances, or strangers to say all the right things to us. Each of us parents reacts differently, just as every person responds differently, so there is no one pat answer that can serve all needs. All of this is just more reason why life is so interesting.

Such was some of the philosophy that prompted statements I made when it was my turn at the PEP meeting to rise as spokesman for the group of parents who had children in high school. I had listened to criticisms about physicians not having recognized learning disabilities, and about teachers dealing heartlessly and impatiently with parents and students, and vice versa. I told the attending parents and educators that as a nurse and a wife of a physician, I knew that doctors cannot know all the answers. And as a parent who had close communication with teachers through the years, I recognized that neither teachers nor parents could know all the answers, either; nor can they always have unlimited amounts of patience. But there is a solution. The formula for that solution is: Respect plus Cooperation equals Success. Without the first quality, we cannot effectively attain the other two. If we show respect for one another, we automatically open the path to good communication, and anything is possible after that.

As those of us at that meeting were striving to shape niches on this earth for our special children, so, too, was nature continuing to reshape the earth. Mount St. Helens erupted in Washington state, and it was fitting that, if that volcano was going to erupt anyway, it happened in the month of May 1980. An unintended grand salute to Jenny's accomplishments! Her graduation month!

The last day of Jenny's training at Community College, Dad and I treated her to luncheon at the Hatchcover Restaurant. She was pleased to be so honored. Then we went home, and Jenny baked cookies to be served at Katie's piano recital.

Jenny's school didn't have a Baccalaureate service, so we attended the one at Katie's school and pretended Jenny was one of those graduates. It was a lovely service, especially so when the dads of the seniors sang "You'll Never Walk Alone." I wished that Jenny could have the beautiful graduation ceremony that I was sure that school would offer.

Jenny eagerly looked through the mail every day and claimed her congratulatory cards, letters, and gifts. Some of the well-wish-ers mentioned that they still baked the brownies from the recipe she had given them. Aunt Alice sent a rosary that was blessed by Pope John Paul II. Jenny loved the treasures her friends and relatives sent, and she also liked the cash gifts. She asked to be taken to Pike's Peak Community College so she could use gift money to buy a PPCC tee shirt, and to ask her kitchen friends to sign her yearbook.

Jenny wrote thank-you notes promptly and kept a list of the mail and gifts Paul received so he could acknowledge them, whenever that might be.

While we lived out graduation, the moving company came to make an estimate of our household furnishings and dropped off packing boxes. We started the process of ridding out, giving Goodwill any unneeded item. Never would we throw anything away that could still be used — especially now that we understood Goodwill's purpose. Would Charleston have a Goodwill Rehabilitation Center or any kind of a vocational training opportunity for Jenny? We could only trust that Jenny would find a niche no matter where we chose to live, and that it would benefit her in a special way.

Jenny was excited that Katie's friend Jenifer Kohout, who now lived in Washington, D.C., was going to join us for moving and summer travel. We could not offer Jenifer city experiences like those her parents showed Katie, but we could offer the experience of small towns and farms.

While we finalized plans, the boys called from "a bend in the trail" and said they had only about twenty-one hundred more miles to hike. They asked about Jenny and were told that we had gone dress shopping but that she would, after all, wear the red print dress she had worn for Confirmation. She felt comfortable in it. Her gown was pressed, and rehearsal was to be held the morning of graduation at Garry Berry stadium.

From afar her brothers cared about her, and that pleased her.

Finally it was May 28th. Jenny's graduation day had arrived!

It was a beautiful, cloudless morning for rehearsal at 8:45. Jenny made her way to the mingling students to learn where she was to stand in line. I chose a seat in the empty bleachers and made some notes in a tablet. As I remembered, tears blurred my eyes. There had been so many emotional struggles through the years, but we had survived. There were many people who deserve thanks even now, like Mr. Ammons, one of Jenny's teachers who caught my eye and indicated that all was as it should be.

I thought of the past years. I thought of the past days. I thought of yesterday when the doorbell rang and it was the florist with a delicate bouquet of daisies for Jenny. And who was it from? Her former guidance counselor, Mrs. Barker, from Limestone, Maine — Mrs. Barker, who cared about her students so and had eased Jenny's transition from the cocoon of Edgerton to a new, challenging world.

As I sat in that stadium, I thought about Jenny's dependencies and how there always seemed to be special people who rallied to her needs. The world was full of special people. It seemed we all need help, and we are all special people who can help one another in one way or another.

I also thought about percentages of people. Twenty years before, when Jenny was born, seven percent of our population were farmers; now only four percent were. I wondered what percentages were listed twenty years before for mentally handicapped persons. Now two percent of the population were. Had our new understanding about environment and health had an effect? I felt gratified that better education and improved technology were bettering the lives of handicapped people. It spoke well for our nation. It spoke well for our individual people. It spoke well for our recognition of the value of our less-than-perfect members.

Jenny's graduation was taking place in a world full of turmoil. The oil situation was critical. Everyone wanted electric power, but no one wanted a power plant in his backyard. Communist leaders seemed intent on dominating the world. Castro in Cuba was ejecting its human problems onto the United States, and we were consequently bursting our refugee facilities; Miami was having race riots. Mount St. Helens' volcanic ash was causing devastation to agriculture, vehicles, and health. California was having earthquakes. Not only that, but my Uncle Leo died.

The personal suffering in knowing that Uncle Leo had died was more traumatic than knowing about all the terrible things that were happening around the world.

I think we must never forget that the personal suffering of individual men should affect us, no matter what kind of suffering that is. When we learn to care enough about one another, we will then be able to solve the big problems.

Despite the world's problems, Jenny's Big Day had arrived.

And now the afternoon had arrived.

Daddy came home from work early, and the five of us drove to the football stadium.

Wearing her blue cap and gown, Jenny left us to make her way to the group of graduating students. We watched as she confidently claimed her place in line.

She would be seated on the west side, so we chose bleacher seats on that side. There were hundreds of graduating seniors, and more hundreds of relatives and friends.

The music rose. The blue-gowned young men and women started to walk toward rows of seats on the football field. Catcalls issued from the crowd to attract the attention of certain seniors. We watched as Jenny walked up the field, entered her row, and stood in front of her chair.

It seemed so natural, what she was doing.

"The Star Spangled Banner" sounded from the horns as the flag flowed in the whispering breeze. The invocation prompted heads to bow. The graduates settled onto their chairs.

Then the commencement addresses were given by students. No longer could the graduates contain their emotions. Movement rippled through those seated honorees.

I watched with dampened emotions as some of them threatened their own dignity. One male graduate, prominently visible on the outside aisle, carelessly tried to prove that he was wearing nothing, or little, underneath his gown. "For that he spent twelve years?" I thought. I felt sorry for him. I caught myself comparing him to Jenny. And yet, why should I compare anyone to Jenny? She was an individual; others were individuals.

After the speeches, the principal of the school formally presented the class for their diplomas. The superintendent of schools gave an acceptance. Now the names were called, and the graduates made their way row by row to the raised temporary stage. Occasionally the announcer urged graduates and guests to maintain a quiet dignity, so that each graduate could be honored as he deserved to be.

As he continued to announce the names, the crowd increased its response. One shrill whistle seemed to cue another. Though many families sat in subdued respect, others caused more nagging comparisons. I wondered if their children had learned the discipline that Jenny had needed to survive the years. Not only to survive the years but to rise above them.

The alphabetical announcements droned on and I looked at my dwindled family. Sometimes their faces were pensive. We each held a deep respect for our special child.

There were many names still to be announced before they got to the P's. I thought of teachers Jenny had had through the years.

The flag fluttered gracefully as a student staggered along in the otherwise respectable line and was sometimes supported by those near him. When he got near the stage steps, he lurched to the ground, retching. Teachers escorted him behind the scenes. My heart cried, "For that they offered their years to a student?"

Clouds drifted, and I thought of Mark and Paul. Were they remembering that their sister was, at that hour, in a stadium in Colorado Springs finally receiving recognition for her years of accomplishment? They said they would be, and knowing them, I was sure they were.

The N's! We poked one another. "Pretty soon it's her!"

Jenny was standing. Jenny was moving in the line. My goodness the line moved fast! Had it moved that fast during all those dozens of other names?

Then the ten O's.

Was it all real?

Had there really been any concerns through all those years? Jenny looked just like any of those other boys and girls. Had I perhaps been dreaming all those years? What was her Dad thinking? I looked at him with deep love in my heart and knew that lots of husbands and dads would never have been that supportive.

"Paul Anthony Paquette."

I looked at Katie and Sarah. They were sitting erect and alert on their bleacher seat. Sarah had a look of expectation. Katie had a distinct look of satisfaction.

"Julianna Joyce Parks."

I fastened my eyes on Jenny.

"Clifton Parsons."

She was near the steps.

"Barry James Patterson."

As I watched the next young lady make her way up the steps, I whispered, "Thank you, God."

"Jennifer Pavlik."

challenging world • 259

She crossed to the center of the stage, reached for her diploma, accepted the handshake, and continued on.

"Paul Pavlik."

She descended the steps.

The announcer went on to the next name.

"Clara Toth Pegler."

She returned to her row.

"Robert Joseph Peloso, Jr.."

She remained standing with her rowmates.

"Edward A. Penick."

In her own way, Jenny was one of them.

... two tributes from Katie ...

I was very startled when it struck me that my retarded sister may be the supreme example of holiness, since existing as God wants one to exist is the ultimate holiness. Jenny definitely does not seek to control her existence. Whatever directions her life takes she accepts without concern. Today my very own sister has become an example of holiness to me! So many qualities I have Jenny cannot have because of her handicap, but here is a quality of Jenny's that I cannot imagine ever coming close to having.

Katie Pavlik
April 25, 1983
Excerpt from college essay

PAIN WITHSTOOD

There is one whom I have
    Hated in girlish rage,
    Scorned for persisting in oblivious oddity,
        (silent mouthing, fanatic notation),
    Slapped in frustration,
    Prodded through impatience,
    Ignored in self-defense
        from incessant chatter,
    Slighted for more capable company,
    Manipulated to serve me.

I pretended to be free.
        She did not remember,
        understand, judge
        from her laggard realm.

One of Them

She loved me.

        Can you wonder why now
I love all and forever?

Katie Pavlik
1984
Copyright © 1988

... postscript ...

Beyond graduation from high school, Jenny's years have been happily productive. She continues to develop into a caring, capable, knowledgeable credit to society, self, and God. In Charleston, South Carolina, she trained daily with Vocationcal Rehabilitation, and at home learned to prepare complete meals. After two years she enjoyed an extended bus trip to New England with her sister Katie. It ended at her family's relocation in a small Nebraska village. There she did odd jobs around the community and earned the "Volunteer of the Year" award at the nursing home. Two years later her family's move to El Centro, California, again made available daily training through the Regional Center for Developmentally Handicapped. She was also a member of the Special Olympics team and competed in district and state swimming meets at San Diego, Berkeley and Los Angeles. Jenny now lives in Verdigre, Nebraska, where her father is meeting the medical needs of his hometown.

Mark graduated from Gonzaga University and Western Washington State University. He and his wife, Terilyn, are presently volunteer teachers at St. Bonaventure Mission in New Mexico. Paul, a graduate of Creighton University, is serving as social-work volunteer also at St. Bonaventure Mission. Katie graduated from Creighton University and is volunteer librarian at Our Lady of Lourdes School in Porcupine, South Dakota, and Pine Ridge Indian Reservation. All of them have done extensive short-term social-service work, bicycling, and backpacking. Sarah is finalizing plans to be a foreign exchange student with Youth For Understanding.

This is 1988, eight years after Jenny's graduation. Each year seems to bring its new happenings, and relocations for one or another of us. Jenny continues to learn. She has not yet met the limit of her potential.

Our Sunday Visitor titles are available at fine religious bookstores everywhere. Titles can be ordered direct from OSV by writing or calling. When writing, include the following information: title(s), stock number(s), and quantity(ies) along with your name and address plus your payment and $2.00 for shipping and handling.

VISA and MasterCard orders may be placed anytime by calling toll-free 1-800-348-2440. From Indiana and Alaska call 1-219-356-8400. Call or write for OSV's free full-line book catalog. *Our Sunday Visitor / 200 Noll Plaza / Huntington, IN 46750.*

You will find our latest line of titles on the following pages.

Classic Catholic Poetry, compiled and edited by Thomas P. McDonnell, no. 494-9, casebound, $12.95, 144 pp. Dante, Chaucer, Merton, and Pope John Paul II are among the famous poets found in *Classic Catholic Poetry*. Includes explanatory notes on both the poets and their works.

1989 Catholic Almanac, edited by Felician A. Foy, O.F.M., and Rose M. Avato, no. 259-8, kivar, $13.95, 600 pp., no. 262-8, cloth with dust jacket, $18.95, 600 pp. The unique resource of current, accurate information on the Church around the world. Like its predecessors, the *1989 Catholic Almanac* includes many features that will expand your understanding of Catholicism. An annual best seller.

Pocket New Testament — Revised New American Bible, no. 222-9, leatherette, $4.95; no. 223-7, red bonded leather, $12.95; no. 249-0, white bonded leather, $12.95, 640 pp. Take God's Word with you wherever you go with the *Pocket New Testament*. This convenient New Testament now comes in three editions: red leatherette, red bonded leather, and white bonded leather.

Stepfamilies: A Catholic Guide, by Paul J. Cullen, no. 508-2, paper, $4.95, 168 pp. Answers questions on such topics as finances, disciplining stepchildren, and interfaith marriages for Catholic stepfamilies. Includes a list of books for further reading.

A Celebration of Padre Pio, no. 190-7, VHS videocassette, $49.95, 58 minutes. Experience the remarkable life of Padre Pio on this new videocassette. *A Celebration of Padre Pio* includes motion-picture footage of Padre Pio working and saying Mass, firsthand accounts of miraculous events, readings from his writing, and much more.

Strangers at Your Door: How to Respond to Jehovah's Witnesses, the Mormons, Televangelists, Cults, and More, by Albert J. Nevins, M.M., no. 496-5, paper, $6.95, 144 pp. *Strangers at Your Door* gives you the background and beliefs of many evangelistic religious groups and appropriate Catholic responses to their challenges. A valuable resource for those who must explain their Catholic faith.

The Sword and the Cross: A History of the Church in Lithuania, by Dr. Saulius Suziedelis, no. 416-7, paper, $9.95, 264 pp. *The Sword and the Cross* reveals the strong Catholic Faith of the Lithuanian people, one of the many ethnic groups currently feeling the effects of Soviet restructuring.

The Life of Brother André: The Miracle Worker of St. Joseph, by C. Bernard Ruffin, no. 492-2, paper, $6.95, 228 pp. From the author of *Padre Pio: The True Story* comes the inspirational story of Brother André Bessette, a small, quiet, humble man who believed in and used the healing power of intercessory prayer.

I Am with You Always, by Fr. Berard Doerger, O.F.M., no. 414-0, paper, $5.95, 144 pp. Written for both the clergy and laity, *I Am with You Always* clearly explains the background, beauty, and significance of the Catholic Church's liturgical year.

The Catholic Living Bible — Four Editions, no. 218-0, Confirmation (deluxe imitation white leather), $14.95; no. 219-9, Gift (deluxe imitation white leather), $14.95; no. 220-2, Gift (deluxe imitation black leather), $14.95; no. 221-0, Gift (deluxe imitation red leather), $14.95. Give a friend or loved one the special gift of God's Word as clearly presented in *The Catholic Living Bible*.